Living
with the
Qur'an

Also by Aliyah Umm Raiyaan

The Power of Du'a
Ramadan Reflections

Living
with the
Qur'an

A yearlong journey to falling
in love with Allah's Words

Aliyah Umm Raiyaan

R
RIDER

RIDER

UK | USA | Canada | Ireland | Australia
India | New Zealand | South Africa

Rider is part of the Penguin Random House group of companies
whose addresses can be found at global.penguinrandomhouse.com

Penguin Random House UK
One Embassy Gardens, 8 Viaduct Gardens,
London SW11 7BW
penguin.co.uk
global.penguinrandomhouse.com

Penguin
Random House
UK

First published by Rider in 2025
1

Typeset 10/13.75 pt Optima LT Pro by Six Red Marbles UK, Thetford, Norfolk
Printed and bound in Great Britain by Clays Ltd, Elcograf S.p.A.

The authorised representative in the EEA is Penguin Random House Ireland,
Morrison Chambers, 32 Nassau Street, Dublin D02 YH68

A CIP catalogue record for this book is available from the British Library

ISBN 9781846048197

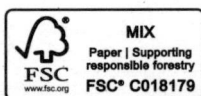

MIX
Paper | Supporting
responsible forestry
FSC
www.fsc.org   FSC® C018179

Penguin Random House is committed to a sustainable future
for our business, our readers and our planet. This book is made
from Forest Stewardship Council® certified paper.

For the lovers of Allah who seek to be close to Him.
May this book be a means of living with His Book as
your closest, most intimate companion. Ameen.

CONTENTS

Introduction XI

PART 1:

PREPARING YOUR HEART 1

Week 1: Setting Out 3

Week 2: The Best Route Is Your Own 8

Week 3: Pack Light 14

Week 4: Pack Right 20

Week 5: One Day at a Time 26

Week 6: Awaken Your Heart First 31

Week 7: The Time is Now 37

PART 2:

DRAWING NEAR 45

Week 8: Making Him Your First Priority 47

Week 9: Excuses 53

Week 10: The Possessor of Mercy 59

Week 11: Humility 66

PART 3:

WHEN FAITH IS TESTED 73

Week 12: Injustice 75

Week 13: Despair 81

Week 14: An Angry Salah 87

Week 15: Balancing 93

Week 16: Tests 99

Week 17: The Timing of Tests 104

PART 4:

PAIN 109

Week 18: Sickness 111

Week 19: Loss 117

Week 20: Dilemmas 122

Week 21: Absence 130

Week 22: Unwanted Decree 137

Week 23: Surrender 142

Week 24: Worry 147

Week 25: One Step at a Time 152

Week 26: Turning Back 157

Week 27: Repetition 162

PART 5:

RELATIONSHIPS 169

Week 28: Your Heart is Understood 171

Week 29: Bias 176

Week 30: Ihsaan 182

Week 31: Trust 187

Week 32: The Relationship You've Been Waiting For 193

CONTENTS

PART 6:

A JOURNEY FOR LIFE 199

Week 33: The Training You Need 201

Week 34: Ilm 206

Week 35: Guidance 212

Week 36: Leave Your Comfort Zone 217

Week 37: Submission 222

Week 38: Barakah 228

Week 39: Go with His Flow 233

Week 40: Salah 238

Week 41: Vigilance 243

Week 42: Joy 248

Week 43: Learning Arabic 253

Week 44: Losing the Qur'an 258

Week 45: Two Pages Daily 263

Week 46: Find Your LWQ Tribe 269

Week 47: Gratitude 274

PART 7:

AKHIRAH 279

Week 48: The Grave 281

Week 49: The Throne Verse 286

Week 50: Roadmap 292

Week 51: Endless Devotion 297

Week 52: Arriving Home 303

Conclusion 309

Glossary 311

Bibliography 317

Gratitude 319

Introduction

Dearest reader, I almost didn't write this book.

Not because I didn't want to, but because I felt the immense weight of writing a book about Allah's Book – the Qur'an. The responsibility felt heavy, and I began to experience imposter syndrome – that I'm not a scholar nor have I studied at length in Islamic institutes. I really questioned whether I was the right person to write this at all.

But then I sat with that thought, and what came to me was a profound lesson that reshaped my intention and guided every page that I wrote in the book you are now reading.

It was this: the Qur'an was revealed for everyone. The learned and the layperson. The believer and the disbeliever. The righteous and the sinner. The one on the straight path and the one who has lost their way. It wasn't revealed for a select few – it was revealed for hearts, for seekers. It was revealed by the Lord of the Worlds for you and me.

You may be someone I know personally, or someone I will never meet in this world, reading this in a quiet moment, tucked away in a corner of your own life. Whatever your current state, whatever your relationship with faith, wherever you are with Allah: the Qur'an is for you too.

This book, *Living with the Qur'an*, is a humble invitation to spend a year with Allah's Perfect Words – not just reading or reciting them, but truly living with them.

Structured in a manner that provides you with the space to reflect, apply and connect with Allah 'azza wa jal and His Words, each week includes:

1. a verse to anchor your reflections;

2. a personal story that brings the lessons to life;

3. a 'Pause and Reflect' section to draw out meaning;

4. three practical ways to 'Live with His Words';

5. a 'Question for Your Heart' to stir inner thought; and

6. a final invitation to get to know and 'Fall in Love with The Author' (Allah 'azza wa jal).

So I invite you to take your time on your first read through it, following each week in consecutive order and letting the words and practices sink in.

You can read this book all the way through, in one sitting, within a few days or weeks, if you like. But, if you do, I encourage you to return to it, to go week by week when the time is right. That slow, deliberate pace will allow for a gradual spiritual build-up – because change doesn't always happen in big leaps. Sometimes it happens quietly, steadily, with one ayah (verse) at a time. Thereafter, you can dip in and out as you wish.

You can also read this book on your own or with your 'tribe' – your nearest and dearest – or even as part of a book club. If you are embarking on this journey with others, before you start Part 1, be sure to read 'Week 46 – Find your LWQ Tribe' for some guidance.

As the Qur'an was revealed in the Arabic language, I have included the original verses in Arabic, which is to be read from right to left, as well as the transliteration and English translation. Various volumes of tafsir by scholars such as Ibn Kathir, Sayid Qutb, Razi, As-Sadi and others have been referred to in the writing of this book.

Along this journey, I'll share stories: my own and those of others – of people who have clung to the Qur'an through grief, hope, heartbreak and transformation. These stories are from ordinary people who became lovers of Allah and His Book, showcasing that there is always a backstory to our peek into the current life chapter of people who we deem to be a 'success'. The stories I have included in this book are real, raw and full of heart. My prayer is that through them, you'll see yourself, and more importantly, you'll see how the Qur'an speaks to your life too.

This book is a little different from my previous ones. You'll still find depth, compassion and honesty here – but you'll also be met with gentle yet firm challenges to increase in faith and submission. I want your heart to feel seen and held, but I also want you to take brave steps forward in your connection with Allah and His Book. My du'a (personal supplication) is that this becomes a turning point in your journey through life and faith.

Unlike my previous books, I've chosen not to include many inspirational quotes from others in this book. Not because they aren't valuable, but because I wanted to centre the verses of the Qur'an themselves. Often, we reach for Islamic quotes to feel inspired and to give us that emaan (faith) boost, but the Qur'an, subhanAllah, is the most powerful boost of all to faith. It is The Quote. And your Rabb's Words speak to you directly, without needing to be dressed up or explained away.

As the wife of the Prophet ﷺ, Aisha (may Allah be pleased with her), said, the first verses of the Qur'an to be revealed were about the afterlife and accountability – verses that connected directly to the heart and softened it. That is what this book seeks to achieve: to develop your heart's connection to the Book of Allah. Not just studying the Words of Allah, but deeply living with them.

I am a writer who is no more than an imperfect soul trying to navigate this life, often failing, sometimes getting it right. But I believe deeply in the power of reflection and in pausing. I believe there is great power in discovering the context behind why a verse was revealed, the linguistic depth of carefully selected Words of an intentional Creator, and asking what a verse means for you in your moment. The moments of your life are precious, because this life is not the end – there is eternity to strive for.

And I believe the Qur'an is the best guide we have to journey through this life to the next.

If you allow it to, this book will help you make the Qur'an

personal again. Not just a sacred book on a shelf, but a trusted companion through every season of your life. I pray that by the end of this journey, your heart will whisper what mine has come to know:

The Qur'an is a gift.

And it is a gift meant for you.

By Allah, for Allah and with Allah – it is time to experience the depth of the following verse, which I pray embodies what you will encounter through this book:

قُلْ إِنَّ صَلَاتِى وَنُسُكِى وَمَحْيَاىَ وَمَمَاتِى لِلَّهِ رَبِّ ٱلْعَٰلَمِينَ ١٦٢

Qul inna ṣalātī wa nusukī wa maḥyāya wa mamātī lillāhi
rabbil-'ālamīn

Say, 'Surely my prayer, my sacrifice, my life, and my death are
all for Allah – Lord of all worlds.'

Surah Al-Anam 6:162

Aliyah Umm Raiyaan

PART 1:

Preparing Your Heart

وَتَزَوَّدُواْ فَإِنَّ خَيْرَ ٱلزَّادِ ٱلتَّقْوَىٰ ۚ وَٱتَّقُونِ يَـٰٓأُوْلِى ٱلْأَلْبَـٰبِ ١٩٧

wa tazawwādū fa-inna khayra az-zādi at-taqwā,
wa-ttaqūni yā ulī al-albāb

'. . . and take provisions, but indeed, the best provision is
taqwa (God-consciousness). So be mindful of Me,
O people of reason.'

Surah Al-Baqarah 2:197

1

WEEK 1:

Setting Out

Verse(s) of the Week
Your Rabb's Words for Your Soul

وَوَجَدَكَ ضَآلًّا فَهَدَىٰ ٧

Wa wajadaka ḍāllan fa-hadā

'And He found you lost and guided [you].'

Surah Duha 93:7

My Story

In May 2024, I stood facing the kabah and one du'a escaped
my lips more than any other:

Rabbi (my Lord), I feel far from You. Grant me the biggest,
most profound turning point in my faith so that my heart
becomes firmly attached to You, knows You, loves You and

worships You. Grant me knowledge of You and draw me close to Your Book.

Why this particular cry to my Lord? Because I was suffering from an emptiness that just wasn't being filled, despite everything I tried so hard to fill it with. I felt lost and incomplete despite my life being rooted in activities very much connected with my deen (way of life): my work as CEO of my charity, Solace, supporting women who have embraced Islam and find themselves in difficulty; my books; speaking engagements; even being blessed with friends who were also striving to be beloved to Allah and our hours-long conversations together. But still there was something missing. I carried on being busy, even adding things to my plate with the hope that the void would disappear. But these things were like a plaster over a wound that, in fact, needed surgery.

I had made du'a with heart and tongue in sync. I had turned to the One above the seven heavens with my empty soul pleading to be filled.

If you've read my second book, The Power of Du'a, *you will know of my absolute belief in the extraordinary things that come to be when a yearning heart calls upon the One who makes the impossible possible. So, deep inside, excitement was brewing. I had an expectation that my Lord was going to answer my du'a in an exceptional way and that He would revive my dying heart.*

Exactly two months later, it came in the form of a WhatsApp message. I was offered a free place on a two-year course that would take students through the entirety of the Qur'an – in tafseer (exegesism or interpretation of text), in tadabbur (contemplation of the Qur'an), reflection and application. I knew instantly this was my du'a being answered.

Pause and Reflect

Dear lover of Allah, I know your heart yearns to feel a closeness to your Lord. I know, from time to time, your soul feels dehydrated. But know this: the gaping hole within your soul and the fact you are aware of it, are gifts from your Lord. He wants to show you what is missing so that you may begin your search.

In this week's verse, we find Allah reminding the Prophet ﷺ how He found him searching and granted him divine guidance.

In every verse of the Qur'an – it does not matter whether Allah is addressing the prophets, the disbelievers or even the hypocrites – there is a message in there for you too.

And so, when your Rabb specifically used the verb 'wajada', which means 'to find', it is to remind you that whenever you feel lost and you sincerely search to be close to your Lord, He will intentionally find you. Wajada is not passive; it is deeply personal. Allah, ﷻ (Glorious and Most High is He), is drawing attention to His Active Care in your life, like a parent finding a lost child – but more so. This is how Allah receives the sincere, seeking heart.

The verse continues: '. . . and guided you'. Hadā (هدى) is His Perfect guidance, carefully leading you to the destination you seek.

This verse is a description of your story – of everyone's story, of souls that are seeking truth. Feeling lost is never the end – it is the beginning of being found.

When your soul feels empty, when you feel deep within that something is missing, there is absolutely nothing that can fill you deeply except the Words of your Lord.

This is the journey.

Get ready, because journeying through life with the Qur'an, with the humble efforts of my book as your aid, will, by His Permission, change you and your life in ways you cannot imagine! Through the stories and reflections in this book, I cannot wait to prove to you the transformation that is awaiting you, insha'Allah (God willing)!

Live with His Words . . .

Here are three steps to live with this week's verse(s):

1. As you go about your week, choose to focus deeply on parts of Allah's Creation. It might be the sky as you walk to the shops, the birds flying above or a fallen leaf from a tree. Reflect on Allah's Creation and notice how your reflections, in turn, make you feel – perhaps guided and grounded.

2. Acknowledge the times you've felt lost in your life and how Allah looked after you and guided you to better, to ease, to solutions – to Him.

3. Turn to the Owner of your soul and tell Him: Al-Khaliq, the Creator of my soul, there are times I feel so lost. Rabbi, I am like that child who has been wandering around scared, confused, longing to return Home. Ya Rabb, find me. I know my soul's peace lies in being close to You. And I know the only possible way to be close to You is by attaching myself to that which You have left of You tangibly in this dunya (the life of this world): Your Perfect Unchanged Words.

A Question for Your Heart

Have you ever paused to reflect on the moments you felt lost, only to realise Allah's Guidance was actually always finding its way to you?

Fall in Love with The Author

Your Lord is Al-Hadi, The One Who Guides, who never leaves a sincere seeker without direction. Every void, detour, delay and every difficulty are pathways leading you back to His Book and, ultimately, to Him.

WEEK 2:

The Best Route Is Your Own

Verse(s) of the Week
Your Rabb's Words for Your Soul

وَعَلَى ٱلثَّلَٰثَةِ ٱلَّذِينَ خُلِّفُواْ حَتَّىٰ إِذَا ضَاقَتْ عَلَيْهِمُ ٱلْأَرْضُ بِمَا رَحُبَتْ وَضَاقَتْ عَلَيْهِمْ أَنفُسُهُمْ
وَظَنُّوٓاْ أَن لَّا مَلْجَأَ مِنَ ٱللَّهِ إِلَّآ إِلَيْهِ ثُمَّ تَابَ عَلَيْهِمْ لِيَتُوبُوٓاْ إِنَّ ٱللَّهَ هُوَ ٱلتَّوَّابُ ٱلرَّحِيمُ ١١٨

Wa 'ala ath-thalāthati alladhīna khullifū ḥattā idhā ḍāqat
'alayhimu al-arḍu bimā raḥubat wa ḍāqat 'alayhim anfusuhum
wa thannū allā malja'a mina Allāhi illā ilayh, thumma tāba
'alayhim li-yatūbū; inna Allāha huwa at-Tawwābu ar-Raḥīm

'And 'Allah has also turned in mercy to' the three who had
remained behind, 'whose guilt distressed them' until the
earth, despite its vastness, seemed to close in on them, and
their souls were torn in anguish. They knew there was no
refuge from Allah except in Him. Then He turned to them in
mercy so that they might repent. Surely Allah 'alone' is the
Accepter of Repentance, Most Merciful.'

Surah At-Tawbah 9:118

I have lost count of how many times I have been asked whether it was difficult for me to write my books so openly and vulnerably. The answer has always been no. My life's journey has brought me to this point – to write as my raw, imperfect self. When I interviewed Romina, a British-Afghani friend of 20 years, I smiled as she recounted a chapter from her life that was a means to her living closely with the Qur'an. I smiled because the best route to a beautiful relationship with Allah's Book is one that is uniquely your own.

Romina's Story

I had been practising Islam for about three to four years. I went to this circle and the sister leading the circle asked everyone: 'What is your favourite book?'

One of the first sisters to answer said: 'I'd like to be able to say the Qur'an, but it isn't my favourite.'

I sat there and my mind screamed, Oh my God! How did she just say that out loud?! It was the most dreadful thing anyone could say in a gathering like that. But then I sat with it and thought, Actually, that was really brave. Because I also wanted to tell everyone the Qur'an was my favourite book – but was it? Was it the book I actually picked up and looked forward to spending time with?

No, the Qur'an was not my favourite book. I shied away from it. I didn't enjoy being with it. I felt there was a barrier between me and its words. If I really wanted to change this, I needed to do something to break down the barrier.

I thought perhaps the answer was in learning how to recite it correctly with tajweed rules (science of reciting the Qur'an correctly) instead of the way my mum had taught me. Maybe that was why there was no enjoyment or connection with it. That went on for a while. I remember looking at my teachers and thinking, Well, they do love the Qur'an, but they either know or are learning Arabic properly. So maybe I need Arabic to really access it. *So, I started lessons: what this word means, this is how you interpret it, this is what the Qur'an is going to do for you, this is what Allah meant. It helped – but the way Arabic was taught back then was very dry. It didn't immediately connect with me.*

By this point, I was married and had small children, and I went to a talk where the sister was speaking about parenting. In that talk, she told me something that changed the course of my life. She shared that the Prophet's character ﷺ was the Qur'an and the people closest to you should feel the benefit of your good character due to your relationship with the Qur'an.

I immediately thought about how I was with my children, and I felt ashamed. I had three children under the age of five. I did not like how I was with them. It was far from the character of the Qur'an. If somebody put up a camera, recording how I was outside in the world and how I was inside at home, they would see that I definitely did not have the character of the Qur'an. I wasn't sure what the character of the Qur'an was, but it definitely did not match with mine.

I knew I had to make a choice: to choose the Prophet's character ﷺ and therefore choose the Qur'an. All the tajweed in the world and all the Arabic in the world hadn't changed me. I started making du'a to Allah, ﷻ, that He uses the Qur'an to transform my heart. And then, finally, something clicked.

I internalised that I needed to have this personal journey with the Qur'an. From there, an appreciation in my heart grew for it and a profound sense of awe for it was embedded deep within – that this was a book that was going to transform my heart, if I brought my heart to it. And so, I took that route – and that's when the true transformation began.

Pause and Reflect

Allah 'azza wa jal has decreed and written that you, exactly as you are – with all your imperfections and shortcomings – should have access to His Book. Yes, you! Every verse within the Qur'an is relevant to you, even if your Lord is talking about the Pharaoh at the time of Musa (Moses, alayhis-salam), the disobedience of Banu Israel (the people of Moses) or the life of one of the prophets. These are not just stories. The Qur'an has been revealed for you to live personally with it, finding yourself and your own story through His Words.

It does not matter where you are on your Qur'an journey – whether you can recite with perfect tajweed or not, whether you know the Arabic language or not. Yes, Allah 'azza wa jal chose to reveal the Qur'an in Arabic for a reason – but your Rabb is not one that would prevent a person from experiencing an intimate relationship with His Words and therefore Him, simply because of the time and place they were born in.

Allah, ﷻ, wants to have a relationship with you and He wants you to have a personal relationship with Him. This journey can only be a personal one – with all your individual qualities, imperfections, strengths and unique experiences, both good and bad.

Never underestimate what Allah can and will do with an intense longing for Him. He sees your heart. Your internal yearning will not only transform your relationship with His Book, but transform your heart that sincerely seeks it.

The verse of this week's chapter is from Surah (chapter) At-Tawbah, where Allah, ﷻ, talks about the three men of the Ansar (tribe of Madinah at the time of the Prophet Muhammad, ﷺ) – including Ka'b ibn Malik (radiAllahu anhu, may Allah be please with him) – who made excuses to the Prophet ﷺ for not joining the Muslim army as it prepared for battle. This led them to be known as 'those who remained behind'. Ka'b ibn Malik was beside himself for a long time – guilty and ashamed that he had not accepted the call. Allah later revealed this verse, showing that this heart-rending regret and yearning of Ka'b ibn Malik to be better and beloved to Him 'azza wa jal was sincere. Allah received his repentance and turned to all three men with His Rahma (Mercy). Cementing His Forgiveness for them, He recorded their story in the Qur'an for all of humankind.

It does not matter who you are, what you have done or where you are in your journey with the Qur'an. Your Rabb wants you to know that He turns to those who take that sincere personal route back to Him. Every time.

Knowing this, there is nothing stopping you from experiencing a personal relationship with His Book – one that will, insha'Allah, lead you to proclaim: yes, the Qur'an is my favourite book!

Live with His Words . . .

Here are three steps to live with this week's verse(s):

1. Read the story of Ka'b ibn Malik (radiAllahu anhu).

2. What are the lessons from Ka'b ibn Malik's story for your own life? Journal your thoughts.

3. Turn to The All Forgiving and tell Him: Rabbi, my sins are many. You continue to bless me every day despite my repeated mistakes. My Lord, I need Your Help. Use the Qur'an to transform my heart, my character and my life.

A Question for Your Heart

When the world around you feels restricted, and your soul is restless despite all you have, could it be that your heart is being called back to the one place it will never feel suffocated, the Qur'an?

Fall in Love with The Author

Your Lord is Al-Wasi – The All-Encompassing. He wants you to know, no matter how tight the walls of despair may feel, His Mercy is more vast than the heavens and He always makes space for you when you turn back to Him exactly as you are.

WEEK 3:

Pack Light

Verse(s) of the Week
Your Rabb's Words for Your Soul

وَلَقَدْ يَسَّرْنَا ٱلْقُرْآنَ لِلذِّكْرِ فَهَلْ مِن مُّدَّكِرٍ ١٧

Wa laqad yassarnal-Qur'āna li-dh-dhikri fa-hal min muddakir

'And We have certainly made the Qur'an easy for remembrance, so is there any who will remember?'

Surah Qamar 54:17

Several people in my life have a truly admirable relationship with the Qur'an. May Allah 'azza wa jal bless them and increase them in goodness. Ameen.

But I can't help comparing their relationship with the Book of Allah to my own. I feel they possess knowledge, I don't. They recite beautifully, I don't. They are righteous, I'm a struggling sinner. In my mind, this is why they have been in relationship with Allah's Book and I have struggled.

So, you can imagine how apprehensive I was when I interviewed

Sheikh Wasim Kempson, a graduate from Madinah University, who holds a master's in Islamic law. I was sure that his story would support my self-limiting beliefs. But if anything, it wonderfully demonstrated what Allah can do when you feel you are at zero.

Wasim's Story

Before I embraced Islam, the only access I had to the Qur'an was through the Marmaduke Pickthall translation, which I used to pick up from time to time.

After I became Muslim, I had access to three translations: Pickthall, Yusuf Ali (which had lots of footnotes and felt off-putting as there was so much information) and the Noble Qur'an printed in Saudi Arabia.

I didn't feel I was able to engage with the translation of the Qur'an due to the language used. It seemed so dry. And unlike the Bible, which I'd been taught to pick sections from here and there, as a Muslim I was taught to read the Qur'an from cover to cover to really grasp its message. But I was unable to do that because of the language barrier.

Three years after becoming Muslim, I still didn't have a solid relationship with the Qur'an, nor did I realise the importance of studying it.

That changed when during a dars (religious class) I bumped into a brother who had studied in Madinah. He told me I could study Islam full-time at university. I thought to myself, If I do that, I'll be able to understand the Qur'an in its original language.

And so, I left London and arrived at the prestigious Madinah University in Saudi Arabia. But there was a problem. The weekly schedule showed a regular Qur'an class in which we had to recite. Only knowing a few Arabic letters at that point, to me it felt like climbing Mount Everest.

On the very first day of the class, the teacher approached me and in Arabic said: 'Read.' In the little Arabic I knew, I said, 'I can't.' I could hear and understand him saying, 'Try, try.' There was a brother who could speak better Arabic, and I turned to him and pleaded, 'Please can you tell him – even if I had something of a foundation to work with, I would try. But I literally don't have anything to work with to try to read.' He translated it into Arabic for the teacher. The teacher listened and looked at me and said: 'Read.'

I was so frustrated, I walked out, thinking to myself, Okay, I need to seriously find a solution.

There was a brother in his final year and I told him: 'Not only can I not read, but also, if I don't memorise from Surah Duha to Surah An-Nas, I'm off the course. I need to pass this to go to the next level. I need to learn how to read!'

He calmed me down and said: 'Every Saturday, Sunday, Monday and Tuesday after Asr (the third prayer), I'll teach you, one-to-one, how to read, and I'll help you memorise Surahs (chapters) Duha to Nas and read the whole of Juz Amma (the 30th part of the Qur'an).'

We did that four days a week until I started to grasp how to read and recite. As I became more fluent, there was such enjoyment in its recitation. Before that, I would recite using the transliteration (converting text into another language, but concentrating on pronunciation rather than meaning), but now, I was able to look at the letters and the vowels and this was such a boost to my emaan (faith). I started having a real relationship with the Qur'an because I was able to speak the very words that my Creator, Allah Himself, said. That's the root of everything.

Pause and Reflect

All journeys require you to pack a suitcase. Your journey with the Qur'an is no different.

If I were to ask you to draw up a list of things you would need for your Qur'an journey, you'd probably say that a course, a teacher, the Qur'an in Arabic, a translation of the Qur'an, notebooks, pens, highlighters, bookmark tabs were all necessary items.

But the suitcase on this journey is not one that contains tangible items. The journey with the Qur'an is an intimate internal journey of your soul and the suitcase is your heart – the home of your thoughts and feelings and the governor of your actions.

The Prophet ﷺ said:

> Truly in the body there is a piece of flesh which, if it is sound, the whole body is sound; and if it is corrupt, the whole body is corrupt. Truly, it is the heart.

Bukhari and Muslim

Before you can pack, you need to empty your heart of anything that is no longer needed. Create space for what will truly move you forward with the Book of Allah. This requires you to be completely honest. You may need to remove grudges, envy, bitterness, arrogance – and something else. You need to release the belief you are not enough to live life with the Qur'an.

Any belief that makes you feel you need to be someone else, have something else or exist somewhere else, my dearest reader, those beliefs have got to go. As well as anything that reinforces those beliefs – social media searches and all external voices that aim to keep you paralysed by your feelings of inadequacy.

Allah 'azza wa jal does not require you to be a certain person, with certain knowledge or free of all shortcomings, in order to be in relationship with Him. The Qur'an was for the disbelievers and hypocrites of Makkah and Madinah. It is also for you.

What I love about Wasim's story, apart from the fact that Allah 'azza wa jal took a new Muslim who knew nothing and turned him into a sheikh, is that Allah presented him with an invitation to the Qur'an exactly where he was, as he was. And you too can start with who and where you are: your level of practice of Islam, your sins, mistakes, issues, trauma – the lot. When you do, your relationship with the Qur'an will lead you to realise that you, in fact, are enough, paving the way for beautiful possibilities within you and around you.

So let go of self-imposed limitations and instead focus on the abundant possibilities of how Allah 'azza wa jal, in His Infinite Wisdom, can draw you close.

You may be at the beginning of your journey, having just started to string together letters of the Arabic alphabet. You may have recited the Qur'an for years but wish to understand its meanings more deeply and live by them. Whatever your situation is, this week's verse is a message of love from the Lord above. The journey with the Qur'an is not only a beautiful one but also an easy one, made accessible for all, for you, by Him.

Live with His Words . . .

Here are three steps to live with this week's verse(s):

1. Take a piece of paper and list all the limiting beliefs you have about yourself, your relationship with Allah and your relationship with His Book.

2. Shred or burn that piece of paper, visualising the suitcase of your heart becoming lighter, making room for that which Allah knows you need for this journey.

3. Turn to Allah with a sincere heart and tell Him: Rabbi, I come to You and Your Book, just as I am. I have searched for acceptance from others but I realise I will only ever feel whole and complete with You. Al-Fattah – The One Who Opens the way – open my heart to all that You know I need to truly live with Your Words.

A Question for Your Heart

What if the only thing standing between you and the Qur'an are the beliefs that you are not enough and that this journey will be difficult, when Allah already treats you as enough and has already made it easy for you?

Fall in Love with The Author

Al-Fattah – The One Who Opens the way – wants you to always know that the greatest barriers are not in the Qur'an's accessibility, but in the limits you place on yourself. He wants you near. He tells you He is near. When you take one step towards His Guidance, He opens the rest of the way for you. Trust Him.

WEEK 4:

Pack Right

Verse(s) of the Week
Your Rabb's Words for Your Soul

فَقُلْتُ ٱسْتَغْفِرُوا رَبَّكُمْ إِنَّهُ كَانَ غَفَّارًا ١٠ يُرْسِلِ ٱلسَّمَاءَ عَلَيْكُم مِّدْرَارًا ١١ وَيُمْدِدْكُم بِأَمْوَالٍ وَبَنِينَ وَيَجْعَل لَّكُمْ جَنَّاتٍ وَيَجْعَل لَّكُمْ أَنْهَارًا ١٢

Fa-qultu istaghfirū rabbakum innahu kāna ghaffārā

Yursili as-samā'a 'alaykum midrārā

*Wa yumdidkum bi-amwālin wa banīna wa yaj'al lakum
jannātin wa yaj'al lakum anhārā*

'So I said, "Seek forgiveness of your Lord. Indeed, He is ever
Forgiving. He will send rain to you in abundance, and provide
you with wealth and children, and make for you gardens and
make for you rivers."'

Surah Nuh 71:10–12

20

My Story

Remember the gifted Qur'an course I mentioned in Week 1 – the one I signed up for after making du'a? Just hours before the first lesson, I was buzzing with excitement! I truly believed I was about to be instantly transformed – that I'd become this deeply devoted servant, brought closer to my Rabb.

Of course, that's not what happened. Little did I know that I would need something special to open that path.

When I stopped practising Islam within the first few years of becoming Muslim, a close friend who had been part of my journey to Islam felt crushed. (There is more about this in my first book, Ramadan Reflections.) I understood at the time why she was sad, but it was not until recently – when another dear friend, Maryam, began to lose her own way in faith – that I fully comprehended the extent of my friend's grief back then on my behalf. When you choose to live your life with the akhirah (eternal life) as your goal, you don't just want that for yourself. You deeply desire it for your loved ones too.

The scary thing is, losing our way is something that can happen to any of us.

Maryam went from studying the Qur'an, teaching it and reminding others about Allah to not wanting to engage in conversations about Allah ﷻ or her deen at all. She had lost her connection to her deen and Allah, and began to live a completely different lifestyle – far from Islam. She stopped reading the Qur'an and teaching it. It was very hard for me to witness this. A sister I loved for the sake of Allah, who once deeply loved the Book of Allah, was no longer living with it, nor was she interested in it. I felt a tightness in my chest as I saw her drift further and further away.

21

Time passed and our distance grew. This is what happens when souls seek different goals. Finally, we lost touch altogether.

When we re-established contact, I met Maryam in a coffee shop and her face was simply a source of light. We sat for hours as we sipped our tea, as she told me what had transpired in her life – difficult tests and an internal battle between what her soul knew to be true and an alien version of herself that she had become. As we sat and caught up on the happenings in each other's life, I noticed her ring, whose button she kept tapping at whenever I spoke and she was listening. With each tap, her lips parted and closed, as she sought forgiveness from her Lord. It was a dhikr (remembrance of Allah) counter that I like to call an istighfaar ring.

Allah had gifted her the understanding of the power of istighfaar – the act of seeking forgiveness from Allah, bringing your soul back to the path of seeking Him 'azza wa jal. She had returned home – to istighfaar – which then led her back to life with the Qur'an, which superseded the relationship with it she had previously encountered. My dear Maryam began to live life again, with akhirah as her priority.

Shortly after that meeting, I rummaged through a drawer in my desk and retrieved my own ring. And I began – 300, 500, 1000, 2000 – no particular number, just as much istighfaar as I could. And then it came: sitting in one of my Qur'an course lessons, we covered a verse that seemed to latch onto my heartstrings and pull until my heart split open. And that was the beginning of experiencing the Qur'an like never before.

Pause and Reflect

Aside from sending salawaat (peace and blessings) upon the Prophet ﷺ, there is nothing more aiding and valuable for your Qur'an journey than istighfaar. This is the key item to pack into your heart. Why? Because Allah is Al Quddus – the Holy One. By default, His Words are pure. The more you engage your soul in istighfaar, the more your heart will become pure and the more insight and blessings you will encounter on your journey with Allah's Book.

Many times, in the Qur'an, Allah 'azza wa jal uses the metaphor of rain and water to depict the abundant effects of the Qur'an. In light of this week's verse, we see that istighfaar allows that beneficial rain to descend.

When you find yourself in life desperately needing a sign, a message and guidance from The Most High, and He gently guides you to read a verse you have read many times before, but this time it hits the right spot – calming and soothing you, shifting your perspective – that is your abundant rain.

It is relieving, refreshing and makes you feel renewed. And when you taste this level of abundance and thank Allah for it, the returns just keep increasing. The more you come to istighfaar, the more you can come to the Qur'an. And the more you come to the Qur'an, the more it gives you.

This relationship cannot be understood by the laws of nature in which what is used diminishes in quality. The Book of Allah does not originate from this world, and neither does your soul. You enter a new dimension of spirituality where you become excitedly curious and ask yourself: What more is the Qur'an going to offer me? Your curiosity is honoured by Ar-Raheem (The Especially Merciful). A priceless cycle ensues – constant increased nourishment filling you to your core.

Romina from Week 2's story shared something her teacher once told her, which I feel is right to share with you now. He said:

'Your body is made from this earth and so it is nourished by the food of the earth. Your ruh (soul) is from Jannah (Paradise), so it cannot be nourished by things from this dunya. It must be fed by Allah with something from outside this dunya. The nourishment of the soul and the heart is the Qur'an. It can only come from Allah.'

Live with His Words . . .

Here are three steps to live with this week's verse(s):

1. If you don't have one already, get yourself a dhikr counter or you can use your fingers – whichever allows you to increase in seeking Allah's Forgiveness.

2. Say AstaghfiruAllah 100 times a day as part of your morning and evening adhkaar (supplication and remembrance). Really zone into the memory of things for which you are seeking forgiveness as you repeat it. Once you have established the prophetic minimum, increase and aim to make abundant istighfaar with sincerity. Connect your istighfaar to your personal needs and to your desire to live with the Qur'an.

3. Turn to the One who loves to forgive and tell Him: Rabbi, I fall before You with a mountain of sins seeking Your Forgiveness. As my tongue moves in sync with my heart and I utter AstaghfiruAllah, with each call for forgiveness, erase my sins one by one with Your Mercy. Indeed, You are The Most Forgiving, The Most Merciful.

A Question for Your Heart

If your Rabb is a Lord who provides you with abundance when you ask for forgiveness for your sins, what levels of abundance await you when you take righteous, intentional steps towards faith, Him and His Book?

Fall in Love with The Author

Al-Ghafur – The Most Forgiving – as told by the Prophet ﷺ in Sahih Muslim, is a Lord who would replace a people with those who sin just so that He may forgive them. He loves to forgive so much that His Forgiveness not only leads to the erasure of sins, He also envelops you within His Mercy and opens doors, showering you with blessings without measure, simply because you sincerely turned back to Him.

WEEK 5:

One Day at a Time

Verse(s) of the Week
Your Rabb's Words for Your Soul

وَٱلَّذِينَ جَـٰهَدُوا۟ فِينَا لَنَهْدِيَنَّهُمْ سُبُلَنَا ۚ وَإِنَّ ٱللَّهَ لَمَعَ ٱلْمُحْسِنِينَ ٦٩

Walladhīna jāhadū fīnā lanahdiyannahum subulanā, wa inna Allāha la-maʿa al-muḥsinīn

'And those who strive for Us – We will surely guide them to Our ways. And indeed, Allah is with the doers of good.'

Surah Ankabut 29:69

After I lost my way in the early years after embracing Islam, I'll never forget the first few steps back – steps gently guided by my Loving and Compassionate Lord. They paved the path of my return to Him, 'azza wa jal.

It started with something incredibly simple: reading just one page of the Qur'an translation every day, no matter what. I would sit in the park opposite my flat in Hendon, North London, reflect on its verses, and let the words settle in my heart. That quiet, consistent act slowly rekindled my connection to the worship of Allah.

It reminds me of the beautiful saying of the Prophet ﷺ:

Take up good deeds only as much as you are able, for the best deeds are those done regularly, even if they are few.

Sunan Ibn Majah

Allah loves sincere, simple deeds, especially when they are done with consistency. I was reminded of this through Saleha's story.

Saleha is a Shaykha who grew up in the same London borough that I lived in as a child. And from her presence and advice, you might assume she's spent her entire life close to the Qur'an. But as you'll discover in the chapters to come, her journey tells a different, powerful truth: it doesn't matter when or where you begin.

Saleha's Story

I remember looking at other brothers and sisters who had the Qur'an in their hands, in their hearts and on their lips. I remember thinking, They have such a close relationship with Allah and I don't have that. That yearning turned into a du'a. Alhamdulillah, it was answered at a much later age in life. Ever since my relationship with the Qur'an began to take shape, I realise that prior to this, I was not truly living.

Living is found when you read the Qur'an, reflect over its verses or study it. It is then that you will always experience barakah (blessings and divine favour) in it.

There needs to be regular interaction with the Words of Allah – from beginning your day with a few verses to reciting in the evening. Through this, you experience contentment and sukoon (tranquillity) descending upon you and your heart as you recite the Words of your Creator with beautification just as our Prophet 鏊 taught us. This method of recitation has been passed on from the Prophet 鏊 through a sanad (chain). That's why we have this tradition of ijazat (authorised licence). We recite it exactly as it was recited from Allah to the Angel Jibreel (alayhis-salam) to the Prophet 鏊 and passed onto us. When we recite in this manner and recite loudly, though alone, we find ourselves in a beautiful gathering of angels that fills the space around us with tranquillity and peace.

Pause and Reflect

I often think about the things we do daily without fail – eat and sleep being the main two. Without both, our bodies would begin to decline and fail, and this would eventually lead to death.

Your soul is no different. Your soul needs daily sustenance just as your body does. In fact, the sustenance of your soul is more important than that of your body because you were a soul first. One day, your body will cease to function and will be wrapped in its final garment and lowered into the ground, where it will begin to disintegrate. I don't tell you this to frighten you. I tell you this to remind you that it is your soul that will continue to live on before Resurrection, and thereafter when it is reunited with the body. And so, your soul's food is priority. What spiritual nutrients does it need?

I always find it fascinating to hear about men and women who've been lost in the wilderness, or been stranded or adrift in boats for days and weeks, and have survived. Having hardly eaten for so long, upon being found, they are not instantly loaded with food. It would be too much for their system – so overwhelming it could actually lead to harm rather than benefit. So they are given a little, and then a little bit more.

This is exactly what your soul needs. I love the following piece of advice, shared by Ruzi, who I first met 26 years ago as a very new Muslim: 'Establish a daily habit of having physical contact with the Qur'an – of holding the actual mushaf (written version of the Qur'an in Arabic) – and reciting just one verse. Do not belittle this regular act. Let the Qur'an be displayed in your living space so that you can reach out for it when you need it. Doing so keeps you connected like a rope to Allah.'

In this week's verse, Allah 'azza wa jal tells us that He sees you and your efforts, however small. Never underestimate the seemingly small daily steps you can take towards living with His Book.

Live with His Words . . .

Here are three steps to live with this week's verse(s):

1. Take your mushaf, or a copy with a translation, and place it in your living room in your home.

2. Set an alarm twice a day (once in the morning and once in the evening). Commit to reading a minimum of one ayah (verse) daily. If you already have your daily wird (regular portion), establish an absolute minimum number of ayat you will always read and never fall below.

3. Turn to the One who appreciates your effort and rewards you for it and tell Him: My Lord, make me among those who strive for Your Sake even if all I can do is so very little. Rabbi, guide me to paths that lead me to Your Love.

A Question for Your Heart:

What next 'meal' will you prepare for your soul?

Fall in Love with The Author

Ar-Rashid – The Perfectly Wise Guide – is a Lord who leads those who seek Him with sincerity. Every moment spent with the Qur'an is one where He Lovingly leads you towards clarity of mind, purpose of heart and a life aligned with His Wisdom.

WEEK 6:

Awaken Your Heart First

Verse(s) of the Week
Your Rabb's Words for Your Soul

إِنَّمَا ٱلْمُؤْمِنُونَ ٱلَّذِينَ إِذَا ذُكِرَ ٱللَّهُ وَجِلَتْ قُلُوبُهُمْ وَإِذَا تُلِيَتْ عَلَيْهِمْ ءَايَـٰتُهُ زَادَتْهُمْ إِيمَـٰنًا
وَعَلَىٰ رَبِّهِمْ يَتَوَكَّلُونَ ٢

Innamā l-mu'minūna alladhīna idhā dhukira llāhu wajilat qulūbuhum wa-idhā tuliyat ʿalayhim āyātuhu zādat-hum īmānan wa-ʿalā rabbihim yatawakkalūn.

'The 'true' believers are only those whose hearts tremble at the remembrance of Allah, whose faith increases when His revelations are recited to them, and who put their trust in their Lord.'

Surah Al-Anfaal 8:2

31

My Story

My youngest child, aged 12, recently told me that the mother of one of her closest friends, also a revert, showed her a picture of herself before she became Muslim. My daughter's eyes were wide with shock as she recounted how different her friend's mother looked and that she once rode a motorbike! She couldn't believe it.

My daughter begged me to share one of my pictures before Islam with her so she too could show her friends. I pulled out a few photos on my phone. My daughter couldn't stop giggling at the remarkable difference between how I dressed back then and the way I dress today. And sometimes I too forget the remarkable transition that has taken place since I embraced Islam.

To go from carefree party animal to a Muslim woman seeking closeness to Allah, aiming to love what He loves even when that pushes against the desires of my ego, was not, and at times is still not, an easy journey. It's a lifelong battle between the callings of the self and choosing the calling of Allah. Sometimes the former wins and sometimes the latter wins. But what I have noticed is this: the latter tends to win when my heart is tender and soft – softened by Allah, for Allah and with Allah 'azza wa jal. Over the years this has come in the form of an Islamic reminder, being of service to my sisters in faith, contemplation, prayer in the last part of the night and deep conversations with close friends.

But now, there is nothing that softens my heart more than understanding the meanings of the Qur'an, finding the linguistic gems within the Arabic and applying lessons from contemplation to my own life.

In my early years as a Muslim, I came across the following words of the wife of the Prophet ﷺ, Aisha (radiAllahu anha).

Yusuf ibn Mahak reported that Aisha, may Allah be pleased with her, said:

> Verily, the first verses to be revealed were from the shorter chapters at the end of the Qur'an. In them is mentioned Paradise and Hellfire, until people were firmly established upon Islam and verses of lawful and unlawful were revealed. If the first verse to be revealed was 'do not drink wine,' they would have said, 'we will never stop drinking wine.' And if the first verse to be revealed was 'do not commit adultery,' they would have said, 'we will never stop committing adultery.'

Sahih Bukhari

Pause and Reflect

What strikes me here is how savvy and remarkable Aisha (radiAllahu anha) was. She spotted that the very first verses that Allah 'azza wa jal revealed were from the Qur'an's shorter chapters that had nothing to do with the halal and haram – permissible and impermissible. In other words, they weren't about rules, rituals and obligations. They were emotional verses that would directly impact the core – the heart of a person, which transforms his or her perspective, capacity, attachment and actions.

After that, once the heart is aligned and softened, there is space to teach and to challenge. But the awakening of the heart must come first.

When I first read these words and even as I read them today, I felt warm inside, knowing I have a Lord who knows how we operate as human beings and deals with us with great understanding.

Abu Salih reported that Abu Huraira, may Allah be pleased with him, said:

The heart is king and its soldiers are the limbs. If the king is set right, his soldiers will be set right. If the king is corrupted, his soldiers will be corrupted.

Shu'ab al-Iman

Your Lord who created you and knows you better than you will ever know yourself, knows that change is only ever possible when He takes your heart and transforms it, which is why the Prophet ﷺ made the following du'a:

O Turner of the hearts, keep my heart firm upon Your religion!

Sunan Tirmidhi

The melting of your heart is necessary for your limbs and life to follow. True worship is the beautiful alignment of the submission of the heart and the limbs. You can read all the self-development books in the world, you can get a coach, you can attend classes and courses, but until your heart is jolted and moved, you will struggle to change.

If you're reading this, questioning whether you need to change, let me firmly and lovingly tell you, yes, you need to change. We all do. You need to change because the breath you just took in and exhaled may be one of your last. You need to change because the only thing guaranteed in this life is, in fact, death. How you seek Allah's Mercy here will make all the difference in the only thing that matters – your position in the eternal life.

When I looked at the old photographs of me, I knew such a transformation both inwardly and outwardly was only possible because Allah took my heart and softened it. As someone who used to look upon Muslim women with pity for having to cover to now loving my hijab, I know I changed because He flipped my heart.

Allah knew that the men and women of Quraysh would need to hear verses of the Qur'an that would instil fear: such that their hearts would tremble and hope, such that their hearts would somersault in love. This beautiful balance is described by the scholar Ibn al-Qayyim as a bird with love as its head, and fear and hope as its two wings. When the head is healthy, then the two wings fly well. When the head is cut off, the bird will die.

With this, the hearts of the companions of the Prophet ﷺ melted and were ready to absorb lessons that were alien and new to them, but were also the beneficial medicine Allah knew they needed for their souls.

Live with His Words . . .

Here are three steps to live with this week's verse(s):

1. Make a decision to live with the Qur'an. Make wudu (ablution before prayer), wear your best clothes, pray two rakat (units of prayer) and speak to your Lord of your intention to seriously embark upon this journey.

2. However much you read this week, let each word and phrase evoke emotion, bringing you closer to Allah. When you feel your heart soften, recognise the honour and blessing of being in the presence of His Words.

3. Turn to the One who has placed His Book within your reach and tell Him: My Lord, I am only one among billions, but I know that does not matter, for You treat me as the individual that I am. You are a Lord who comes to me running when all I have taken is a single step towards You. I take this step towards living with Your Qur'an. Bless this journey for me. Allow this to be one where my heart experiences Your Light, Guidance and Mercy.

A Question for Your Heart

What is the state of your heart when you bring it before the Words of Allah – are you truly taking it in and listening, or are you merely reading and hearing?

Fall in Love with The Author

Al-Wadud – The Most Loving – is a Lord who pours His Mercy into every verse of the Qur'an, calling you with love to return to Him, soften your heart, and find peace in His Words.

WEEK 7:

The Time is Now

Verse(s) of the Week
Your Rabb's Words for Your Soul

ٱعْلَمُوٓا أَنَّمَا ٱلْحَيَوٰةُ ٱلدُّنْيَا لَعِبٌ وَلَهْوٌ وَزِينَةٌ وَتَفَاخُرٌ بَيْنَكُمْ وَتَكَاثُرٌ فِى ٱلْأَمْوَٰلِ وَٱلْأَوْلَٰدِ
كَمَثَلِ غَيْثٍ أَعْجَبَ ٱلْكُفَّارَ نَبَاتُهُ ثُمَّ يَهِيجُ فَتَرَىٰهُ مُصْفَرًّا ثُمَّ يَكُونُ حُطَٰمًا وَفِى ٱلْءَاخِرَةِ
عَذَابٌ شَدِيدٌ وَمَغْفِرَةٌ مِّنَ ٱللَّهِ وَرِضْوَٰنٌ وَمَا ٱلْحَيَوٰةُ ٱلدُّنْيَآ إِلَّا مَتَٰعُ ٱلْغُرُورِ ٢٠

I'lamū annamā al-ḥayātu ad-dunyā la'ibun wa lahwun wa
zinatun wa tafākhurun baynakum wa takāthurun fī al-amwāli
wa al-awlādi, kamathali ghaythin a'jaba al-kuffāra nabātuhu
thumma yahīju fatarāhu muṣfarran thumma yakūnu ḥuṭ
āman, wa fī al-ākhirati 'adhābun shadīdun wa maghfiratun
mina Allāhi wa riḍwānun, wa mā al-ḥayātu ad-dunyā illā
matā'u al-ghurūr

'Know that this worldly life is no more than play, amusement,
luxury, mutual boasting, and competition in wealth and
children. This is like rain that causes plants to grow, to the
delight of the planters. But later the plants dry up and you
see them wither, then they are reduced to chaff. And in
the Hereafter there will be either severe punishment or

37

forgiveness and pleasure of Allah, whereas the life of this world is no more than the delusion of enjoyment.'

Surah Al-Hadid 57:20

My eldest daughter keeps reminding me playfully but honestly that I've officially entered my 'aunty era'. I've had to sit with that. She's right. I was around her age when I gave birth to her. SubhanAllah, how quickly time flies. It feels like just yesterday I was a teenager, trying to make sense of the world. And yet, when I look ahead, death doesn't feel so far. Such is the nature of this life.

When I interviewed Ahmed, an Arab-American mosque director, I was reminded that time is like sand, slipping away faster than we realise. In truth, all we really have are the present moments – precious moments to seek His Mercy.

Ahmed's Story

During the first two years after I migrated to the United States, I was this new immigrant trying to get my education situated and my medical licence into practice. I was also focused on getting myself financially settled. It was a hectic two years, and nothing short of a rat race – running around and trying my best to get things going on. I did not have much time available to connect with the Qur'an. This seems to be very common – life gets so busy and it takes away precious moments from our days to connect with the Qur'an. I felt really disconnected at that time.

And for me, it wasn't going so well. My licence to practise was delayed by another six months. I lost the temporary job I had been doing. I was living in a shared house but had issues with my roommates that made home feel unwelcoming. Life seemed to be getting darker and darker. Every hiccup and delay felt like a huge obstacle.

To clear my mind, one day, I decided to go for a drive. I went outside and my car was gone. It had been stolen.

On top of everything else, the loss of my car just felt too much. I retreated to my bedroom and sat on my bed. A verse from the Qur'an came to my mind:

أَلَمْ يَأْنِ لِلَّذِينَ آمَنُوا أَن تَخْشَعَ قُلُوبُهُمْ لِذِكْرِ اللَّهِ وَمَا نَزَلَ مِنَ الْحَقِّ وَلَا يَكُونُوا كَالَّذِينَ أُوتُوا الْكِتَٰبَ مِن قَبْلُ فَطَالَ عَلَيْهِمُ الْأَمَدُ فَقَسَتْ قُلُوبُهُمْ وَكَثِيرٌ مِّنْهُمْ فَٰسِقُونَ ١٦

Alam yāni lilladhīna āmanū an takhsha'a qulūbuhum li-dhikri Allāhi wa mā nazala mina al-ḥaqqi wa lā yakūnū kalladhīna ūtu al-kitāba min qabl faṭāla 'alayhimu al-amadu faqasat qulūbuhum wa kathīrun minhum fāsiqūn

Has the time not yet come for believers' hearts to be humbled at the remembrance of Allah and what has been revealed of the truth, and not be like those given the Scripture before – ˹those˺ who were spoiled for so long that their hearts became hardened. And many of them are ˹still˺ rebellious.

Surah Al-Hadid 57:16

I sat there and reflected over the verse. Allah was addressing the believers who were disconnected from the Words of Allah. In essence, in this verse He is saying: Has not the time come for you to wake up?!

I felt as though Allah was talking directly to me: It's time! Wake up! Let your heart be humbled by the Words of Allah.

It's a powerful verse – so much so that the companions would hear it and cry because of how detached they felt they were from the Words of Allah. That's how I felt. Allah was bringing me to account for my busy life. He was saying

to me: It's about time you come and connect with My Words and have your heart be humbled by them.

That evening I decided to walk 45 minutes to the masjid to pray. I certainly couldn't drive there anymore! I remembered the darkness Prophet Yunus (alayhis-salam) was in at the bottom of the ocean. The Prophet ﷺ said that if you make the du'a of Yunus (alayhis-salam) in your sad moments, Allah would replace your sadness with joy. I put myself in the situation of Prophet Yunus and kept repeating the du'a:

$$\text{لَّآ إِلَٰهَ إِلَّآ أَنتَ سُبْحَٰنَكَ إِنِّى كُنتُ مِنَ ٱلظَّٰلِمِينَ}٨٧$$

Lā ilāha illā anta subḥānaka innī kuntu mina athālimīn

There is no god worthy of worship except You. Glory be to You! I have certainly done wrong.

Surah Al-Anbiya 21:87

I arrived at the start of Esha (the fifth prayer) and the Imam was reciting beautifully. Immediately, a serene feeling spread through my heart, and I thought to myself, I like this. I need this. I need to start going to the masjid again. *From that day onwards, I started going every night, which then led me to revisit anything I had previously memorised. The best feeling was capturing meanings of verses that went straight to the heart. I began to review and revise my hifdh (memorisation of the Qur'an). Shortly after, I put together a plan to memorise the Qur'an.*

That is how my relationship with the Qur'an really started. One of the most challenging days of my life ended up becoming one of the best, because it brought me back.

Sometimes you get closer to Allah through difficulties and sometimes through blessings. That was a moment of difficulty that brought me closer to Allah. Alhamdulillah.

Pause and Reflect

This week's verse beautifully describes the stages of life that we go through. We need to pay attention to the fact that none of them lasts forever. Nothing will last – not materialism, not consumerism, not individualism. Nothing except the good things that we are doing.

We are being prepared for that which will never end and never disappear.

Remember Ibn al-Qayyim's analogy of the believer being like a bird with two wings of hope and fear. I feel we have lost our balance. I am the biggest proponent of moving through life with hope, seeking out Allah's Mercy. But we need to have the hard conversations too. We need a reality check. This life is passing by in the blink of an eye and our eternity depends on how much we've sought Allah's Mercy, hoping for His Pardon, His Forgiveness and Grace so that we may enjoy the wonders of the eternal life.

Take stock of the preparation you have undertaken in the past seven weeks. Regardless of where you are at in your Qur'anic journey, you have

- acknowledged your soul's need for the Qur'an;

- recognised the ways in which Allah gently manages your yearning to be close to His Book;

- let go of feeling that you are not enough and come to believe you can have this beautiful relationship;

- packed the right things in your heart for this journey;

- established small consistent steps with the Qur'an that are ever so beloved to Allah;

- recognised that your heart needs to be softened in order to be awakened; and

- been reminded that you are passing quickly through stages of life – and the time to connect with your Rabb's Words is now.

With all of that, the next organic step is entering the realm of deep contemplation about His Verses in the context of you and your life. The Qur'an is not simply for reading and study. It is for living.

Live with His Words . . .

Here are three steps to live with this week's verse(s):

1. Schedule masjid moments in your weekly schedule. Choose one day or night a week to go to the masjid. Sit for a while after salah (ritual daily prayers) and just be. Reflect. Let the stillness settle into your heart. Do this to reset your spiritual rhythm and remind your soul of where it truly feels at home. If you're a brother reading this and you're already accustomed to praying in the masjid, stay that little bit longer after salah to reflect.

2. Adopt the 'Du'a of Darkness' – the du'a of Prophet Yunus (alayhis-salam) when he was in the belly of the whale, as your anchor. Memorise and regularly recite it during your moments of overwhelm and difficulty.

3. Turn to your Creator who wants you always to remember this dunya is deceptive and fleeting and tell Him: My Lord, do not make this worldly life my greatest concern. I know I am here only to worship You. Never let me forget that. Never let this dunya be the goal of my desires. Place this dunya in my hands but never in my heart.

A Question for Your Heart

When your time here comes to an end, what will your soul carry with it: regret for what was wasted or relief for what was preserved?

Fall in Love with The Author

Ar-Raheem – The Especially Merciful – is a Lord who you can return to at any time. Only by His Special Mercy, can His believing servants make up for lost time and missed moments.

PART 2:

Drawing Near

يَـٰٓأَيُّهَا ٱلَّذِينَ ءَامَنُوا۟ ٱتَّقُوا۟ ٱللَّهَ وَٱبْتَغُوٓا۟ إِلَيْهِ ٱلْوَسِيلَةَ وَجَـٰهِدُوا۟ فِى سَبِيلِهِۦ لَعَلَّكُمْ تُفْلِحُونَ ٣٥

Yā ayyuhalladhīna āmanū ittaqū Allāha wa ibtaghū ilayhi al-wasīlah wa jāhidū fī sabīlihī la'allakum tuf'lihūn

'O believers! Be mindful of Allah and seek what brings you closer to Him and struggle in His Way, so you may be successful.'

Surah Al-Maidah 5:35

WEEK 8:

Making Him Your First Priority

Verse(s) of the Week
Your Rabb's Words for Your Soul

قُلْ يَٰعِبَادِىَ ٱلَّذِينَ أَسْرَفُواْ عَلَىٰٓ أَنفُسِهِمْ لَا تَقْنَطُواْ مِن رَّحْمَةِ ٱللَّهِ ۚ إِنَّ ٱللَّهَ يَغْفِرُ ٱلذُّنُوبَ
جَمِيعًا ۚ إِنَّهُۥ هُوَ ٱلْغَفُورُ ٱلرَّحِيمُ ٥٣

*Qul yā 'ibādiya alladhīna asrafū 'alā anfusihim lā taqnṭū min
raḥmati Allāh; inna Allāha yaghfiru adh-dhunūba jamī'an;
innahu huwa al-ghafūru ar-raḥīm*

*'Say, 'O Prophet, that Allah says, ` "O My servants who have
exceeded the limits against their souls! Do not lose hope in
Allah's Mercy, for Allah certainly forgives all sins. He is indeed
the All-Forgiving, Most Merciful." '*

Surah Az-Zumar 39:53

47

We all need realignment at different points in our lives. Sometimes, we're walking a straight path – focused, intentional, heading in the right direction. And then, almost without noticing, we veer off course. We look up one day and wonder how we ended up so far from where we're meant to be.

That's happened to me more times than I can count. And each time, it is only by His Mercy that I found my way back. Sometimes it's been through an external event – but often, it began with a quiet internal nudge, a subtle feeling that something's just not right.

Allah draws us back in the most beautiful ways – through Jumu'ah (Friday prayers), an unexpected invitation to the pilgrimages of Umrah or Hajj, the beautiful months of Ramadan and Dhul Hijjah. And sometimes, through something deeply personal and tailored to exactly what your soul needs. Your Rabb does this out of pure love, because He wants you to succeed in the next life. He gently redirects you to where you need to be, reorienting your focus so that your soul's journey to Him becomes your highest priority.

Let me introduce you to Nadia, a friend of mine, whose story never ceases to amaze me. Her story is an invitation to pause, to reflect honestly and to ask: *What is truly taking priority in my life?*

Nadia's Story Begins

I was always connected to the Qur'an through my mum. I have memories of her always reciting the Qur'an. I would come home from school or work and she would be reciting. I know she had a wird (regular portion of recitation) but I don't know how many pages it consisted of. All I know is whenever she was free, she was reading. She wanted me to have that connection too, but I never did because I had so many negative stereotypes related to Islam. I did maintain one connection with the Qur'an to please her. Every

Thursday (as per her non-sunnah-related habit), I would read certain chapters like Surahs Yaseen and Al-Waqiah.

I kept that up all the way through my university degree and my master's – I felt I had to. So long as I did this, I thought I hadn't lost my way.

Except, I had. My priorities were completely off. My focus was my career – I wanted to be successful in what I was doing. More than that, I wanted to be someone different and unique. I couldn't relate to anything that was happening back home. To me, this was my mission: to show the world that Muslims can be excellent in any field and give people a good impression about Islam and Muslims. What I didn't realise was I was really compromising Islam in so many ways. I was oblivious to this fact. I thought I was doing okay – praying five times a day, knowing what's right and wrong and maintaining basic connection to my deen (religion). The reality was I was increasing in everything else but not in my deen. Everything else was on an upwards trajectory, except my practice of Islam.

Every Friday when I read verses 103–104 in Surah Al-Kahf, I would panic. Allah ﷻ says:

قُلْ هَلْ نُنَبِّئُكُم بِٱلْأَخْسَرِينَ أَعْمَلًا ١٠٣ ٱلَّذِينَ ضَلَّ سَعْيُهُمْ فِى ٱلْحَيَوٰةِ ٱلدُّنْيَا وَهُمْ يَحْسَبُونَ أَنَّهُمْ يُحْسِنُونَ صُنْعًا ١٠٤

Qul hal nunabbi'ukum bil-akhʾsarīna aʿmālan Alladhīna ḍalla saʿyuhum fī al-ḥayāti ad-dunyā wahum yaḥsabūna annahum yuḥsinūna ṣunʿā

Say, ˊO Prophet,ˋ 'Shall we inform you of who will be the biggest losers of deeds? They are those whose efforts are in vain in this worldly life, while they think they are doing good!'

This ayah (verse) scared me and it still does. I only found relief when I read the following ayah 105, where Allah specifically mentions who these people are:

49

أُوْلَٰٓئِكَ ٱلَّذِينَ كَفَرُوا۟ بِـَٔايَٰتِ رَبِّهِمْ وَلِقَآئِهِۦ فَحَبِطَتْ أَعْمَٰلُهُمْ فَلَا نُقِيمُ لَهُمْ يَوْمَ ٱلْقِيَٰمَةِ وَزْنًا ١٠٥

Ulā'ika alladhīna kafarū bi-āyāti rabbihim wa liqā'ihi fa ḥabiṭ
at a'mālahum fa-lā nuqīmu lahum yawma al-qiyāmati waznan

They are those who denied the signs of their Lord and the
meeting with Him, so their deeds have become worthless,
and We will not assign them any weight on the Day of
Resurrection.

I can breathe again, alhamdulillah, *I thought. Because
despite all this, I was still a believer.*

*Every Thursday, despite how far I was from Allah, I would
read those surahs and after reading Surah Waqiah, I would
ask Allah to make me of the muqarabeen (those closest to
Allah) and the saabiqoon (the forerunners in doing good
deeds), although I was nowhere near such states. I knew I
wasn't worthy of my du'a being answered but I kept making
that du'a. AstaghfiruAllah (may Allah forgive me).*

Pause and Reflect

Never underestimate the power of du'a. Even if it is made in a regret-
ful or sinful state, it embodies belief. At the moment it is made, the
servant of Allah declares their faith that Allah exists and is listening,
and that He alone can help.

We will find out in a later chapter how this would impact Nadia's
future life.

In this week's chapter, I will not ask you to deprioritise what is
important to you. Rather, consider how you can bring your priorities
in line with your soul's journey to Allah.

Begin to navigate the journey with your priorities through the
Qur'an. To relieve the stress that comes with trying to establish yourself in your career and your life, go to Allah's Book and ground

yourself. For your dilemmas and the decisions you need to make, turn to the Qur'an to find guidance. To truly acknowledge the blessings you experience from that which you have prioritised, learn of the level of gratitude Allah describes in His Book.

In this way, your priorities will align with the priority of your soul – one that knows it came from Him and is returning to Him.

Live with His Words . . .

Here are three steps to live with this week's verse(s):

1. This week's verse reminds you that despite how you perceive yourself, Allah is telling you He is not done with you. Push away shame, distance and feelings of unworthiness and come to your Lord just as you are, telling Him: Rabbi, I want to come back to You.

2. Draw a table in your journal with two columns: 'My Priorities' and 'Making Them the Real Priority'. Add your current priorities to the first column and write down one action you can take to bring them in alignment with your desire to come close to Allah and His Book. Look over that list once a week and aim to take daily action.

3. Turn to the One who looks upon you and interacts with you with priority and tell Him: O Allah, turn to me with an acceptance of my repentance that purifies my heart, washes away my sins and raises me beautifully towards You.

A Question for Your Heart

What part of you still believes you're too broken to be embraced by the One who created you from nothing? What would your life look like if returning to Him became your ultimate priority?

Fall in Love with The Author

Al-Awwal – The First – is a Lord who never tires of inviting you to make Him first in your heart again – before your desires, your distractions, your plans. His Forgiveness isn't just a fresh start – it's a reordering of what truly matters: Him becoming your starting point, your centre and your ultimate destination.

WEEK 9:

Excuses

Verse(s) of the Week
Your Rabb's Words for Your Soul

وَقَالَ ٱلشَّيْطَٰنُ لَمَّا قُضِىَ ٱلْأَمْرُ إِنَّ ٱللَّهَ وَعَدَكُمْ وَعْدَ ٱلْحَقِّ وَوَعَدتُّكُمْ فَأَخْلَفْتُكُمْ ۖ وَمَا كَانَ لِىَ عَلَيْكُم مِّن سُلْطَٰنٍ إِلَّا أَن دَعَوْتُكُمْ فَٱسْتَجَبْتُمْ لِى ۖ فَلَا تَلُومُونِى وَلُومُوٓا۟ أَنفُسَكُم ۖ مَّآ أَنَا۠ بِمُصْرِخِكُمْ وَمَآ أَنتُم بِمُصْرِخِىَّ ۖ إِنِّى كَفَرْتُ بِمَآ أَشْرَكْتُمُونِ مِن قَبْلُ ۗ إِنَّ ٱلظَّٰلِمِينَ لَهُمْ عَذَابٌ أَلِيمٌ ٢٢

*Wa qāla ash-shayṭānu lammā quḍiya al-amru inna Allāha
wa'adakum wa'da al-ḥaqqi wa wa'adtukum fa akhlaftukum
wa mā kāna lī 'alaykum min sulṭānin illā an da'awtukum fa
istajabtum lī, fa lā talūnī walū anfusakum, mā anā bi muṣriḥi-
kum wa mā antum bi muṣriḥiyya, innī kafartu bimā ashraktum
min qabl, inna al-ẓālimīna lahum 'adhābun alīm*

*'And shaytaan will say ˈto his followers˗ after the judgment
has been passed, "Indeed, Allah has made you a true promise. I too made you a promise, but I failed you. I did not have
any authority over you. I only called you, and you responded
to me. So do not blame me; blame yourselves. I cannot save
you, nor can you save me. Indeed, I denounce your previous*

association of me with Allah in loyalty. Surely the wrongdoers
will suffer a painful punishment."'

Surah Ibrahim 14:22

For the longest time, I've told myself I have the worst memory. It became the excuse I clung to for not memorising much Qur'an since embracing Islam. Of course, I'd never accept such a limiting belief from my own children on their own journeys with memorisation. But for me, it became a quiet crutch – a reason to stick mainly to recitation.

Excuses and beliefs can become so deeply rooted that they feel like permanent truths, etched into our hearts. That is, until we decide to face them head-on and trace them back to their origin.

Aminah, an English revert of 15 years, shared her own story about confronting the excuses that held her back, and how everything changed once she did.

Aminah's Story

I am so embarrassed to admit that I have only periodi-cally picked up the Qur'an in my journey since embracing Islam. The Qur'an led me to Islam but thereafter, I was not consistent.

I have always known how super-important engaging regularly with the Qur'an is for my relationship with Allah. Every Ramadan, I've read the Qur'an's translation cover to cover. And every time, I get so much benefit from it. I learn something new about myself and am able to draw parallels between experiences and the verses I have read. There is this tremendous growth I experience through that one month of active reading. I can read one verse and it feels like I have never read it before, and my entire perspective changes.

But what follows post-Ramadan has always been the same. I make intentions that I'm going to stick with it this time. I'm going to open the Qur'an regularly every day. I'm going to definitely read at least one verse per day. Or at least one per week. It's fascinating because the benefit is so apparent and the feeling is so positive; yet it starts to feel like such a chore. And pretty soon, what I experienced in Ramadan becomes a distant memory and the Qur'an becomes a book on the shelf or a phone app I've not opened in weeks.

I believe my resistance to the Book of Allah comes from the fact that I have always wanted to learn Arabic. But I am not a person who picks up languages easily at all – so I've used this as an excuse. Yes, I definitely want to learn Arabic so that I can understand the Qur'an in its best form – in Allah's Original Words – but it would be so hard for me. As a result, for years and years I haven't even tried. The result is a feeling of shame that I'm not worthy of the Qur'an yet.

It's interesting how we self-impose these conditions, criteria and feelings of worthiness. Actually, it's not just interesting, it's insane, because Allah revealed the Qur'an for everyone. It's not just for the most pious. Not even just for the believers. The Qur'an was revealed for the disbelievers to find faith.

And that's the trick of shaytaan, where he will try to use any tools he can find to keep you away from the word of Allah. Because without a relationship with it, you will always feel disconnected – right where he wants you to be.

Then I met a revert sister from the Philippines and heard that she was in a difficult financial situation. I and some sisters decided to help her and her children with food and funds for her basic needs. She was a proud woman and refused to be a charity case. She wanted to work. She was fluent in Arabic, and so the idea came to hire her as a teacher. She gets paid *and I get to learn how to read and recite the Qur'an – a win-win situation.*

That's how my lessons started. Oh my, was it difficult at first. It was months before I really felt I was getting somewhere. But gradually, I felt more confident. I could take one step at a time and a willingness to approach the Qur'an grew within me. Allah knew that the gentle encouragement of my teacher gave me the confidence I needed to continue. I am still on a journey of building a relationship with the Qur'an, but I now know possibilities are endless. When Allah presents you with an opportunity, you need to seize it.

Pause and Reflect

Where are you currently on your journey with the Qur'an? What is the next milestone for your journey? What excuses have you been leaning on, allowing shaytaan to keep you where you are, stagnant, unable to progress and move forward?

Dear reader, remember, one of shaytaan's most subtle whispers is making you think that your negative thoughts are true and your excuses are valid.

But there's even more to this week's verse. Allah is telling you that you are responsible for your own choices. You can either accept your thoughts and excuses as truth or you can challenge them. You must challenge them! Shaytaan will do all he can to persuade you to choose other than Allah, and as soon as you make that choice, he will drop you and walk away smiling – mission accomplished – never accepting any blame for the consequences.

In the akhirah, you will wish you could return to the dunya and do better, strive harder and overcome the thoughts and excuses that held you back. Those excuses won't hold any weight on the Day of Judgment.

This is real. This is truth. This is haqq (absolute truth). This is your battle.

Your journey with the Qur'an has to come with a battle plan against your limiting thoughts and against shaytaan. Remember shaytaan is actually limited. He calls you, but it is you without the shield of Qur'an who chooses to respond and follow.

Live with His Words . . .

Here are three steps to live with this week's verse(s):

1. Keep a journal or voice memo where you record moments you delay doing good deeds, especially living with the Qur'an. Note what you told yourself in those moments. Was it 'I'm too tired' or 'I'll do it later' or 'It won't make a difference'? Shaytaan's invitations often come masked as harmless thoughts. Naming them reveals their roots and weakens their power.

2. Practise the One Breath Rule: when you remember an obligation or good deed, especially a sudden call to read the Qur'an, do it within one breath. 'I need to pray' – get up right away. 'I want to sit with the Qur'an' – immediately open the mushaf or app on your phone. This disrupts the excuse-making process before it begins. Remember, shaytaan works in delay.

3. Turn to the One who wants you to live as an empowered believer and tell Him: Al-Hadi – guide my heart to see truth as truth and falsehood as falsehood. Help me reject the whispers of shaytaan and take responsibility for what I do.

A Question for Your Heart

How many times have you called something 'impossible' when in truth it was simply inconvenient to your nafs (lower self)?

Fall in Love with The Author

Al-Haqq is a Lord who is The Truth and calls you to the truth. He wants you to stop hiding behind excuses and face yourself with honesty, remembering that it was He, Al-Haqq, The Absolute Truth, who was always guiding you back to what truly matters.

WEEK 10:

The Possessor of Mercy

Verse(s) of the Week
Your Rabb's Words for Your Soul

وَرَبُّكَ ٱلْغَفُورُ ذُو ٱلرَّحْمَةِ ٥٨

Wa rabbuka al-ghafūru dhu ar-raḥmah

'Your Lord is the All-Forgiving, the Possessor of Mercy.'

Surah Al-Kahf 18:58

In both of my previous books, something remarkable happened as I wrote the first draft – real-time incidents that felt divinely ordained by Allah. I remember it clearly with *Ramadan Reflections*: I was sitting in a coffee shop, completely stuck while trying to write a chapter. Then an idea came to me, and that very writer's block became one of my favourite chapters in the book, on the topic of acceptance. It happened again with *The Power of Du'a*, when I made du'a for Allah to send me people with amazing du'a stories. Not long after that I met Marcia, and her story ended up closing the book, in my opinion, perfectly.

59

So, I have to admit, I secretly wondered whether something similar would happen with this book.

And lo and behold, just after Eid in 2025, I found myself writing in East London Mosque. The prayer hall, packed during Ramadan, was now quiet – only a few sisters scattered around, reciting the Qur'an. One sister in particular caught my attention. She had her back to me; her voice was soft but audible, steadily reciting for over three hours with no break! Every so often, I'd glance over at her.

As she began to walk away upon finishing, I felt a sudden urge to talk to her. I hurried to catch up and called out, 'Sister, sister!'

She turned around.

'I'm writing a book about the Qur'an,' I said, slightly out of breath. 'And I've been watching you, mashaAllah. Don't worry, I'm not a weirdo,' I added quickly, smiling. 'I just – I wanted to know what your story is, if you wouldn't mind sharing it.'

And she did share.

Her story gently reminds your heart that Allah 'azza wa jal is always taking care of it, even in ways you don't yet see, and guiding you to where you need to be.

Umaymah's Story

I grew up in Lagos, Nigeria, and my dad often travelled on business. He used to bring us presents, and one time he got me and my brother a reading pen – a device that reads the Qur'an aloud when you place it on a verse.

It fascinated me. I spent so much time playing with it and listening that before I knew it, I had memorised Juz Amma — just from using the reading pen. Looking back, I feel like that pen was the sabab (cause) of my love for the Qur'an.

My parents loved that we could read the Qur'an, but they weren't pushing for hidfh (full memorisation) because, for them, Western education was the main priority.

Then, I started going to a tuition class where I met some-one who'd memorised the whole Qur'an. I'd never seen someone like that before. And the sons of a family friend were also close to completing their hifdh. Seeing that made me realise that hifdh was actually possible.

I joined my uncle's madrasah, and that was a turning point for me. It really motivated me and made me want to learn more about my religion. By then, I had already memorised about six to seven ajzaa (parts) of the Qur'an.

After primary school, I was homeschooled. It made me a bit reserved and feel disconnected from my environment, but at the same time, it gave me a really fast-paced second-ary school education. My private teacher instilled in me the importance of excelling in Western education without losing my religion and morals.

So when I finally got to university in Nigeria, I had a strong background in both my religion and my academics. I thought everything there would go well, but instead I found life very difficult. I began to struggle, and then to feel quite depressed. I was in an environment completely different from what I was used to. Seeing opposite genders casually hug or shake hands, women dressed in ways I wasn't familiar with – it was all overwhelming. My academic work also took up all my time. I didn't have the same balance between Islamic stud-ies and my course work anymore, and that imbalance really affected me. The university was a non-religious space, and I struggled to feel I belonged.

I started to understand something about myself: the Qur'an was what made me feel close to Allah. It was my anchor. An environment that didn't allow me to read or memorise it left me feeling lost. That was the cause of my depression.

So I had to find a way to hold on to my faith. Every weekend, I returned to my hometown to go to my uncle's madrasah. It became my detox, my way of realigning my mind and hearing about Allah. Then on weekdays, I would go to the university's masjid early in the morning for my hifdh. And during term breaks, I attended intensive hifdh classes.

By the time I left Nigeria, I had memorised 16 ajzaa of the Qur'an.

My brother had moved to the UK, and he encouraged me to come over to complete my studies, hoping that I would have more time to focus on both my academics and my hifdh. But when I got here, things didn't go as planned.

I've had to start working to pay my university fees. This takes a toll on my hifdh schedule, and destabilises me. I've started to feel that same emptiness I felt before, but this time I know why. It's disconnection from the Qur'an which always affects my heart.

I'd promised myself that I would complete my hifdh before my 19th birthday. But here I am now, almost 20 in a few days, and I still haven't finished.

That's why I've committed to going to the masjid daily to do my hifdh. No matter what, I have to be consistent. I pray that Allah grants me the strength to complete it soon.

Pause and Reflect

Dearest reader, when you are convinced that your heart is precious to your Lord, when you internalise that fact, the eyes of your heart will open and see the constant ways in which He is looking after you and drawing you near. You'll find more and more evidence. And the more evidence you find, the stronger your belief becomes that He, in fact, loves and cares for you. And the more strongly that belief embeds itself, the more you will perceive qadr – your decree – through the lens of your Lord caring for you, supporting you, protecting you and showering you with His Love.

And why should your Lord look after your heart in this way? Well, the answer lies in a verse that most Muslims read every Friday and it is one that always jumps out at me whenever I read Surah Al-Kahf. It is:

وَرَبُّكَ ٱلْغَفُورُ ذُو ٱلرَّحْمَةِ ٥٨

Wa rabbuka al-ghafuru dhu ar-rahmah

Your Lord is the All-Forgiving, the Possessor of Mercy.

Surah Al-Kahf 18:58

As is always the case, the translation never does justice to the eloquence found within the Arabic language.

From the very beginning of this short verse alone, Allah 'azza wa jal reminds you that He is Rabbuka – Your Lord. He wants you to know that this relationship between you and Him is personal. It's special. Allah tells you that 'Your Lord is The All-Forgiving, The Possessor of Mercy.' That short word 'Dhu' translates to 'possessor' or 'owner'. But in Arabic, it also denotes One Who is Constant.

There is something in the way He has ordered His Attributes that will melt your heart. First, He takes your mistakes and wipes them away. And then showers you with His Mercy to support you to recover from all the ways in which you are feeling guilty and ashamed for disappointing Him. Not only is He removing the stains of your heart, He is tenderly supporting you because you made the choice to turn back to Him 'azza wa jal.

Allah then follows that up with the reminder that He is The Possessor of Mercy.

Allah looks after your heart because He has to. He has made it incumbent on Himself to be the Perpetual Owner of Mercy – not just here and there, in various moments, but constantly. The use of Dhu'l Rahma (The Possessor of Mercy) is Him reminding you that mercy isn't something He just does. Mercy is something He owns, controls and showers upon you perfectly.

Umaymah's story did not involve disappointing Allah. But she felt she'd lost her way and felt far from Him. She chose to turn back towards Him, to reset her destination. And what did He do? He showed her that He is Dhu'l Rahma and enveloped her in His Mercy with no greater medicine for her sadness than her relationship with Him through His Words. This is one of the many ways that He ﷾ looks after the heart.

He takes what is empty and fills it. He takes what is torn and fixes it. He takes what is weighing it down and lightens it. He takes you and gives you all that He knows you need to reach the place you need to be – close to Him.

Live with His Words . . .

Here are three steps to live with this week's verse(s):

1. The Messenger of Allah ﷺ said,

   The merciful will be shown mercy by the Most Merciful. Be merciful to those on the earth, and the One in the heavens will have mercy upon you.

   Sunan Tirmidhi

   To live with the awareness that Allah is Dhu'l Rahma invites you to be a vessel of mercy. This week take hold of all opportunities to show mercy to other people. Whisper to your Lord: For the ways I am merciful to others, Rabbi, be Merciful towards me.

2. Turn to the Qur'an right now and continue from your wird or go to your favourite surah and read each verse, absorbing the many ways Allah is The Possessor of Mercy. You may wish to journal your thoughts.

3. Turn to the One who has bound Himself by Mercy and tell Him: O Possessor of Mercy that encompasses all things,

have mercy on me; a mercy that mends what is broken within me, purifies my heart, draws me closer to You and makes me of those who truly attain Your Love and Your Pleasure.

A Question for Your Heart

If Allah, the Possessor of Infinite Mercy, were to open the gates of His Nearness to you this very moment, what would He find occupying the space in your heart that was meant only for Him? What do you now need to do about that?

Fall in Love with The Author

Ar-Raheem is a Lord who is Especially Merciful. In a world quick to condemn and slow to forgive, Allah is One whose mercy is constant and all-encompassing. He welcomes your return not because you are flawless, but because you are worthy of His Mercy as His honoured servant, created with purpose and loved with infinite compassion.

WEEK 11:

Humility

Verse(s) of the Week
Your Rabb's Words for Your Soul

وَلَا تَمْشِ فِى ٱلْأَرْضِ مَرَحًا ۖ إِنَّكَ لَن تَخْرِقَ ٱلْأَرْضَ وَلَن تَبْلُغَ ٱلْجِبَالَ طُولًا ٣٧

*Wa lā tamshi fī al-arḍi maraḥ; innaka lan takhriqa al-arḍa wa
lan tablugh al-jibāla ṭūlan*

*'And do not walk on the earth arrogantly. Surely you can neither
crack the earth nor stretch to the height of the mountains.'*

Surah Al-Isra 17:37

We all chase success in one way or another. But what is *true* success? Is it in what we accomplish or how the world responds to us? Or is it something much deeper? Real success, the kind that endures, is the success of the soul. Anything related to the soul cannot be tied to this world. True success lies in something far beyond recognition or applause. Only the soul can attain it. It is our best and truest destination.

If you've read either of my first two books, you'll know that I once told Allah, with complete conviction, that I believe in His Ability to make what feels impossible possible. I told Him that if something was truly good for me, He would bring it into my life in the most remarkable of ways.

So when Allah 'azza wa jal brought the largest publisher in the world to my door, I was stunned – but at the same time, I wasn't. Because when Allah wills a thing, all He has to say is 'Be', and it is.

Shortly after my first book was printed, I held it in my hands for the first time. It was a surreal moment. I turned to Allah and whispered: 'This is from You. Accept this effort of mine. But O Allah, do not place this achievement in my heart – keep it only in my hands.' Because I knew that people would congratulate me and might praise me for my achievement, something every human heart welcomes. But at the same time, I knew that my first book existed because Allah answered my du'a. It was by His Permission. Only He had made it possible.

Let's return now to Ahmed's story. He faced many setbacks as he was striving to build himself up as a successful young man. But it was later, when Allah granted him real success, that he came to realise that the greatest lessons sometimes come wrapped in the hardest moments. And sometimes, those moments are the beginning of a different kind of success altogether, and the first steps on a journey to a very different destination.

Ahmed's Story Continues

In general, I consider myself a successful person in life. But sometimes you get carried away, thinking your success is because of your strength and intelligence. As if these qualities got you to where you are.

There is a verse that puts me in my place and has completely changed my perception towards success. It is verse 78 of Surah Qasas, where Allah ﷻ says:

قَالَ إِنَّمَا أُوتِيتُهُ عَلَىٰ عِلْمٍ عِندِيٓ ۚ أَوَلَمْ يَعْلَمْ أَنَّ ٱللَّهَ قَدْ أَهْلَكَ مِن قَبْلِهِ مِنَ ٱلْقُرُونِ مَنْ هُوَ أَشَدُّ مِنْهُ قُوَّةً وَأَكْثَرُ جَمْعًا ۚ وَلَا يُسْـَٔلُ عَن ذُنُوبِهِمُ ٱلْمُجْرِمُونَ ٧٨

Qāla innamā ūtītu 'alā 'ilmin 'indī, awalam ya'lam annallāha qad ahlaka min qablīhi mina al-qurūni man huwa ashaddu minhu quwwatan wa aktharu jam'an, wa lā yus'alu 'an dhunūbihim al-mujrimūn

He replied, 'I have been granted all this because of some knowledge I have.' Did he not know that Allah had already destroyed some from the generations before him who were far superior to him in power and greater in accumulating ˈwealthˈ? There will be no need for the wicked to be asked about their sins.

This verse relates to a man in the time of Musa (alayhis-salam) called Qaroon. He bragged about his success and wealth. When people told him, take it easy, be careful with what you're doing, be grateful and thank Allah for what you have, Qaroon's reply was: 'I am successful because of my own knowledge. I'm successful, rich and wealthy because of my intelligence.'

The consequence was severe. Allah punished him for that arrogance. This verse is a clear example of the arrogance many people have.

This verse was a turning point for me in my mindset. I changed from thinking everything I had was from myself to knowing that everything I have is only by Allah's Permission. I became much more humble and grateful to Allah for everything I have. Even if I see that my intelligence has led to success, it is Allah who gave me my brain. It is Allah who put me in situations where I could learn, revise, take exams, pass those exams and develop in my career.

Alhamdulillah, I went from too much ego and self-confidence to humility in front of Allah. Be humble. It is all from Allah.

Pause and Reflect

When Ahmed shared this part of his story with me, I could not help but think, *Ya Allah, look at us. We're all the same.* We are insaan (human beings), and that word comes from the root word ن-س-ي, noon-seen-yaa, which means 'to forget'.

What a befitting word for us. We forget Allah, forget our purpose, forget where we have come from and forget how we were once so fragile and in need of Him. Ya Allah – forgive us.

Ahmed's story reminded me how we often forget where we once were – without, lonely, in pain, ill, broken, lost, alone, struggling. And how Allah carried us through all of it.

Arrogance is when we consider ourselves better than others or look down upon others. But arrogance can also be found in subtle things that go unnoticed to a soul that is not connected to Allah – such as attributing blessings to our efforts alone, instead of recognising they were only by His Permission, His Generosity. This can become one of the greatest obstacles on the journey towards Him 'azza wa jal.

Using the imagery of nature, your Lord tells you in this verse: 'Surely you can neither crack (open) the earth' – because you don't have the strength. 'You will never reach the mountains' – because you don't have the stature. So why act like you are more than what you were created to be? In truth, you are a fragile creation.

I want to end this section of this week's chapter with a reminder that Allah's Mercy towards you does not just manifest through overt love, care and compassion. Allah cares for your heart by developing you at your very core, removing anything that should not take residence there and replacing it with that which must become rooted within. When you embark upon a journey towards Allah through engagement with His Book, expect lessons that don't always taste sweet, but whose medicine will cure the illnesses of your soul – permitting you to draw near to Him.

Live with His Words . . .

Here are three steps to live with this week's verse(s):

1. Sometimes deeply rooted arrogance is difficult to detect. So start by walking and speaking with grace, not in a way that seeks to assert superiority. Notice how you enter a room, how you speak to someone you disagree with or how you behave when praised. Let gentleness reflect humility.

2. When you reach a goal, succeed in something or are complimented, remind yourself it is only by Allah's Permission. Attribute anything you own, have achieved or enjoy to Allah. The best way to do that is to find ways of using these things in the way of service to others that no one sees: cleaning a masjid far from where you live, and helping others quietly, seeking no recognition.

3. Turn to the One whom you are indebted to and tell Him: My Lord, do not place pride in my heart or arrogance in my steps. Plant within me a humility that pleases You and a character that brings me closer to You.

A Question for Your Heart

If true greatness belongs only to Al-Mutakabbir, the Supremely Great, then what illusion of greatness might you still be clinging to – and what might your heart become if you let it break in humility before Him?

Fall in Love with The Author

Al-Khabeer is a Lord who alone is worthy of exaltation. He wants your heart to recognise that He is greater than everything and that you are honoured simply by being His Servant.

PART 3:

When Faith Is Tested

لَا يُكَلِّفُ ٱللَّهُ نَفْسًا إِلَّا وُسْعَهَآ

Lā yukallifu Allāhu nafsan illā wus'ahā

'Allah does not burden a soul beyond what it can bear.'

Surah Al-Baqarah 2:286

WEEK 12:

Injustice

Verse(s) of the Week
Your Rabb's Words for Your Soul

يَـٰٓأَيُّهَا ٱلَّذِينَ ءَامَنُوا كُونُوا قَوَّٰمِينَ بِٱلۡقِسۡطِ شُهَدَآءَ لِلَّهِ وَلَوۡ عَلَىٰٓ أَنفُسِكُمۡ أَوِ ٱلۡوَٰلِدَيۡنِ وَٱلۡأَقۡرَبِينَ ۚ إِن يَكُنۡ غَنِيًّا أَوۡ فَقِيرًا فَٱللَّهُ أَوۡلَىٰ بِهِمَا ۖ فَلَا تَتَّبِعُوا ٱلۡهَوَىٰٓ أَن تَعۡدِلُوا ۚ وَإِن تَلۡوُۥٓا أَوۡ تُعۡرِضُوا فَإِنَّ ٱللَّهَ كَانَ بِمَا تَعۡمَلُونَ خَبِيرًا ١٣٥

*Yā ayyuhalladhīna āmanū kūnū qawwāmīna bil-qisṭi
shuhadā'a lillāhi walaw 'alā anfusikum awi al-wālidayni wal-
aqrabīn, in yakun ghanīyan aw faqīran fa-llāhu awlā bihimā,
falā tattabi'ū al-hawā an ta'dilū, wa in talwū aw tu'riḍū fa-inna
Allāha kāna bimā ta'malūna khabīran*

*'O believers! Stand firm for justice as witnesses for Allah even
if it is against yourselves, your parents, or close relatives. Be
they rich or poor, Allah is best to ensure their interests. So
do not let your desires cause you to deviate 'from justice'. If
you distort the testimony or refuse to give it, then 'know that'
Allah is certainly All-Aware of what you do.'*

Surah An-Nisa 4:135

The Qur'an is the best guide. There is always a verse from Allah waiting just for you. A verse that speaks to your exact test, your specific moment, your hidden need. But it won't always appear immediately. You have to seek it. Sit with the Qur'an. Persist. And when you find it, you will know: it was always meant for you.

Babar Ahmad learned this truth through the most severe of tests. I came to know about his story through his sisters, who lived in my local area in South London. Born and raised in London by Pakistani parents, in 1992, at the age of 18, he travelled to the war in Bosnia as an aid worker. The persecution and genocide he witnessed there compelled him to join the Bosnian Army in the defence of their people. After the war, he returned to his university studies in London and set up a website paying tribute to those lost in that conflict. His website went on to cover news from Chechen forces fighting Russian troops during Russia's invasion of Chechnya in the 1990s. He shut down this website in 2002 but, one year later, Babar was arrested at his London home by UK police, who subjected him to a brutal ordeal of physical, verbal, religious and sexual abuse. He was then released without charge after the Crown Prosecution Service declared that there was no evidence that he had broken any UK law.

Before his story begins, I must tell you that it starts in a place of deep trauma, so I am sharing a trigger warning.

Babar's Story Begins

In 2003, I had been married for two and a half years. We had bought a new place and were doing it up. Life was pretty much routine – going to work and coming back home.

Then suddenly, my house was raided by the police. For 40 minutes, I was subjected to an ordeal of physical, verbal, religious and sexual abuse. One police officer put me in a chokehold, then he let go. During the second chokehold,

I thought I was going to die and I started to try to say my shahadah (declaration of faith). I was completely powerless. They tortured me, twisting the cuffs on my arms until I was screaming like an animal.

I got to the police station, and I was bleeding from my ears and there was blood in my urine. That first day, I couldn't really feel much pain – it must have been the adrenaline. But later on that night, I was in extreme pain and my head felt like it was broken, like a flask when it breaks. It's like I could feel the internal bleeding. My wrists were on fire. I couldn't walk because they had stamped on my feet. I would limp to the sink, at the far end of the corridor to make wudu (ablution).

While I was in that state, I asked for a Qur'an and they came and gave me one. I was trying to find comfort in various surahs. There was something I was looking for, but I didn't find it. But then I finally found it in verse 27 in Surah Muhammad that reminded me that Allah saw my horrific ordeal and I would achieve justice, if not in this life, then most certainly in the next.

فَكَيْفَ إِذَا تَوَفَّتْهُمُ ٱلْمَلَـٰٓئِكَةُ يَضْرِبُونَ وُجُوهَهُمْ وَأَدْبَـٰرَهُمْ ٢٧

Fakayfa idhā tawaffathumu al-malā'ikatu yaḍribūna
wujūhahum wa adbarahum

Then how ˹horrible˺ will it be when the angels take their
souls, beating their faces and backs!

I'm able to talk about my ordeal now as I've had extensive therapy to process it. I was completely helpless and defence-less. But Allah was comforting me and telling me: Wait, there will be a day they will face what they have done, when full retribution will be meted out.

I began to recite that surah on a loop in that police station cell until I was released a few days later.

Little did I know this was just a taster of how the Qur'an would support me, of how I needed to live with it, as a preparation of what was to come. I was out of custody for the next eight months. I tried to rebuild my life. Then I was rearrested. This time, although I didn't know this at the time, I was going to be in prison for 11 years.

That's when the real journey of the Qur'an began and became alive for me. It was no longer a book in which I read about something that happened to people over one thousand years ago or about some abstract future. It was for me. It was and is about me. It talks directly to me. It guides me.

Pause and Reflect

This week's verse is about justice and injustice. At the time of writing this book in 2025, I am sickened by the lack of justice towards the Palestinian people. The bias of the media headlines when they report on the 'killings' or 'loss of life' of Palestinian people, versus the reality of murder and genocide, makes me feel sick to my stomach. Their dehumanisation and the arrests, deportations and harsh sentences against protestors are the essence of injustice.

This week's verse is a call to stand on the side of justice. And that is a test of this dunya. You may often think of a trial or a test as something inflicted upon you, where you are the recipient or the one struggling. But a test of this dunya is also all that you bear witness to and whether you remain silent or speak up and do something about it.

This week's verse is powerful. It falls within a surah that talks about justice towards the most vulnerable members of society.

As much as Allah is Merciful, He is also The Most Just and so this week's verse is a wake-up call. Whenever a verse starts with Ayyuh'aladhina amanu (O you who believe), take notice, because after the address is a call to uphold a certain characteristic or do something that will set you firmly upon the siraat-ul-mustaqeem (the straight path). This is a central part of your journey with the Qur'an.

In this verse, Allah tells you that in the face of any type of injustice you must be 'qawwamin', which is the plural intensive form of qama. This means someone who is constantly standing upright, standing firm; not just once, not occasionally, but always standing upright with justice, even when the world is against you.

Your Lord knows your human condition. He knows it is hard to step away from the masses and to stand on the side of truth – to be in a minority. But part of the journey of your soul to Allah is journeying with moral courage and a stand for truth and justice that must transcend your own interests, feelings or emotions.

There are times when you will need to be on the receiving end of Allah's Mercy, Care and Love. And there are other times when you will need to gather yourself and stand tall, upright, a voice for the oppressed. This is you choosing your own soul but also saving the souls of others. And your Lord says in Surah Al-Maidah, verse 32:

$$وَمَنْ أَحْيَاهَا فَكَأَنَّمَآ أَحْيَا ٱلنَّاسَ جَمِيعًا$$

Wa-man aḥyāhā fa-ka'annamā aḥyā n-nāsa jamī'ā.

Whoever saves a life, it will be as if they saved all of humanity.

Live with His Words . . .

Here are three steps to live with this week's verse(s):

1. When you speak out – in meetings, family discussions or community spaces – do so as a witness for Allah, not to win or please people. Let justice be your intention, even when it is uncomfortable.

2. Turn away from bias during conflict and just pause. Ask yourself: Am I being fair to both sides, or swayed by emotion, loyalty or status? Stand with the truth, even if it means disagreeing with someone you love or admire.

3. Turn to the One who loves justice and tell Him: Al-Adl, The Most Just, place truth above my ego, integrity above my fear, and justice above all loyalties. Let my heart stand firm knowing I am within Your Sight even when it is hard to speak. Make me a witness for You alone – honest, courageous, and sincere in all that I say and do.

A Question for Your Heart

As you continue in your journey with the Qur'an, answer this – it requires radical honesty: In the course of my day-to-day life, when truth demands sacrifice, whose voice do I honour – my ego's, other people's or my Rabb's?

Fall in Love with The Author

Al-Adl is The Absolutely Just. He is a Lord whose justice is never flawed, never delayed, never influenced. He is the source of all fairness. He is a Lord who sees every silent truth, weighs every hidden injustice and gives every soul its due with perfect balance and mercy.

WEEK 13:

Despair

Verse(s) of the Week
Your Rabb's Words for Your Soul

كِتَـٰبٌ أَنزَلۡنَـٰهُ إِلَيۡكَ مُبَـٰرَكٌ لِّيَدَّبَّرُوٓاْ ءَايَـٰتِهِۦ وَلِيَتَذَكَّرَ أُوْلُواْ ٱلۡأَلۡبَـٰبِ ٢٩

Kitābun anzalnāhu ilayka mubārakun liyaddabbarū āyātihi wa liyatadhakkara ulū al-albāb

"This is` a blessed Book which We have revealed to you 'O Prophet` so that they may contemplate its verses, and people of reason may be mindful.'

Surah Sad 38:29

'll never forget the moment I discovered that there was a practice in Islam called tadabbur. As someone who had always been naturally reflective, it felt like a breath of fresh air – divine permission, even an invitation, to engage deeply with the Qur'an. To question. To ponder. To explore the layers of meaning. The idea that Allah – the Lord of the Worlds – invites you to reflect on His

Words and apply them personally in your life was both comforting and empowering.

Tadabbur isn't academic or detached. It's personal. It's intimate. It's opening yourself – heart and soul – to the Words of your Rabb, letting them speak to the rawest parts of your life when you are close to giving up.

Because, in the words of Babar who we met in last week's chapter and whose story will continue here, 'It's okay to despair. It's okay to lose heart.' Eight months after his first traumatic arrest, he was arrested again, but this time on an extradition request from the US government, which alleged that the information on his website about the wars in Bosnia and Chechnya amounted to 'support of terrorism'. He had no idea for how long he would be held. He began a legal case to fight his extradition.

Babar's Story Continues

I'll repeat – it's okay to despair. It's okay to break because the Prophets broke and Allah values their breaking moments by recording them in the Qur'an. Nothing in the Qur'an is there by chance or to fill space. Allah does not do that. He does not fill space. Everything that is there – every story, every verse – is there for a reason and a purpose. The Qur'an is a collection of stories and it has your personal story in there too.

Verse 214 of Surah Al-Baqarah came up several times when I randomly opened the Qur'an in my cell during that terrible time to find comfort and guidance. In my dreams, I saw this verse. Allah 'azza wa jal says:

أَمْ حَسِبْتُمْ أَن تَدْخُلُوا ٱلْجَنَّةَ وَلَمَّا يَأْتِكُم مَّثَلُ ٱلَّذِينَ خَلَوْا مِن قَبْلِكُم ۖ مَّسَّتْهُمُ ٱلْبَأْسَاءُ وَٱلضَّرَّاءُ وَزُلْزِلُوا حَتَّىٰ يَقُولَ ٱلرَّسُولُ وَٱلَّذِينَ ءَامَنُوا مَعَهُ مَتَىٰ نَصْرُ ٱللَّهِ ۗ أَلَا إِنَّ نَصْرَ ٱللَّهِ قَرِيبٌ ٢١٤

Am ḥasibtum an tadkhulū al-jannata walammā
ya'tikum mathalu alladhīna khalaw min qablikum,
massathumu al-ba'sā'u wa ḍ-ḍarrā'u wa zulzilū ḥattā yaqūla
ar-rasūlu walladhīna āmanū ma'ahu matā naṣru Allāh; alā
inna naṣra Allāhi qarībun

Do you think you will be admitted into Paradise without
being tested like those before you? They were afflicted with
suffering and adversity and were so ˈviolentlyˈ shaken that
ˈevenˈ the Messenger and the believers with him cried out,
'When will Allah's Help come?' Indeed, Allah's Help is
ˈalwaysˈ near.

*We are often told to 'be positive!' or to 'never give up!' But
what is said less often is that positivity itself can be toxic. A
particularly painful example of such toxic positivity is telling
women being subjected to domestic violence to 'just have
sabr (patience)' or that 'this is what Allah wants from you'.*

*No, He does not want that from you. Allah tells us –
reassures us – that it's okay to feel despair in moments that
are almost too hard to bear. The despair of the believer is
not doubting Allah, it's just a moment of human weakness.
We can find it in the story of Yaqub (alayhis-salam) who
despaired in deep grief over the loss of his son, Yusuf, and
cried until he lost his eyesight.*

*The believer cries out to Allah in earnest – and this is
ibadah (worship) too.*

Pause and Reflect

Dearest reader, take every verse from the Qur'an and read it as a
verse that is about you. Ask yourself: What is Allah telling me? What

does Allah want from me? What does He want to convey to me by this verse from His Book?

That's why it is said:

> If you want to talk to Allah, pray salah (ritual daily prayers).
> And if you want Allah to talk to you, then recite the
> Qur'an.

Unknown author

And when you recite the Qur'an, in the words of Al-Hasan (rahimuAllah), aspire to the ways of the companions who would

> ... approach the Qur'an as messages from their Lord so
> they used to reflect on them at night and follow them during
> the day.

Al-Nawawi, *al-Tibyan*

On this journey of yours with the Qur'an, the best guides to accompany your tadabbur journey are the volumes of tafseer written by lovers of the Qur'an. They did not know how their efforts in disseminating knowledge would provide a depth of understanding and connection for later Muslims, who would read their works about the Words of Allah in a printed book or on a screen. But their work was made possible by Allah to guide us all on our personal Qur'anic journeys.

If there is one thing you take away from this book, let it be this: whatever the season of your life, whether it is deep sadness or even despair, take the Qur'an personally. There are no barriers between you and Allah's Words.

The Qur'an is a personal letter for you. It is the address of the King of Kings to you. Reflect on this. Bring everything you have of your past, circumstances of your present and concerns for your future to your sittings with the Qur'an. Allow your Rabb's Words to penetrate your heart. Take your time with it. Do not rush. Allow your Lord's Words to change you and heal you deeply.

Live with His Words . . .

Here are three steps to live with this week's verse(s):

1. Stationery lovers, you will be happy! Go and invest in a journal for your personal reflections.

2. As you recite or read a translation of the Qur'an, pause at each verse and ask: What is Allah teaching me here? What does He want from me? Contemplate and journal.

3. Turn to the One who invites you to ponder and reflect and tell Him: My Lord, the One who is Most Wise, open the doors of understanding of Your Book for me and grant me the ability to reflect deeply on its verses. Plant wisdom in my heart and grant me the profound understanding that draws me closer to You.

A Question for Your Heart

Tadabbur of Qur'an has the potential to hold up a mirror to you and your life. What might it reveal about the circumstances of your life, the depths of your heart and your connection to the One who revealed the Qur'an?

Fall in Love with The Author

Al-Aleem – The All-Knowing – is a Lord who revealed the Qur'an as a source of wisdom. As you reflect upon it, you will find your heart illuminated by the Knowledge of your Creator, who knows the deepest secrets of your soul.

WEEK 14:

An Angry Salah

Verse(s) of the Week
Your Rabb's Words for Your Soul

لَّقَدْ صَدَقَ ٱللَّهُ رَسُولَهُ ٱلرُّءْيَا بِٱلْحَقِّ ۖ لَتَدْخُلُنَّ ٱلْمَسْجِدَ ٱلْحَرَامَ إِن شَآءَ ٱللَّهُ ءَامِنِينَ مُحَلِّقِينَ
رُءُوسَكُمْ وَمُقَصِّرِينَ لَا تَخَافُونَ ۖ فَعَلِمَ مَا لَمْ تَعْلَمُواْ فَجَعَلَ مِن دُونِ ذَٰلِكَ فَتْحًا قَرِيبًا ٢٧

Laqad ṣadaqa Allāhu rasūlahu ar-ru'yā bil-ḥaqqi
latadkhulanna al-masjida al-ḥarāma in shā'a Allāhu āmīnīna
muḥalliqīna ru'ūsakum wa muqaṣṣirīna lā takhāfūn, fa'alima
mā lam ta'lamū faja'ala min dūni dhālika fatḥan qarīban

'Indeed, Allah will fulfil His Messenger's vision in all truth:
Allah willing, you will surely enter the Sacred Mosque, in
security – ˹some with˺ heads shaved and ˹others with˺ hair
shortened – without fear. He knew what you did not know, so
He first granted you the triumph at hand.'

Surah Al-Fath 48:27

atching the film *The Message*, which documents the seerah (life of the Prophet Muhammad ﷺ), around the time I embraced Islam left a lasting mark on me. It changed the way I read the Qur'an. Scenes from the film brought certain verses to life, and my imagination led me to reflect deeply on what life might have been like for the first Muslims.

This connection became even more meaningful as I began navigating my new life as a Muslim – often in the face of disapproval from friends and family. As I mentally linked verses to scenes, a curiosity began to grow within me: I wanted to understand the historical backdrop – the unfolding events across the 23 years the Qur'an was revealed.

That growing interest deepened after I listened to Babar speaking of his experiences in prison when he turned to the Qur'an, remembering the specific circumstances of its revelation.

Babar's Story Continues

The lowest point for me while I was in prison was when I thought that my deen was in danger. I remember the day – it was 17 May 2005. That was the first-stage hearing of my extradition proceedings against the United States.

I was 100 per cent sure the judge was going to rule in my favour and that I was going to walk out of there. Why? Because that's how ridiculous my extradition case was, and he was surely going to see through it. There had been protests and much campaigning and it had been all over the news. I had been in prison by then for 10 months. I had made a lot of du'a. My family had gone on Umrah and made a lot of du'a there. I just thought with all this effort, Allah was not going to disappoint me.

When the ruling was delivered and it was against me, I couldn't believe it. I was angry at Allah. I questioned Him – why did You do this? I had made du'a! I had done so much. I was like a child upset with their parent.

That evening, as the doors to my cell were shut, I stood on my prayer mat and prayed, but it was an angry prayer, an angry salah.

By morning, at the time of Fajr prayer, I read a verse from Surah Al-Fath. I had read this verse many times before and I knew the story and the context well. Surah Al-Fath was revealed at the time when the Prophet ﷺ and his companions had been driven out of their homes and land. He ﷺ wanted to go and perform Umrah with his companions as he had seen this in a dream, but they had to turn back, unable to do it.

But Allah called that outcome a victory. In His Plan, according to His Schedule, this was something He wanted to grant later. The Prophet ﷺ was bewildered, and could not see what Allah's Purpose could be.

That's when the realisation hit me: I made tawbah (the return to Allah through repentance) to Allah. I realised Allah wasn't giving me what I so badly wanted now, because He wanted to give me a greater victory at some point in the future.

Doubting Allah's Decree was the lowest point of my ordeal. It happened at a time when I most needed Him, when I had lost everything – my liberty, career, money, marriage, being with my family, reputation. The only thing I had left was my deen. And then I almost lost that too, due to my own weakness of faith.

But just as with the Prophet ﷺ, there was wisdom in the delay and a beautiful victory was awaiting me.

Pause and Reflect

For the next eight years, Babar was held without charge in UK high-security prisons while he fought extradition. No other British citizen in modern history has been detained without charge for as long as he has. His indefinite detention without trial became a cause célèbre and was raised repeatedly in parliament and by politicians and celebrities.

During his imprisonment, Babar counselled other prisoners, helped them with their legal work and mediated between warring prison gangs.

Anyone who has read my second book, *The Power of Du'a*, will know that I am a strong believer in the precise ways Allah beautifully and perfectly answers du'a. I believe His Response is perfect – every single time. Even the responses where He says 'no'. Or when He says 'not yet, wait'.

Babar received the very opposite response of what he had hoped for. And his very human heart was shattered, disappointed and pained. But Allah 'azza wa jal turned to him with a verse he had read many times before, about how the Prophet ﷺ too yearned for an opening, a solution and an outcome. But in Allah's Infinite Wisdom, it was delayed for a greater wisdom and purpose.

I know the delays to the yearnings of your heart are heavy to bear. I know they weigh down heavily on you. I know you secretly wonder and question: When, ya Allah, when?! Rabbi, I've been trying. I really have.

Please know this: His Delays are intentional because He is the Owner of your future. He knows all that is yet to come. His Delays are to set you up for what He has prepared for you, and often it is to give you even more.

Babar was able to see that the Prophet's ﷺ pain was natural and human, which gave him permission to be human too. And Babar remembered the Prophet's ﷺ response of acceptance – a lesson in surrender and trust of Allah. And in it, Babar saw the light and beauty of Allah's Wisdom and Timing.

Ibn Al-Jawzi shares a beautiful quote on the topic of delays that made me smile. He said:

Yahya al-Bakka saw his Lord in his dream and he asked Him, 'Rabbi, I always call upon You but You do not answer my supplications.' So Allah said to him, 'O Yahya, I like to hear your voice calling upon Me.'

Sayd al-Khater

In Babar's story, as you will come to discover, Allah 'azza wa jal was smiling upon him as he found himself caught up in an internal whirlwind. Because not only did The Lord of Humankind know what was round the corner, but He was gifting him something else – a calling deep within Babar's heart that hadn't yet surfaced to du'a.

Live with His Words . . .

Here are three steps to live with this week's verse(s):

1. Train your heart to trust in Allah's Delay. Each time you feel frustrated with a delay in your life, pause and recite: Hasbi Allahu wa ni'ma al-wakeel – Allah is sufficient for me, and He is The Best Disposer of my affairs. Look back at your life at a time when Allah delayed a response to something you had asked for. What might have been the reason(s) and wisdom behind the delay? Journal your thoughts.

2. Set aside one day per week where you will add an entry to a qadr (decree) journal and write down instances of how something didn't happen when you wanted, but later, Allah granted you something better. This will help you recognise His Perfect Wisdom over time.

3. Turn to the One who interacts with your life with precise guidance and timing and tell Him: O Allah, I trust in Your Wisdom and know that Your Plan for me is always better than my own. Grant me certainty that fills my heart, patience that lights my path and openings of goodness I

never expected. Indeed, You are Al-Fattah (The Opener) and Al-Aleem (The All-Knowing).

A Question for Your Heart

If everything in your life were taken away, would your faith in Allah still remain intact? If your answer is 'no', what needs to change so you can answer, 'yes, bi'idhnillah (by His Permission)'?

Fall in Love with The Author

Al-Fattah – the Supreme Opener – is a Lord who unlocks doors you never knew existed, turning delays into divine timing, full of blessings and barakah, and your perceived setbacks into the very path to victory.

WEEK 15:

Balancing

Verse(s) of the Week
Your Rabb's Words for Your Soul

إِنَّهُمْ كَانُوا يُسَارِعُونَ فِي ٱلْخَيْرَاتِ وَيَدْعُونَنَا رَغَبًا وَرَهَبًا ۖ وَكَانُوا لَنَا خَٰشِعِينَ ٩٠

*Innahum kānū yusāri'ūna fil-khayrāti wa yad'ūnā rāghaban
wa rahaban wa kānū lanā khāshi'īn*

'Indeed, they used to race in doing good, and call upon
Us with hope and fear, totally humbling themselves before Us.'

Surah Al-Anbiya 21:90

One of my favourite Islamic quotes is by the scholar Ibn al-Qayyim Al Jawziyyah (may Allah have mercy on him). I love it so much that I have already mentioned it, back in Week 6.

The heart, in its journey to Allah ﷻ, is like that of a bird: love is its head, and fear and hope are its two wings. When

93

the head and two wings are sound, the bird flies gracefully. If the head is severed, the bird dies. If the bird loses one of its wings, it then becomes a target of every hunter or predator.

I realise I have spent my entire journey in Islam trying to be that bird – trying to find the roadmap that would lead me to my Lord – when all along, the path has been the study, contemplation and application of the Qur'an.

My Story

When I became Muslim, 26 years ago, I did so as a result of the dawah (calling people to Islam) of an Islamic group. But they gave me a strange piece of advice: to worship Allah without emotions and instead with reason, logic and rationale. Quite literally, I was advised to remove all feelings from my journey with la ilaha illAllah (there is no God worthy of worship, except Allah).

It will come as no surprise that within no time at all, I experienced a religion that felt rigid and dry. There was a misalignment between who I was as a human being and this religion that was presented to me in such a black and white manner.

Desperate to feel again, desperate to find connection with my Creator again, I gravitated towards another Islamic group whose focus was tawheed – the oneness of Allah, perfecting prayer and upholding Islamic rulings. But its black-and-white one-rule interpretations of how to observe Islam meant no grey areas, no understanding of the journey of the human being within faith and life itself. And so once again, I found myself feeling distant, burdened by religion.

The beauty of the faith I had embraced seemed to be disappearing fast!

I wanted to find a middle path, with people who practised Islam compassionately and understood that the path to reach ihsaan (the highest level of faith) was by worshipping Allah as though you see Him with all the feels: passion, love and hope. And with committed steadfastness to living life with a reverent fear, being careful, knowing that He sees you.

I thought I was on that middle path, until I started studying the Qur'an deeply. That's when I understood: the becoming of that bird described by Ibn al-Qayyim is found in knowing and understanding what Allah wants from you and living by that as outlined by Him, in His Book.

I truly believe, from experience as well as observing the lives of others, that our tests and trials are specifically picked by Him 'azza wa jal because you and I, and everyone else on the face of the earth, needs recalibration. Hearts need to be rebalanced. And the method for that is found within His Book.

I ask that you do something for me before you read the rest of this chapter. Step away from your ego and instead process what I am about to say with all of your heart. Bismillah (in the Name of Allah).

Pause and Reflect

It is not enough for you to worship Allah in light of His Love and Mercy alone. This week's verse captures the full flight of your heart towards Allah in a manner that is balanced, devoted and deeply aware.

Some of you reading this may have been raised to worship Allah with fear only. This experience may have completely ruined your perception of Him – for it is far from the reality of Him. He is One whose Mercy outweighs His Wrath.

A balance is required, beautifully explained by Allah in this week's verse.

Look how your Lord starts with the manifestation of a heart that is balanced by using the word 'يُسَارِعُونَ' (yusāri'ūna), which comes from sara'a, which means to race or compete, not just to do good, but to rush eagerly and compete in goodness. The plural form 'الخيرات', al-Khayrāt, indicates all kinds of good deeds, big and small. They are racing in any way they can – grabbing hold of every opportunity, big and small – as they run towards the ultimate goal.

Allah explains how they are able to do this and, more importantly, how you can do this too. He ﷾ says they call upon Him and therefore are in relationship with Him with 'رَغَبًا' (raghaba): hope, longing, a deep desire for reward and closeness to Allah; and 'رَهَبًا' (rahaba): fear, awe, and dread of His Displeasure and Punishment. The 'hal' in this verse indicates how they made du'a, how they were in relationship with Allah. They came to Him with a balanced heart steeped in both hope and fear of Him 'azza wa jal.

This is the path to the peace you seek in life. It is the path to goodness reaching you. It is the path to Allah being pleased with you. It is the path to a journey to Him that is sound and balanced.

Allah describes that once the balance of the heart is established, the heart is then able to prostrate with 'خَاشِعِينَ' (khāshi'īn), a deep humility with fear and presence, producing a brokenness before Him 'azza wa jal. It is the sunnah (tradition) of life that beauty always emerges from everything that goes through a breaking process. The seed breaks for the flower to emerge. The rainbow appears through the cracks in the stormy sky. The grain is split for wheat to grow. Your heart, when balanced, will then break in humility, so that true faith and submission flows. And finally, look how Allah placed 'لَنَا' (lana), to Us, before 'خَاشِعِينَ' (khāshi'īn). This balance, this brokenness before Allah, was only possible because they sought Him and Him alone.

True worship is rooted in emotional presence: love, hope and fear. If you want to experience the closest relationship in this dunya that will complete you in every way, check your heart: how balanced is it? And how might Allah be placing you through situations so that you are lovingly guided to restore your heart to equilibrium, for Him?

Live with His Words . . .

Here are three steps to live with this week's verse(s):

1. Balance your heart between hope and fear. In every du'a, include something you hope for (Ya Allah, grant me ease, joy, reward) and something you fear (Ya Allah, protect me from arrogance, misguidance, punishment). Use both in sujood (prostration): whisper your longings and your worries to Him. Let your heart stretch in both directions, engaging your heart in humility, reminding yourself that you are in relationship with the King of Kings.

2. Race to be the first. Be the first to volunteer, forgive, give or help when an opportunity arises. Set a personal challenge: How can I beat my own delay? Even if it's replying to a message kindly, giving charity quickly or praying early.

3. Turn to the One who wants beautiful balance for you and tell Him: Ya Allah, make my heart rush to what pleases You and make my soul race towards every good You love.

A Question for Your Heart

Ask yourself: Am I too hopeful (assuming forgiveness without accountability)? Or am I too fearful (thinking my sins are unforgivable)?

Fall in Love with The Author

Allah is Al-Mujeeb – The One Who Answers, not just your words, but the state of your heart when you call upon Him in hope and fear. He sees you race towards good, and He responds to you with mercy, power and perfect timing.

WEEK 16:

Tests

Verse(s) of the Week
Your Rabb's Words for Your Soul

أَوَلَا يَرَوْنَ أَنَّهُمْ يُفْتَنُونَ فِي كُلِّ عَامٍ مَّرَّةً أَوْ مَرَّتَيْنِ ثُمَّ لَا يَتُوبُونَ وَلَا هُمْ يَذَّكَّرُونَ ١٢٦

Awalā yarawna annahum yuftanūna fī kulli 'āmin marratan aw marratayn thumma lā yatūbūna wa lā hum yadhakkarūn

'Do they not see that they are tried once or twice every year? Yet they neither repent nor do they learn a lesson.'

Surah At-Tawbah 9:126

You might remember from Week 5 that Saleha is a Shaykha who shared some beautiful advice about maintaining a daily relationship with the Book of Allah. But it's easy to forget that even a person who seems spiritually grounded or successful has a story, and more often than not, it's a story shaped by pain.

Take a moment to revisit Shaykha Saleha's words from Week 5. Then, as you read her story in this week's chapter, reflect on how Allah often awakens our souls through hardship. Every test, then, becomes a form of preparation – a quiet unfolding of future blessings, both for ourselves and for those we're meant to serve.

Saleha's Story Continues

As a child, I was taught the basics of Islam, and I used the surahs in my salah. Aside from that, my relationship with the Qur'an was non-existent.

I didn't really meet any real challenges until adulthood. When the tests and trials started coming, it was then that I realised I needed a lifeline. That's when I noticed the absence of the Qur'an from my life.

My mum suddenly died. It was the first time I had lost someone in my immediate family. Shortly after her death, I stood by her graveside in deep grief. I desperately wanted to do something for her: pray for her or pass something on to her in the form of sadaqa jariah (ongoing charity that you are rewarded for beyond death). In the end, I decided to try to recite the Qur'an for her.

Except I wasn't sure where to start my recitation, nor where to stop. I had no idea if I was pronouncing the words correctly. I stumbled to read every word in every verse. And it dawned on me that my whole life up until that point had never included a relationship with the Qur'an.

At the time of a death, we say: 'Inna lillahi wa inna ilayhi rajioun' (indeed we belong to Allah and indeed to Him we will return). But I never questioned why. It wasn't until I experienced my mum's death that I realised the depth of its meaning: that whatever test or loss you go through, you are being tested to give something up to Allah. Nothing belongs to us. Not even those we love the most.

Just prior to that verse, Allah ﷻ says:

وَلَنَبْلُوَنَّكُم بِشَىْءٍ مِّنَ ٱلْخَوْفِ وَٱلْجُوعِ وَنَقْصٍ مِّنَ ٱلْأَمْوَٰلِ وَٱلْأَنفُسِ وَٱلثَّمَرَٰتِ
وَبَشِّرِ ٱلصَّٰبِرِينَ ١٥٥

*Wa-lanabluwannakum bishay'in mina l-khawfi wa-l-
jū'i wa-naqṣin mina l-amwāli wa-l-anfusi wa-th-thamarāt,
wa-bashshiri ṣ-ṣābirīn.*

And We will surely test you with something of fear and
hunger and a loss of wealth, lives, and fruits, but give glad
tidings to the patient.

Surah Al-Baqarah 155

*In this verse, He was telling me that the reward was for the
saabiroon, the ones who are patient.*

*But I was in so much pain. I didn't want to be patient. It
was the last thing I wanted to be. That's when it hit me. What
does it mean to be from the saabiroon? What does it mean
to be a believer? What does Inna lillahi wa inna ilayhi rajoun
really mean?*

*I finally understood: the difficulties will keep coming. My
mum's death wasn't going to be my only trial. There was
going to be more. So I had to have a relationship with the
Qur'an. Tests were inevitable and the only way I would get
through whatever Allah had decreed for me was to learn
how to be a believer, and a patient one at that. And I could
only learn that through the Qur'an.*

Pause and Reflect

This week's verse is a powerful one. Allah ﷻ begins with a
rhetorical question to shock your soul so that it awakens from its
dunya-sleep. *Do they not see?* grabs the soul. But what is it that He
'azza wa jal wants you to see?

'يَرَوْنَ' (yarawna) isn't just physical seeing – it includes inner perception, awareness and recognition. Your Lord wants you to win in the next life and so He is making you aware of the blindness of the heart that needs to be fixed and refocused on the akhirah, not the eyes.

Allah is asking, Do their hearts not see that 'يُفْتَنُونَ' (yuftanūna), 'they are tested'? This comes from the root ف-ت-ن (fa-ta-na), which originally refers to the refining of gold in fire, achieved by purification through applied pressure. The use of the passive verb form emphasises the very subtle, ongoing way they are being tested – by divine design, without them necessarily knowing it, and only once or twice.

Your Lord sends you major divine tests, only once or twice a year, reminding you that you have a Lord who sends tests in a way that is measured by His Mercy, designed to awaken your soul and never to break you.

The verse ends with Allah saying, despite all this, there are many who never take the lessons. Do not be that person. Your tests are whispers, calling your soul back to where it needs to be.

Live with His Words . . .

Here are three steps to live with this week's verse(s):

1. Keep a 'trial + lesson' journal. Each time you face hardship, whether small or large, journal:

   - What happened?

   - What could Allah be teaching or reminding me?

   - What part of my heart or behaviour needs to realign?

2. Think back to your most recent test or one that you're experiencing right now: to what might Allah be awakening your soul?

3. Turn to the One who wants your soul to awaken and align with all that will make it win eternally, and tell Him: My Lord, when You test me, let it not harden my heart but awaken it. Let every difficulty draw me closer to You, not further away.

A Question for Your Heart

Ask yourself: If the pain I'm experiencing right now isn't enough to awaken my heart, then what will it take? How much more must I go through and lose before I finally return to Ar-Raheem, who is calling me back with mercy?

Fall in Love with The Author

Al-Lateef is a Lord who sends tests and trials to touch your life. They are, from His Care and Mercy, awakenings to stir your soul when He sees you drifting away too far.

WEEK 17:

The Timing of Tests

Verse(s) of the Week
Your Rabb's Words for Your Soul

ثُمَّ أَنزَلَ عَلَيْكُم مِّنۢ بَعْدِ ٱلْغَمِّ أَمَنَةً نُّعَاسًا يَغْشَىٰ طَآئِفَةً مِّنكُمْۖ وَطَآئِفَةٌ قَدْ أَهَمَّتْهُمْ أَنفُسُهُمْ يَظُنُّونَ
بِٱللَّهِ غَيْرَ ٱلْحَقِّ ظَنَّ ٱلْجَٰهِلِيَّةِۖ يَقُولُونَ هَل لَّنَا مِنَ ٱلْأَمْرِ مِن شَىْءٍۗ قُلْ إِنَّ ٱلْأَمْرَ كُلَّهُ لِلَّهِ ١٥٤

*Thumma anzala 'alaykum min ba'di al-ghammi amanatan
nu'āsā yaghshā ṭā'ifatan minkum, wa ṭā'ifatun qad ahammat-
hum anfusuhum yaẓunnūna billāhi ghayra al-ḥaqqi ẓanna
al-jāhiliyya, yaqūlūna hal lanā mina al-amri min shay'in, qul
inna al-amra kullahu lillāh*

*'Then after distress, He sent down serenity in the form of
drowsiness overcoming some of you, while others were
disturbed by evil thoughts about Allah – the thoughts of ʿ
pre-Islamicʾ ignorance. They ask, "Do we have a say in the
matter?" Say, ʿO Prophet,ʾ "All matters are destined by Allah."'*

Surah Al-Imran 3:154

This week's verse describes a moment of severe distress for the believers after their defeat during the battle of Uhud. Sadness and anxiety engulfed their hearts. But at the precise moment of need, Allah sent down serenity and rest. This is a reminder for you that Allah's Mercy and relief come exactly when needed, not a moment too soon or too late.

I often find myself reflecting on the types of tests I've faced – and the timing of those tests. Once you've come through to the other side, there's a certain clarity. You can look back and observe from a distance, noticing the stepping stones and the subtle signs that were there all along. If you hadn't gone through that particular test, you might not have met that person, learned that lesson or found yourself led to a specific opportunity.

Saleha's story in Week 16 is a powerful reminder of this. The loss of her mother was the catalyst that awakened her soul and called her towards the Qur'an. And then, as if by divine orchestration, another test followed.

Saleha's Story Continues

While I was learning to read and recite the Qur'an, I was introduced by my Qur'an teacher to the Alamiyyah course. The course was four years long – five years if you count the Arabic language-intensive year. Being a mother and wife, I thought to myself, There was no way I was going to be able to study for five years; *but I was really interested in learning the Arabic language and so told myself,* Let me see how each year goes by.

On literally the first day of the course, my youngest was starting secondary school. So I thought this was perfect timing. All the children will be at school and I'll be able to manage my studies.

But on the first day of my course, I got a call from his school that my eldest son had been taken seriously ill. He left school and became bed-bound, unable to walk. I was engulfed in helplessness and was confused, not knowing what to do. This time really tested my reliance upon Allah.

I did question whether I should give up the course and look after my son or carry on. But with every year that passed, I realised more and more how the Alamiyyah course became my lifeline. It put everything into perspective for me. I was comforted, knowing I was within Allah's Sight. Sukoon settled in the midst of so much stress and fear. And in time – in Allah's Time – my son made a full recovery a few months before I was to graduate, which meant he walked to my graduation.

There was this one verse that I often used to tell myself:

أَحَسِبَ ٱلنَّاسُ أَن يُتْرَكُوٓاْ أَن يَقُولُوٓاْ ءَامَنَّا وَهُمْ لَا يُفْتَنُونَ ٢

Aḥasiba n-nāsu an yut'rakū an yaqūlū āmannā wa-hum lā yuftanūn.

Do they think they can say 'I believe' and they will not be tested?

Surah Ankabut 29:2

When a calamity befalls you, a question silently enters your head: why me? It doesn't disappear even if you don't vocalise it. But Allah is the only one Who knows the answer. He knows what is best for all of us. We will never know. That was my constant reminder: to fully trust in Allah.

Pause and Reflect

Dearest reader, I would like to invite you to consider a time of extreme distress when you felt overwhelmed and uncertain.

There is a situation in my life where I experience deep struggle. I have been making du'a for relief for years. I do wonder why it has not been granted yet. But I trust in my Lord's impeccable timing. There is something He wants from me during what I perceive as a delay. I know there is khair (goodness) in what is, in fact, not a delay but Divine Timing, which always paves the way to Divine Blessings.

In this week's verse, Allah 'azza wa jal uses the word 'anzala' (sent down). The serenity and peace that comes with a test is from a Lord who sees you and intentionally intervenes exactly when you need it most. This deliberate act of care and kindness is perfect because it comes from a Lord Who was ever close, Who will not task a soul with more than it can bear.

Relief from our tests is an outcome we so ardently yearn for. Relief, as Allah shows in this verse, is emotional, mental and spiritual – in that calm placed lovingly by Him 'azza wa jal into your heart.

Live with His Words . . .

Here are three steps to live with this week's verse(s):

1. Turn the waiting periods of your trials into a time of productivity. Whenever you are waiting for Allah's Relief, engage in acts of goodness:

   a. Volunteer for something that strengthens your faith or helps others.

b. Seek knowledge that brings you closer to Allah.

c. Engage in increased private worship.

2. Take a moment daily to list three things you are grateful for despite the challenges you face. Allow this exercise to shift your mindset from focusing solely on the difficulty to recognising the wisdom in Allah's Plan.

3. Turn to the One whose sight never leaves you or your situation and tell Him: My Lord, You know my innermost state. I am in need of Your relief, mercy and guidance. You are the Best Planner of my affairs. When I am hit by trials and tribulations, remind me that Your Mercy will always follow, at a time that is Your Choice based on Your Wisdom.

A Question for Your Heart

When you feel lost or uncertain, how can you strengthen your trust in Allah's divine timing, knowing that His Plan for you unfolds exactly when you need it, even if you cannot see the way ahead?

Fall in Love with The Author

Al-Hakim is a Lord whose Wisdom cannot be comprehended by human intelligence. He is Wise in allowing your trials to unfold with purpose and precision, and His Perfect Timing brings serenity to your heart just when you need it most.

PART 4:

Pain

قُل لَّن يُصِيبَنَآ إِلَّا مَا كَتَبَ ٱللَّهُ لَنَا هُوَ مَوْلَىٰنَا ۚ وَعَلَى ٱللَّهِ فَلْيَتَوَكَّلِ ٱلْمُؤْمِنُونَ ٥١

Qul lan yuṣībanā illā mā kataba Allahu lanā huwa mawlānā wa 'alā Allāhi falyatawakkali al-mu'minūn

'Say, "Nothing will ever befall us except what Allah has destined for us. He is our Protector." So in Allah let the believers put their trust.'

Surah At-Tawbah 9:51

WEEK 18:

Sickness

Verse(s) of the Week
Your Rabb's Words for Your Soul

وَنُنَزِّلُ مِنَ ٱلْقُرْآنِ مَا هُوَ شِفَآءٌ وَرَحْمَةٌ لِّلْمُؤْمِنِينَ وَلَا يَزِيدُ ٱلظَّٰلِمِينَ إِلَّا خَسَارًا ٨٢

*Wa nunazzilu mina al-Qur'āni mā huwa shifā'un wa raḥ
matun lil-mu'minīn wa lā yazīdu al-ẓālimīna illā khasāran*

*'We send down the Qur'an as a healing and mercy for the
believers, but it only increases the wrongdoers in loss.'*

Surah Al-Isra 17:82

May Allah forgive me, although I've always believed in everything contained in the Qur'an and the authentic Sunnah, there was a time when I viewed spiritual ailments such as ayn (evil eye) and sihr (black magic) as exaggerated explanations for a weak state of emaan (faith). I never denied their existence, but I suspected many Muslims used them as excuses – blaming unseen forces rather than taking responsibility for their own choices. It wasn't until I was tested with spiritual illness myself, many years ago, that I came to understand: this is haqq – truth. It cannot be explained through science or logic, nor can it be treated except through the healing power of the Qur'an. What I once doubted, I came to experience first hand.

My beloved friend Sumayah's story may come as a shock, especially for those of you who have followed our YouTube show, *Honest Tea Talk*. Her story is a profound reminder: the Qur'an does not only comfort and support, it heals. It is a cure for the body, heart, mind and soul.

Sumayah's Story

I had been healthy and well, but within just two months, I became really sick. I had severe stomach pain, food phobia, headaches, eye pressure, earaches, indigestion, heartburn, weakness, sciatica, cramping, spotting, lower back pain, shoulder and neck pain, and I began to lose my voice. I lost one third of my body weight. The doctors had no idea what was happening to me.

Before I fell ill, I wasn't where I was meant to be. My prayers were empty. I was going through the motions. I felt lost. I was dying inside.

With no medical explanation for the sudden decline in my physical health, I turned to the Qur'an for my healing and began to recite Surah Al-Baqarah. It is the second and longest chapter of the Qur'an, where the Prophet ﷺ said:

Read Surah Al-Baqarah, for reciting it regularly is a blessing and forsaking it is a cause of regret, and the Batlah (magicians) cannot withstand it.

Sahih Muslim

Reciting its verses brought me such comfort. I felt my heart changed. It freed me from negativity and gave me such a sense of serenity. And my health began to improve. Surah Al-Baqarah allows that to happen, and does so rapidly. It changes your priorities and changes your focus without you doing anything. All you have to do is read it.

It literally changed my heart, and then it changed my body. Nowadays, I don't worry about anything else much in my day apart from getting my Surah Al-Baqarah in. If I don't, I start to get symptoms again. So I'm held to it.

There's a verse in the Qur'an that I've held onto:

مَنْ عَمِلَ صَالِحًا مِّن ذَكَرٍ أَوْ أُنثَىٰ وَهُوَ مُؤْمِنٌ فَلَنُحْيِيَنَّهُ حَيَوٰةً طَيِّبَةً ۖ وَلَنَجْزِيَنَّهُمْ أَجْرَهُم بِأَحْسَنِ مَا كَانُوا۟ يَعْمَلُونَ ٩٧

Man 'amila ṣāliḥan min dhakarin aw unthā wa-huwa muʾminun fa-lanuḥʾyiyannahu ḥayātan ṭayyibatan wa-la-najziyannahum ajrahum bi-aḥsani mā kānū yaʿmalūn.

Whoever does righteousness, whether male or female, while being a believer – We will surely grant them a good life, and We will surely reward them according to the best of what they used to do.

Surah An-Nahl 97

Before my illness, I spent my time trying to live a good life through self-development and productivity. But now, I feel clean inside. If I were to die, I'd be less scared now. In verses 2 and 3 of Surah Al-Baqarah, Allah says:

ذَٰلِكَ ٱلْكِتَٰبُ لَا رَيْبَ ۛ فِيهِ ۛ هُدًى لِّلْمُتَّقِينَ ٢ ٱلَّذِينَ يُؤْمِنُونَ بِٱلْغَيْبِ وَيُقِيمُونَ ٱلصَّلَوٰةَ وَمِمَّا رَزَقْنَٰهُمْ يُنفِقُونَ ٣

Dhālika l-kitābu lā rayba fīhi hudan lil-muttaqīn alladhīna yuʾminūna bil-ghaybi wa-yuqīmūna ṣ-ṣalāta wa-mimmā razaqnāhum yunfiqūn.

This is the Book about which there is no doubt, a guidance for those conscious of Allah. Who believe in the unseen, establish prayer, and spend out of what We have provided for them.

These verses anchored me and it only came with the Qur'an. Everything was put in its place.

My condition isn't perfect, of course. I still suffer in many ways – pain and other issues. But where before, I would respond to this with panic and think, Am I dying? *Now if there's a pain, I go to ruqya (recitation for delivery from ailments), to the Qur'an, and it goes away.*

The entire test opened my eyes. How much of our physical ailments, even my period pain, are affliction? I don't know. So many things have changed since Surah Al-Baqarah. It's extraordinary. I didn't think it would touch these things. But it did, and it touched so much more.

Pause and Reflect

Although revelation of the Qur'an ceased with the last verse revealed to the Prophet Muhammad ﷺ, it continues to be 'sent down'. We know this because Allah begins this week's verse with 'nunnazil', a verb in the present tense, which implies continuous revelation and relevance throughout time.

The Qur'an is continuously being 'sent down' in its meaning, light and healing to the heart of the believer – into your heart – even today.

In this week's verse, the Qur'an is described with two powerful attributes: as a shifaa (healing), a cure for doubts, despair, sin, diseases of the heart and any manifestation of spiritual wounds, and as a rahma (mercy) that soothes, nourishes and protects in an intensely gentle way.

What is most apparent in Sumayah's story is the outward physical manifestation of a spiritual illness. And the Qur'an, specifically Surah Al-Baqarah, healed her alhamdulillah. But her story also reveals the emptiness in her heart and the distance she felt from Allah.

Are you able to diagnose the level of health of your heart and soul? The answer is no. Who knows? Only your Lord, your Creator. I've been wanting to book a full body health check for some time. The older I get, the more health challenges I experience. But I ask myself, where is the longing for a full soul health check?

Well, it's available. No booking is required. You don't need to go anywhere. The Qur'an will scan you. It will highlight what illnesses you have, where they are and will cure you while scanning! Can you imagine such a body scan, which detects and heals simultaneously?! But this is the power of the Words of Allah.

All of us are sick to some extent. It may be a physical illness or a spiritual one. Or it may be a state of the heart that is not akin to fitrah (the natural inclination in which we were created, uncorrupted). You will suffer from one of the above at some point in your life. So know that 'nunnazil', He continues to send down the Qur'an as healing. It does not stop. The Qur'an is a cure for it all. May Allah grant us the best of health now and for the rest of our days. Ameen.

Live with His Words . . .

Here are three steps to live with this week's verse(s):

1. Recite with purpose. Read the Qur'an not only for reward, but with the intention of healing. Before opening it, whisper: O Allah, send down healing through Your Words.

2. When ill or overwhelmed by a test, go to the Qur'an first. Replace scrolling or venting with opening the Qur'an – even just one verse. Trust in the power of Allah's Words to hold you and heal you.

3. Turn to the One who holds the keys to all cures and tell Him: Allah, make the Qur'an the light of my heart, the spring of my chest, and a healing for all that weighs down my soul. O Healer of hearts, grant me tranquillity through it. Make every verse a mercy to me, and Your Words a nearness, a guide and a cure for all that no one but You can heal.

A Question for Your Heart

Ask yourself: Which parts of my heart have I tried to heal through the world, that were only ever meant to be restored through the Words of my Creator?

Fall in Love with The Author

Ash-Shafi – The One who heals – has placed in His Revelation a cure for hearts burdened by grief and confusion, and bodies plagued by illness. The Qur'an is not just a recitation, it is His Healing Touch for the soul that turns to Him.

WEEK 19:

LOSS

Verse(s) of the Week
Your Rabb's Words for Your Soul

ٱلَّذِى خَلَقَ ٱلْمَوْتَ وَٱلْحَيَوٰةَ لِيَبْلُوَكُمْ أَيُّكُمْ أَحْسَنُ عَمَلًا ۚ وَهُوَ ٱلْعَزِيزُ ٱلْغَفُورُ ٢

*Alladhī khalaqa al-mawta wal-ḥayāta liyabluwakum ayyukum
aḥsanu 'amalan wa huwa al-'azīzu al-ghafūr*

*"He is the One` Who created death and life in order to
test which of you is best in deeds. And He is the Almighty,
All-Forgiving.'*

Surah Mulk 67:2

recently visited the Gardens of Peace cemetery to spend some
time by the grave of my dear friend Mona Mustafa, whose story
I shared in *Ramadan Reflections*. I sat quietly beside her grave,
looking down at the black granite slab engraved with her name, age
and date of death. Beneath that polished stone, I imagined her body
under the soil. My mind filled with flashbacks – her laughter, her
hugs, the way she used to tease me.

117

Then, I looked again at her name and imagined mine in its place. My age. My unknown date of death. The reality is, we're all somewhere in between life and death, walking each day towards the One who is Ever-Living. Loss is one of the heaviest tests we face. Death is the clearest mirror through which we learn how to live.

The story that follows is a story of life and death. Tahira is a Pakistani sister from Canada who I met many years ago through a mutual friend who lost her child. So I'm putting a trigger warning here for anyone who has been affected by the loss of a pregnancy and may find reading it too difficult.

Tahira's Story

I lost my first baby in 2009. Before that, I had only ever lost my grandmother. I never thought of death as close. Of course I knew I could die at any time; but for my baby inside of me to die? It never crossed my mind. My mum hadn't miscarried in any of her pregnancies. No one I knew had ever miscarried.

My first pregnancy was difficult. I was really ill with morning sickness. But I so looked forward to welcoming my baby. At last my sickness reduced. I had my five-month scan and was told that everything was perfect. Then, just three weeks later, at almost 24 weeks of pregnancy, there was no heartbeat. The angel of death had come and taken my baby from my womb while I, the mother, was left to stay in this world. No one could tell me why.

I asked what was going to happen next, and I was told: we need to induce you. That meant I had to go through labour, to deliver the baby who had died.

Suddenly Surah Mulk, verse 2, came to my mind:

اَلَّذِى خَلَقَ ٱلْمَوْتَ وَٱلْحَيَوٰةَ لِيَبْلُوَكُمْ أَيُّكُمْ أَحْسَنُ عَمَلًا ۚ وَهُوَ ٱلْعَزِيزُ ٱلْغَفُورُ ٢

Alladhī khalaqa l-mawta wa-l-ḥayāta li-yabluwakum
ayyukum aḥsanu ʿamalan, wa-huwa l-ʿazīzu l-ghafūr.

He is the One who created death and life in order to test
which of you is best in deeds. And He is the Almighty,
All Forgiving.

*When my baby entered the world, I got to hold her. She
was only 1lb – tiny fingers, tiny eyebrows, tiny everything. I
was with her for a few minutes and then they took her away.
My pain and loss are hard to put into words.*

*Alhamdulillah, I became pregnant again. But in my sub-
sequent pregnancies, I held my breath at 23 weeks. I felt
such fear. And when that time passed, I felt grateful to Allah.
But I understand now, many years later, that Surah Mulk,
verse 2, was implanted in my mind at that moment for a
reason.*

*In the years since then, things have not always gone
smoothly. There have been times when I have drifted
away from Allah and fallen. But then I think of my lost
baby, waiting for me at the gates of Jannah. What if I don't
make it? It is her death and wanting to meet her in that
place that make me want to be one who is best in doing
good deeds. I need to become better so that I can find her
there – waiting for me at the gates of Jannah. I want to
meet her again and see what she looks like, and be with
her and her siblings.*

*And in that way, she and her death are a gift from Allah.
There is this person I love and who I want to meet again.
There's someone there for me. Allah knew I would need that
constant reminder, and He gave it to me.*

Pause and Reflect

The first thing that jumped out at me when Tahira shared her story was the way in which Al-Aleem, The All Knowing, gifted her a verse that not only comforted her at that precise moment, but which He knew she would need later on down the line, in her future, when she would lose her way.

Your Lord knows all that has come to pass that has led you to who you are now. And because He knows what you are heading towards, He is the Only One who knows how to truly care for you as a result of your past, and how to prepare you for what He knows of your future.

Allah 'azza wa jal in this verse said 'best in deeds', not 'most in deeds'. Let this fill your heart with hope. Sometimes, you'll just about be able to do the basics for Him. You'll be barely surviving. And you have a Lord who understands this. Even if you feel you've wasted years that could have been filled with doing deeds that are beloved to Him, what He is telling you is that it doesn't matter so long as right now you aim to be the best in whatever you can do – here, right now. Just be sincere and do your best, seeking nothing but His Acceptance, His Love, His Reward and His Mercy.

Live with His Words . . .

Here are three steps to live with this week's verse(s):

1. Identify either something or someone you've lost or something or someone you hope to receive/meet in this dunya.

2. Now identify a good deed that your heart inclines towards that you can offer to Allah as your best deed.

3. Talk to your Rabb about the pain that comes with the absence of the person or thing your heart craves for, and tell Him: Ya Allah, the Creator of death and life, You test me to see which of Your servants are best in deeds. Make me among those who do good in secret and in public, in ease and in hardship. Let my life be a testimony for me, not against me, and let my death be a relief from every trial. Make my meeting with You my most beloved moment of all.

A Question for Your Heart

How are you honestly responding to the test of life and death? Are you striving to be among those who excel in good deeds, knowing that this life is only a test from Allah?

Fall in Love with The Author

Al-Hakim – The All-Wise – is a Lord who has created both life and death to reveal which of His servants strive to be the best. Every test is tailored by His Perfect Wisdom to bring out the beauty of your faith.

WEEK 20:

Dilemmas

Verse(s) of the Week
Your Rabb's Words for Your Soul

وَمَن يَتَّقِ ٱللَّهَ يَجْعَل لَّهُ مَخْرَجًا ٢ وَيَرْزُقْهُ مِنْ حَيْثُ لَا يَحْتَسِبُ ۚ وَمَن يَتَوَكَّلْ عَلَى ٱللَّهِ فَهُوَ حَسْبُهُ ۚ إِنَّ ٱللَّهَ بَالِغُ أَمْرِهِ ۚ قَدْ جَعَلَ ٱللَّهُ لِكُلِّ شَيْءٍ قَدْرًا ٣

Wa man yattaqi Allāha yaj'al lahu makhrajan
Wa yarzuquhu min ḥaythu lā yaḥtasib
Wa man yatawakkal 'alā Allāhi fahuwa ḥasbuhu
Inna Allāha bālighu amrihi qad ja'ala Allāhu likulli shay'in qadrā

'And whoever is mindful of Allah, He will make a way out for them, and provide for them from sources they could never imagine. And whoever puts their trust in Allah, then He alone is sufficient for them. Certainly Allah achieves His Will. Allah has already set a destiny for everything.'

Surah At-Talaq 65:2–3

'm not the best at making decisions. But once I do, and I take it to Allah through salatul istikharaa (the prayer of seeking counsel), it's like I've been handed a superpower. There's no stopping me. I move with certainty, eager to see how Allah will respond. Will He open the path and make things fall into place with ease? Or will He gently place obstacles in the way, creating distance between me and what I thought I wanted?

I absolutely love istikharaa. In fact, I've included a chapter or section on it in each of my other books. It's such a beautiful gift. But the real beauty of istikharaa lies not just in how it helps us move forward with clarity, it's in how it shapes us. It builds something in you. It trains your heart to rely on Allah, to trust that He is truly Al-Wakeel – The Most Trustworthy Disposer of Affairs.

Istikharaa isn't just about finding the right answer. It's about being looked after by the One who knows what your heart can handle. Every closed door is a mercy. Every open one, a sign of His Generosity. Through both, Allah shows us that He is the Kindest – The One who never lets us down.

We return now to Babar's story, where one of the most significant decisions of his life unfolded within the walls of a prison. It was there, in that space of desperation, that he turned to Allah with nothing but need. And it was there that Allah 'azza wa jal responded with a verse from the Qur'an that changed everything.

Babar's Story Continues

Between 2004 and 2009, I was involved in legal proceedings in the UK. I was being held in prison, but I had not yet been charged. I was also fighting an extradition case against the US. It was completely exhausting and emotionally draining. In fact, those words don't do justice to the strain and isolation of that time.

And alongside all of this, I was also fighting for justice against the police brutality I experienced when I was first arrested. Those proceedings were coming to a head and there was going to be a trial before a judge.

The police offered me £20,000 to settle out of court. I refused. I made it clear that I was not going to accept unless they admitted liability and apologised.

The trial was due to start on a Monday. My solicitor and barrister came to Long Lartin prison on the Friday to see me. They told me the police had made another last-ditch offer to avoid the case going to trial. This time, they offered me £60,000.

I remember one of them telling me: 'Our advice is you take it. We spoke to your criminal case solicitor as well and she said the same. Look, I know for you this is more than about the money. This is about justice and accountability. But our view is that you should take the money because at your trial, you might lose – the judge might not believe you. Or you may win on some points and lose on other points. It's a big sum of money they're offering you which can help you establish your life when you get out of prison.'

As they had lunch, I was returned to my cell, alone. I had to decide what to do. I sat on my prayer mat and made du'a to Allah ﷻ. I pleaded with Him: I'm so unsure about this. It's an attractive offer. My lawyers – who I trust and know are looking out for me and want to do what's best for me – are telling me to take it. It's a lot of money. The police are offering this to me on condition they will not accept liability. I really don't know what to do. Guide me.

Immediately after I finished making du'a, I opened the Qur'an at random, which I would often do, and I put my finger on a random page and wherever my finger landed, I felt that was what Allah wanted me to read at that given moment.

On this particular occasion, His Book opened on verses 7 and 8 from Surah Anfaal. These verses were from the Battle of Badr that took place at the time of the Prophet Muhammad ﷺ.

Some of the sahabah (companions of the Prophet) wanted the easy way out. They wanted to attack unguarded caravans instead of going to war and fight in battle. They saw it as a win-win.

In this verse, Allah is saying: you wanted the easy way out. But I have My own agenda, which is to establish the truth. 'Remember when Allah promised you one of the two groups (enemy caravans or the army), that it would be yours. But you wished that the unarmed group would be yours, while Allah intended to establish the truth by His Words and to eliminate the disbelievers to the last. So that He may establish the truth and abolish falsehood, even if the criminals dislike it.'

When I read these verses, I knew straight away what my answer would be to my solicitor. I turned to Allah and made du'a: 'You are Al-Razzaq – You are the Provider.'

I was all alone, and now I was gambling £60,000. I prayed the istikharaa prayer and as we reconvened our meeting, I told my lawyers: 'I really appreciate your help getting me to this point. I know it's been four years working on this case. I appreciate everything you've done, but I'm more sure now than I've ever been in my life that I want to reject this offer and I want to go to trial.'

They both looked at me and laughed: 'Okay, at least we're clear.'

I looked back at them and firmly said: 'Even if I lose at trial, unless they admit liability, I will not take any amount of money they offer. I'm prepared to lose the money.'

On day three of the trial, that Wednesday, the police admitted liability and offered me £60,000.

I had wanted them to admit liability, and they did. They paid the same money I had gambled on. The news spread all over the media. I had a friend in Bangkok who later told me that he had seen my name on the front page of the main newspaper with the headline: 'Muslim terrorist suspect wins £60,000 compensation from the police.'

It was a victory. And not only that: it paved the way for us to take further legal action towards the officers responsible. Later, they stood trial.

It was the biggest crisis of my life – at least up to that point. And Allah gave me His Advice. He told me what to do. And I received so much more than I had asked for. My ordeal was not yet over and the extradition hearings still lay ahead of me. But I was comforted and inspired. It gave me hope and trust that Al-Wakeel, The Ultimate Guardian, was with me and would remain with me.

Pause and Reflect

I cried when I heard this part of Babar's story. It reminded me of the times I have found myself in between two hard places, stuck and confused and not knowing which way to turn, desperately wanting someone else to take over and make the decisions for me, to save me from mental confusion.

And guess what, Allah 'azza wa jal knows that. He knows that the greatest relief would be for someone else to tell us what to do, guide us to what's best and just take over in that given moment. And that's why He has gifted us salatul istikharaa. He tells us: You need direction? You want someone to show you the right way? Come, here you go. I am the only One who knows the future. I am the only One who can relieve you and guide you to all that is khair (good) for you. Just turn to Me through istikharaa and I will take care of the rest.

To take that step towards Allah, you need to be certain of a number of things: that He certainly exists. That His Attention never leaves you, even for a second. That He knows where you came from and what you will face in the days ahead. That He is a Caring, Compassionate and Affectionate Lord who wants the best for you and wants you to win in the next life. He wants Paradise for you.

In this week's verses, your Lord tells you, when you have taqwa (consciousness, or pious awareness) of Him, He will make a way out for you from any difficulty. Taqwa is a deep awareness of your Rabb. It's being conscious of who He is and how He interacts with you every day. It's being entirely mindful of Him though you cannot see Him, but you live your life ever aware that He sees you.

In these verses, Allah uses the verb يَتَّقِ (yattaqi), which comes from the root waqa, which means to shield and protect. This verb is in the present tense, which provides a sense of continuous action. Taqwa isn't a one-off action, but a lifelong commitment where you aim to live with consciousness of Allah. One of the greatest ways to live a lifetime of taqwa is to live a lifetime with His Book. So, with this commitment to taqwa, Allah tells you that He will make a way out for you: يَجْعَل لَّهُ مَخْرَجًا (yaj'al lahu makhrajan).

Notice the word 'مَخْرَجًا' (makhraj), which isn't just a way out, but it is a strategic exit – precise in every way, a carefully crafted well-thought-out relief from your hardship, your confusion, your dilemma.

As if this intense mercy is not enough, your Rabb continues: مِنْ حَيْثُ لَا يَحْتَسِبُ (min haythu lā yahtasib), 'from where he does not expect'. Allah uses the verb يَحْتَسِبُ (yahtasib) linked to hisab, calculation, to tell you that He knows you are in great difficulty. He knows you cannot see a way out. But here He tells you that He takes over as The One Who Relieves and Provides.

And then your Lord tells you that He is sufficient. Whenever you feel you are not enough, He is enough for you – completely, absolutely, entirely sufficient for you, your problem and your needs.

فَهُوَ حَسْبُهُ (fahuwa hasbuhu), your heart is comforted. He then seals the deal. Be mindful of Him and He will absolutely and powerfully and precisely make a strategic exit for you in ways that you cannot imagine.

Allah 'azza wa jal tells you: إِنَّ اللَّهَ بَالِغُ أَمْرِهِ (Inna Allāha bālighu amrihi), Allah will accomplish His Purpose.

The word 'بَالِغ' (baligh) denotes something that reaches full extent, nothing can obstruct or limit His will. Your Merciful Lord

tells you He has absolute authority to do what He sets out to do –
to fulfil His Purpose to you. And what is that? Simply, to lovingly
look after you.

Live with His Words . . .

Here are three steps to live with this week's verse(s):

1. Make a list of all the ways that develop your taqwa of
   Allah. What deeds make you mindful of Him? Increase in
   them this week.

2. Grab a Post-It note, a piece of paper or, for the more
   artistic readers, draw or paint the following statement:
   'I will no longer obsess over HOW my problems are
   solved. I will focus on WHO will solve them.' Place this
   somewhere in your home.

3. Turn to the One who says in the Qur'an: 'Remember
   Me, I will remember you.' Tell Him: Rabbi, make me
   among those who are mindful of You. Open for me
   doors of relief from where I do not expect. Plant in
   my heart unshakeable conviction that You alone are
   sufficient for me.

A Question for Your Heart

What burden are you clinging to in fear that was always meant to be
placed in the Hands of the One who never falters?

Fall in Love with The Author

Al-Wakeel is a Lord who wants you to live with Him, in complete trust that He is your Ultimate Guardian. His Wisdom is flawless and His Care is complete. When you entrust your tangled dilemmas to Him, you are placing them within His Perfect Knowledge and His Plan that never errs.

WEEK 21:

Absence

Verse(s) of the Week
Your Rabb's Words for Your Soul

إِنَّ هَٰذَا ٱلْقُرْءَانَ يَهْدِى لِلَّتِى هِىَ أَقْوَمُ وَيُبَشِّرُ ٱلْمُؤْمِنِينَ ٱلَّذِينَ يَعْمَلُونَ ٱلصَّـٰلِحَاتِ أَنَّ لَهُمْ أَجْرًا كَبِيرًا ٩

Inna hādhā al-Qur'āna yahdī lillatī hiya aqwamu wa yubashiru al-mu'minīna alladhīna ya'malūna aṣ-ṣāliḥāti anna lahum ajran kabīran

'Surely this Qur'an guides to what is most upright, and gives good news to the believers – who do good – that they will have a mighty reward.'

Surah Al-Isra 17:9

There's a well-known saying: you don't know what you have until it's gone. As human beings, we're naturally forgetful and prone to taking things for granted, which is why Allah reminds us, time and again in the Qur'an, about the importance of gratitude. Gratitude is not just a feeling; it's the highest expression of faith.

In the past, I often associated gratitude with what had been given to me – the blessings I could clearly see. But true gratitude goes deeper. It's about recognising Allah's Wisdom in all that exists in your life, both what He gives and what He withholds. When something is placed within your reach, and Allah affirms that it is good for your soul, you are called to be grateful in that moment, before it is taken, before it becomes part of the past, before it becomes a test of longing.

As Babar's story concludes, you will find a powerful reminder that appreciation isn't just about holding on; it's about seeing clearly while you still have the gift in front of you. Babar lost more than most of us ever will, confined to prison in terrifying circumstances. There was only one thing he could turn to in that desperate extreme, and that was the Qur'an.

In 2012, after being held for eight years in HMP Long Lartin without ever being convicted of any crime, Babar lost all his appeals against extradition to the US. He was blindfolded, shackled and bundled onto a jet at an RAF Airforce base.

In the US, he was charged with supporting terrorism via his websites and detained for two years in complete solitary confinement alongside death row prisoners in a supermaximum (known as 'supermax') security prison.

Then the help of Allah arrived.

Babar's Story Concludes

In 2011, while I was held in HMP Long Lartin, a prison officer once asked me with quiet bewilderment, 'How do you do it? If I were in your position, I think I would have taken my own life.'

I paused for a moment then replied to him, 'I carry on because I believe there is a Divine Wisdom behind everything I am going through. I may not understand the wisdom right now, but I am certain that one day God will make it clear to me.'

In October 2012, I was taken to the US and put in a supermax prison in complete isolation. No mixing with the other prisoners or gym. You're just in your cell all the time. Part of me was thinking, Well, my case is so high profile, because of the payment the police made to me and the publicity I've received for being imprisoned without trial. They'll be aware of that and make sure not to mistreat me. But they didn't care: as soon as I got there, they stripped me naked on camera and put me in this suit which covered me from my shoulders down to my knees and left my arms bare. They threw me into this cell which was freezing cold and smelled of faeces, which had been smeared all over the walls and window frame. The only thing inside that cell were two little strips of toilet paper next to the toilet with a flush you couldn't operate. You had to tell the officer, and he operated the flush.

Outside the window was a plain concrete wall. I was there with nothing to read and nothing to do. Not a newspaper, not a book. Nothing to write with. No one to talk to. Over the next few days, it became clear to me that one of the officers was inciting other prisoners against me, making up complete lies to make my life hell.

By now, my ordeal had been going on for almost ten years. After so long, I'd almost switched to living in the moment, not thinking beyond the day that I was in. Perhaps it was a protective thing to stop myself from becoming overwhelmed. But on the second day in there, the reality hit me that this was it: I'm in America and I might be here for the rest of my life. I started having a panic attack. I'd never had one before. I felt my chest cave in on itself, and my throat became dry. I was struggling to breathe. It was as though the walls of my cell were crushing in on me.

I was in complete panic and didn't know what to do. I started reciting Surah Yusuf. I didn't have a Qur'an, but I had memorised it. I remembered that the scholars of tafseer had said Surah Yusuf will restore whosoever recites it when going through a difficulty and fill him with hope and comfort. Reciting Surah Yusuf soothed me. My breathing became slower and I felt I was safe again.

I longed for a copy of the Qur'an. But I'd heard about brothers in Guantanamo, where US soldiers had desecrated Allah's Book, throwing it into the toilet bucket and stepping on it. As a result, the brothers decided they would hand their Qur'ans back because they couldn't bear to see His Book humiliated and desecrated in this way. There were several huffadh (memorisers of the Qur'an) among them, and they kept the Qur'an alive even though hundreds of them didn't have a paper copy between them.

In the end, I spoke to the Catholic chaplain. He seemed a really nice man, a man of God, and I asked if he had a copy. All he had was an English translation, but subhanAllah it felt like I had been drowning, and someone had thrown me a rope. All of a sudden, I was able to hold onto it. It was my lifeline.

I would recite the Qur'an by back-translating English into Arabic because I didn't have the original in the Arabic language. I would recite from what I memorised and when I got stuck, I would go to the English and then translate it into the original Arabic.

Having experienced life without access to the Qur'an and then tasted the sweet comfort that the Qur'an brought at that terrible time, I truly understand: you don't know the value of something unless it's taken away from you.

After one year in isolation and nine years in prison without trial, the US government offered me a deal: plead guilty to something and you will be home within 12 months. I accepted the deal and pleaded guilty to posting two articles on my website which broke US sanctions.

At my sentencing hearing in 2014, Judge Janet Hall, chief federal judge for the district of Connecticut and one of the most senior judges in America, concluded after reviewing all the evidence against me that I was not a terrorist. She said: Babar was a 'good person' who was 'not interested in terrorism' and not a security threat to anyone. She ruled that I be released from prison in 12 months and ordered the US government to immediately take me out of isolation.

In 2015, I returned home to my family in London.

Since my release from prison, I have used my experiences to deter young people from crime, gangs, misogyny and terrorism. I speak at schools, youth clubs and places of worship. I deliver guest lectures to universities, think tanks and government audiences in the UK and abroad. In 2018, a radio interview I gave about Ramadan in prison was runner-up in the interview of the year category in the Sandford Saint Martin annual awards, and I was invited to the awards ceremony at Lambeth Palace in London.

You don't know the value of something unless it's taken away from you. Only once the Qur'an was taken from me did I truly understand its worth. And, today, when I look back over my life, I can now recognise the purpose for which Allah was preparing me over the course of 11 long and testing years of absence. At the beginning, I would never have chosen the path I was forced to walk. But standing where I am now, with the clarity of hindsight and the calm that comes from surrender, I am grateful. Truly grateful. Those 11 years shaped me. They deepened me. They enriched me in ways I could never have foreseen.

Such is the Wisdom of Allah: subtle, precise and always unfolding in perfect time. What once felt like punishment now feels like preparation. What once seemed like darkness was, in fact, a concealed light. We may not see it in the moment, but with patience and trust, His Wisdom always reveals itself. And when it does, it leaves us in awe of Him.

Pause and Reflect

Dearest reader, get up and walk over to a physical copy of the Qur'an and hold it. Take a few moments to feel it in your hands. Open it. You are looking at the Words of the Creator who created your eyes, your hands, your loved ones and everything within the heavens and the earth. In this week's verse, Allah 'azza wa jal says إِنَّ هَٰذَا الْقُرْآنَ ; the use of إِنَّ adds emphasis, signifying with absolute certainty that this Qur'an does not just guide. It is a Book that contains His Precise Words.

When the Book of Allah was placed in Babar's hands by the chaplain in that US prison cell, it was as if he was seeing it for the first time. Only then, having been without it, was he able to fully appreciate its blessing and its comfort. But we can see it any time we like, and perhaps that's why we don't always truly see it.

The word يَهْدِي (yahdī), guides comes from هدى (huda), which is a compassionate, step-by-step guide to the most upright, balanced, just and perfect path. Allah uses أَقْوَمُ (aqwamu) in the superlative form of qama, which means upright, just and straight. Look at the word that follows: وَيُبَشِّرُ (wa yubashiru), a glad tiding from the root بشر (bashara), which also means 'skin'. It is as though Allah's Words lead you to such a balanced and good life, that this blessing affects you so deeply that the manifestation is seen on the surface of your skin: in the coolness of your skin, in your hairs lying flat on your arm when you are calm and at peace, in the smile on your face – manifestations of the blessings of comfort that come from His Words. Truly, the Qur'an is the greatest of all the gifts from Al-Kareem, The Most Generous.

This is the book within your hands. This is the power of the Words your eyes are looking upon. His Qur'an guides you to the good life, manifests beautifully upon you and is the very reason why a grand reward is being prepared for you. Allahu akbar!

Live with His Words . . .

Here are three steps to live with this week's verse(s):

1. Before any major decision (work, family, personal), ask: What does the Qur'an say about this? Use it as your moral compass.

2. Before you read, recite or study the Qur'an, thank Allah for His Book.

3. Turn to the One who has generously gifted you the Qur'an and continues to gift you through the Qur'an and tell Him: My Bountiful Lord, to You belongs all praise for the light of Your Book through which You illuminate my heart. O Allah, make me from the people of the Qur'an – those who are especially beloved to You.

A Question for Your Heart

Ask yourself: Is the Qur'an a guest in my life, or a guide?

Fall in Love with The Author

Al-Kareem, The Most Generous, is honouring your soul by permitting it to hear His Words, read His Words and move forward in life with their light so that you may win in this life and the next.

WEEK 22:

Unwanted Decree

Verse(s) of the Week
Your Rabb's Words for Your Soul

ٱلَّذِينَ يُوفُونَ بِعَهْدِ ٱللَّهِ وَلَا يَنقُضُونَ ٱلْمِيثَـٰقَ ٢٠ وَٱلَّذِينَ يَصِلُونَ مَا أَمَرَ ٱللَّهُ بِهِ أَن يُوصَلَ وَيَخْشَوْنَ رَبَّهُمْ وَيَخَافُونَ سُوءَ ٱلْحِسَابِ ٢١ وَٱلَّذِينَ صَبَرُوا ٱبْتِغَآءَ وَجْهِ رَبِّهِمْ وَأَقَامُوا ٱلصَّلَوٰةَ وَأَنفَقُوا مِمَّا رَزَقْنَـٰهُمْ سِرًّا وَعَلَانِيَةً وَيَدْرَءُونَ بِٱلْحَسَنَةِ ٱلسَّيِّئَةَ أُو۟لَـٰٓئِكَ لَهُمْ عُقْبَى ٱلدَّارِ ٢٢ جَنَّـٰتُ عَدْنٍ يَدْخُلُونَهَا وَمَن صَلَحَ مِنْ ءَابَآئِهِمْ وَأَزْوَٰجِهِمْ وَذُرِّيَّـٰتِهِمْ وَٱلْمَلَـٰٓئِكَةُ يَدْخُلُونَ عَلَيْهِم مِّن كُلِّ بَابٍ ٢٣ سَلَـٰمٌ عَلَيْكُم بِمَا صَبَرْتُمْ فَنِعْمَ عُقْبَى ٱلدَّارِ ٢٤

Alladhīna yūfūna bi'ahdi Allāhi wa lā yanquḍūna al-mīthāq

Wa alladhīna yaṣilūna mā amara Allāhu bihi an yūṣala wa yakhshawna rabbahum wa yakhāfūna sū'a al-ḥisāb

Wa alladhīna ṣabarū ibtigā'a wajhi rabbihim wa aqāmū aṣ-ṣalāh wa anfaqū mimmā razaqnāhum sirran wa 'alāniyah wa yadrūna bil-ḥasanati as-sayyi'ah, ulā'ika lahum 'uqbā ad-dār

Jannātu 'adnin yadkhulūnahā wa man ṣalaḥa min ābā'ihim wa azwājihim wa dhurriyyātihim wal-malā'ikatu yadkhulūna 'alayhim min kulli bāb

Salāmun 'alaykum bimā ṣabartum, fani'ma 'uqbā ad-dār

'Those who fulfil the covenant of Allah and do not break their pledge. And those who join what Allah has commanded to be joined, and fear their Lord, and dread the terribleness of reckoning. And those who endure patiently, seeking the pleasure of their Lord, establish prayer, and spend from what We have provided them – secretly and openly – and repel evil with good. It is they who will have the ultimate abode . . . And the angels will enter upon them from every gate (saying): Peace be upon you for the patience you practised. How excellent is the final home!'

Surah Ra'd 20–24

One of the greatest tests of my faith is when the very things I prayed for don't happen. Qadr (decree) is one of the hardest pillars of faith to contend with. It requires submission. It requires total acceptance. It requires total trust. But these states aren't automatic and they certainly aren't easy.

My dear friend Zainab's story is one in which there was no choice.

Zainab's Story

I knew my mum was dying. There's nothing harder than being up against qadr – when there's something you really want and Allah's Decree is the complete opposite. That's hard. It's really hard.

Accepting qadr means you have to surrender. And surrendering to the death of a beloved person is the hardest test of faith and true surrender to Allah's Will.

I kept making du'a for what I wanted: for Mum to still be with me. I made du'a with full conviction. But then I felt torn between making du'a for her health and getting better, or surrendering and instead making du'a for her, for the ease of her passing. It was a struggle; I wanted to save her but I could see that Allah was taking her back.

During the time that she was between life and death, verses from the Qur'an kept coming up as I was reading. What really helped me was just understanding the journey of the believer's soul. They will be welcomed into a better world than this. In our grief, we're distraught at the thought of losing them from our side, when really, we're stopping them from reaching a better place.

The verses from Surah Ra'd verses 20–24 popped up just as my mum died. I'd read them before, but Allah willed that I would read them differently at that time. I know that was Him reminding me and comforting me.

Pause and Reflect

This dunya is heavy. It's hard. It's unrelenting. And it's meant to be that way. It's meant to be that way because it is simply a stop on our journey home. A stop on a journey is for a brief time of rest. It isn't a place to get comfortable, as you're not meant to stay. It's a pause in the movement of your soul to its final resting place.

We are all in one of three states: we've either been tested, are being tested or will be tested. You will always find yourself in one of these three chapters of life: looking back tired at what you've just endured, right in the thick of something now, or moving towards something that will test your levels of sabr (patience), tawakkul (reliance) and faith in who Allah is and can be for you in this new trial.

In Zainab's story, we find the very human internal battle of what you want to be decreed versus what is actually decreed. This battle doesn't lessen your reward in any way. Like a back that has not been accustomed to bowing down in ruku (the bowing position in prayer), it will be stiff, it will feel unnatural, it will even be painful. But the more your back experiences ruku, the easier it becomes. This is how it feels to battle with yourself over Allah's Decree.

Allah sees your difficulty in trying to be patient with your ego screaming at you: *This isn't what I wanted! This isn't fair!* At the end of 2020, my house in Algeria burned down. It was the last test after a series of back-to-back tests. When I found out what had happened, I said to Allah: 'Inna lillahi wa inna ilayhi rajoun', in that moment trying to be a strong believer who was accepting of Allah's Decree.

But the very next second, my human heart cried out: *Allah, now this? I can't take any more!*

Then I remembered sabr (patience, endurance, steadfastness) is the right response at the onset of a test. My aspiring believing self wanted to be trusting of Al-Wali's decree. And then I burst out crying in disbelief this was happening to me.

This was the up and down, the to and fro, that takes place within the heart. That struggle does not go unnoticed by Allah. He sees a Muslim trying to be a mumin (a strong believer) and He receives you by those very aspirations. Such is His Compassionate Care and Generosity.

Your endurance, that active sabr, is rewarded by the angels flocking to welcome you, meeting you with greetings of peace for that very human battle of trying to be a believer.

Live with His Words . . .

Here are three steps to live with this week's verse(s):

1. When facing a difficulty, instead of asking, 'Why me?', ask, 'How is this shaping me for my final home?' Write your answer down. See how your struggles refine your faith.

2. Go through the portrait of the righteous that has been painted in this week's verses. Which of the qualities mentioned in the verse would you like to embody for Allah?

3. Turn to the One who knows your struggle to submit and tell Him: Ya Allah, help me be among those who honour the covenant I've made with You – to worship You, trust You, and remain true to Your Path even when it's hard. Plant patience deep in my heart when I'm tested, and make me constant in my connection to You.

A Question for Your Heart

Acceptance doesn't mean you don't feel pain. It means you turn the pain into a bridge to Allah instead of a wall between you and Him. How can you do exactly that in a situation you are facing right now?

Fall in Love with The Author

Al-Wafiyy – The Most Faithful – is a Lord who wants you to uphold your covenant with Him, even when it is hard, even when it requires sacrifice. And because He is Al-Wafiyy, He sees your steadfastness to keep to your covenant and fulfils His Promise to you.

WEEK 23:

Surrender

Verse(s) of the Week
Your Rabb's Words for Your Soul

أَلَّذِى خَلَقَنِى فَهُوَ يَهْدِينِ ٧٨ وَأَلَّذِى هُوَ يُطْعِمُنِى وَيَسْقِينِ ٧٩ وَإِذَا مَرِضْتُ فَهُوَ يَشْفِينِ ٨٠

Alladhī khalaqanī fa-huwa yahdīnī
Wa alladhī huwa yuṭ'imunī wa yasqīnī
Wa 'idhā maridtu fa-huwa yashfīnī

''He is' the One who created me, and He 'alone' guides me.
'He is' the One Who provides me with food and drink. And
when I am ill, it is He who cures me.'

Surah Ash-Shu'ara 26:78–80

W e first met Nadia in Week 8. Her story continues here.
It is a journey through her deepest vulnerability – the
need to control outcomes to protect the people she
loves. But eventually, she learned what we all must: there's no need
to hold on so tightly, because Allah 'azza wa jal is already holding
everything and managing it all, perfectly.

Nadia's Story Continues

My family was moving house. We were downsizing from a big house to a smaller one, and it was pretty exhausting. On the day we moved, I was unpacking all day and finally went to bed at 11pm. When I woke up, I was unable to move the left side of my face. I thought, That's odd. Did I sleep funny? Maybe it will come back. But it didn't. Immediately my mind went to the thought that maybe I was having a stroke. But at the hospital, CT scans confirmed that it, in fact, wasn't a stroke. It was a condition called facial palsy.

I've seen many people with the condition. It's the one thing I had always made du'a to never be tested with. So when they told me it was indeed this condition, I thought to myself, It can't be. I made du'a! Allah wouldn't test me with this! I was in denial.

I was severely affected. The doctors gave me a huge dose of cortisone to manage the pain and symptoms. I don't react very well to cortisone. I was crippled, I couldn't move. I was in bed all the time. I couldn't even eat.

The hospital neurologist told me: 'It's one of the severe types of the condition. So even if it improves, it's not going to improve that much.'

I remember hearing his words and saying to myself: It's not you who will decide. It is Allah who will decide. The words of the Prophet Ibrahim (alayhis-salam) found in Surah Ash-Shu'ara comforted me like nothing ever has.

For two to three weeks, I remained in that state – unable to eat or talk. But I was with Allah during this time, making du'a and reading Qur'an. And my Rabb was with me.

The old me would have been panicking and going from one doctor to the other, trying to defy the odds, to prove them wrong. There would have been anger and much questioning astaghfiruAllah (may Allah forgive me). But I was calm, although I couldn't eat solid food. I was at peace even though the water I was drinking would escape my mouth and run down the side of my face. I was content despite being unable to sit with my family to eat, out of embarrass-ment at what they would see when I tried to eat or drink. My heart was smiling though I physically couldn't smile. I was with Allah through my relationship with the Qur'an. And He was certainly with me.

SubhanAllah, all that is left of the condition now are minor uncontrollable movements of one of the muscles around the eye. That's it. That is how Allah carried me through. It was He that cured me. But not just in terms of this illness; He cured me to the point of being able to feel at peace during this illness – something I didn't have prior to Him guiding me to live with His Book.

Pause and Reflect

Allah 'azza wa jal gifted Nadia with a verse, this week's verses, uttered by the blessed mouth of Allah's Khalil, Allah's Intimate Friend, the Prophet Ibrahim (alayhis-salam).

The verses are a lesson in surrender. Ibrahim (alayhis-salam) acknowledged Allah's Complete and Absolute Control over all aspects of his life. In this week's verses, he begins by acknowledging Allah's Blessings upon him:

1. Allah created him (26:78)

2. Allah guides him (26:78)

3. Allah provides him with food and drink (26:79)

4. Allah cures him when he is sick (26:80)

These verses indicate complete dependence on Allah for guidance, sustenance and healing.

Your very existence is only by His Will. Your belief is only because He guided you. Your food, drink, car, phone, laptop, even this book is only yours because He gave these things to you. And when you face difficulties, it is He who supports, heals and cures you. In this week's verses are lessons for you: to turn to Allah first for all your needs. Not last, having exhausted all other means, but first, because it is He who knows the best means for your cure or solution to your problems.

And when healing or a solution is delayed, trust in Allah's Wisdom that there is always goodness in His Plan. Often it is because He wants to give you much more than the shifaa (cure) or the positive outcome. He wants your soul to experience the sweetness of surrendering to Him.

Live with His Words . . .

Here are three steps to live with this week's verse(s):

1. We all experience ill health: some are minor ailments like a winter cold, and some are major challenges. Whatever the case, memorise the verse from this week so that you may recite it every time you are ill.

2. Incorporate Qur'anic healing in your routine. Make it a habit to recite verses of shifaa, such as Surah Al-Fatiha, Ayat Al-Kursi, the last two verses of Surah Al-Baqarah and the Mu'awwidhatayn (Surah Al-Falaq and Surah An-Nas). Do this regularly, even when you're not ill, as a means of protection and maintenance.

3. Tell your Rabb: Ya Allah, Ya Shafi, the One who heals seen and unseen pain, I turn to You as the only true source of

healing. Heal me in ways that no doctor or medicine ever could. And if healing is decreed to arrive at a later time, grant me patience. If it comes quickly, grant me humility, remembering it is always from You.

A Question for Your Heart

When faced with illness, whether physical, emotional or spiritual, how might your life change were you to turn to Allah first, with complete certainty that He is The Ultimate Healer and Best Disposer of your affairs?

Fall in Love with The Author

Al-Shafi is a Lord who heals and wants you to be certain, that no matter how deep the wounds are, His Cure is beyond your human comprehension. When you are in pain, whether physical, emotional or spiritual, He wants you to turn to Him for relief. His Healing extends to the heart and soul, restoring you to your fitrah, of being a soul at peace with Him.

WEEK 24:

Worry

Verse(s) of the Week
Your Rabb's Words for Your Soul

وَتَوَكَّلْ عَلَى ٱللَّهِ ۚ وَكَفَىٰ بِٱللَّهِ وَكِيلًا ٣

Wa tawakkal 'alallāh; wa kafā billāhi wakīlā

*'And put your trust in Allah, for Allah is sufficient as a Trustee
of Affairs.'*

Surah Al-Ahzab 33:3

I've started to notice a pattern in my tests. It's rarely about what the test is. Rather, it becomes a test when I'm required to completely let go, relinquish control and place my trust in Allah 'azza wa jal.

Again and again, Allah sends me trials that seem to whisper: *if you truly believe He is the Best Disposer of your Affairs, if you call upon Him as Al-Wakeel – The One who Protects and The Ultimate Guide – then let that trust be visible in your actions.* And when it isn't, He gently, lovingly, sends another reminder, so I can absorb

147

the lesson more deeply: to live a life anchored in tawakkul, in full reliance upon Him alone.

Nadia's Story Continues

I've made a really good recovery from my facial palsy, but seven months ago, my husband was diagnosed with cancer. The one thing that has kept me going are verses 4 and 5 in Surah Sajdah:

ٱللَّهُ ٱلَّذِى خَلَقَ ٱلسَّمَٰوَٰتِ وَٱلْأَرْضَ وَمَا بَيْنَهُمَا فِى سِتَّةِ أَيَّامٍ ثُمَّ ٱسْتَوَىٰ عَلَى ٱلْعَرْشِ ۖ مَا لَكُم مِّن دُونِهِۦ مِن وَلِىٍّ وَلَا شَفِيعٍ ۚ أَفَلَا تَتَذَكَّرُونَ ٤

يُدَبِّرُ ٱلْأَمْرَ مِنَ ٱلسَّمَآءِ إِلَى ٱلْأَرْضِ ثُمَّ يَعْرُجُ إِلَيْهِ فِى يَوْمٍ كَانَ مِقْدَارُهُۥ أَلْفَ سَنَةٍ مِّمَّا تَعُدُّونَ ٥

Allāhu alladhī khalaqa as-samāwāti wal-arḍa wa-mā baynahumā fī sittati ayyāmin thumma istawā 'alal-'arsh(i) mā lakum min dūnihi min waliyyin walā shafī'in afalā tatazakkarūn(a) yudabbiru al-amra mina as-samā'i ilal-arḍi thumma ya'ruju ilayhi fī yawmin kāna miqdāruhu alfa sanatin mimmā ta'addūn(a)

It is Allah Who has created the heavens and the earth and everything in between in six days, then established Himself on the Throne. You have no protector or intercessor besides Him. Will you not then be mindful? He conducts every affair from the heavens to the earth, then it all ascends to Him on a Day whose length is a thousand years by your counting.

Ayah 5 has been my companion. يُدَبِّرُ ٱلْأَمْرَ *yudabbiru al-amr, Allah will manage my affairs. He manages all affairs. Every time I have ever felt I don't know which choice to make, I remember it's not up to me. He has showed me in so many ways that He takes care of us, so why should I ever worry?*

There have been many changes in our lives recently, and when I look back I see that these changes had already begun before my husband received his diagnosis. They were happening to prepare us, to enable us as a family to manage the situation.

Allah put everything in place practically to enable us to cope with what was coming. SubhanAllah.

Allah, ﷻ, directed me to Surah Al-Ahzab 33:3 and it has been my refuge. This is what I have and will continue to hold onto, alhamdulillah.

Before I had a relationship with the Qur'an, I would worry about everything. I would come up with a million scenarios of what could go wrong and the million solutions I'd have to find to protect my loved ones. My father died when I was a child, and this left me with a terror of also losing my mother. I felt a need to do everything to prevent her from dying. I can see now how this transferred into anxiety about other loved ones, and a lot of unhappiness.

But there's a limit to what you can do. It was exhausting to constantly try. Now I've realised, it's not up to me, and that's changed my life. I still worry, but now there's a limit. It stops. That's the way Allah has healed me through the Qur'an. He healed the trauma I grew up with.

Pause and Reflect

يُدَبِّرُ ٱلْأَمْرَ yudabbiru al-amr, Allah manages affairs, Allah, ﷻ, always puts things in their perfect place. He is the One to be trusted completely.

This week's verse was revealed at a time when the Prophet ﷺ was faced with severe trials – some personal and others connected to the community, especially during the Battle of Ahzab. This opening verse prepares the ground for all of these tests. Multiple powerful Arab tribes had united to wipe out the Muslims in Madinah. The Muslims were completely outnumbered. And the hypocrites in Madinah began to try to weaken the morale of the Muslims by sowing seeds of doubt in their hearts that led some to abandon their positions and return home. The Muslims were completely gripped with fear. It was as much an emotional and mental battle as it was a physical battle.

The Prophet ﷺ had to stand firm and hold the Muslims together. He had to execute the strategy, leading and supporting, while he himself was the main target to be killed.

This verse was revealed at that time with a command from Allah: وَتَوَكَّلْ (Wa tawakkal) – a verb that indicates continuous action – reliance that is renewed and constantly repeated. For who? عَلَى اللهِ – ('alallāh). The preposition عَلَى (upon) creates an image in the mind of leaning on someone, placing all your weight on one that will hold you up.

Your Lord wants you to always remember that He is your وَكِيلًا Wakil. His Name and Attribute comes from the root و-ك-ل (wa-ka-la), which means to entrust, hand over and manage your affairs in your absence. Al-Wakeel is your Lord who manages what you cannot see or control.

Live with His Words . . .

Here are three steps to live with this week's verse(s):

1. At the end of a stressful day, journal one thing you need to let go of – and consciously hand it to Allah.

2. Start relying on Allah in the small things: missing the bus, a delayed WhatsApp message, a last-minute schedule

change. Practise surrender in those moments, and your heart will learn to trust Him during bigger storms.

3. Turn to the One who wants you to know you can and must lean on Him and tell Him: Al-Wakeel, I completely hand over the matters of my heart to You. I give You my fears and the burdens that are too heavy for me to carry. I am never able to see the full picture, but I am certain You see all and manage everything with mercy and wisdom.

A Question for Your Heart

Ask yourself: What am I desperately trying to hold together with my own hands that Allah is asking me to surrender, not because I'm weak, but because He is Al-Wakeel (The Guardian, The Best Disposer of affairs)?

Fall in Love with The Author

Al-Wakeel is a Lord who manages all your affairs with power, heaps of mercy, perfect timing and abundant love.

WEEK 25:

One Step at a Time

Verse(s) of the Week
Your Rabb's Words for Your Soul

وَإِذَا سَأَلَكَ عِبَادِى عَنِّى فَإِنِّى قَرِيبٌ ۖ أُجِيبُ دَعْوَةَ ٱلدَّاعِ إِذَا دَعَانِ ۖ فَلْيَسْتَجِيبُواْ لِى وَلْيُؤْمِنُواْ
بِى لَعَلَّهُمْ يَرْشُدُونَ ١٨٦

Wa idhā sa'alaka 'ibādī 'annī fa-innī qarīb, ujību da'wata ad-dā'i idhā da'ān, fal-yastajībū lī wa-l-yu'minū bī la'allahum yarshudūn

'When My servants ask you ˙O Prophet˙ about Me: I am truly near. I respond to one's prayer when they call upon Me. So let them respond ˙with obedience˙ to Me and believe in Me, perhaps they will be guided ˙to the Right Way˙.'

Surah Al-Baqarah 2:186

One of my favourite hadith qudsi (revelation of Allah to the Prophet, narrated in the Prophet's own words) is:

The Messenger of Allah ﷺ said:

Allah Almighty says: Whoever draws close to Me by the length of a hand, I will draw close to him by the length of an arm. Whoever draws close to Me the by length of an arm, I will draw close to him by the length of a fathom. Whoever comes to Me walking, I will come to him running. Whoever meets Me with enough sins to fill the earth, not associating any partners with Me, I will meet him with as much forgiveness.

Sahih Muslim

All Allah wants from you is a step towards Him and He 'azza wa jal turns towards you with so much more. This was definitely the case with my friend Romina, who once had to admit that the Qur'an wasn't her favourite book.

Romina's Story Continues

I had my last child after a big gap. I didn't think I was going to have another baby. So when she came along, it was a huge surprise.

The pregnancy was hard. I suffered with severe sciatic pain. The labour was difficult. I really thought I would just fall into the swing of things, having already had three children. But that didn't happen. I felt I was doing everything wrong and I judged myself harshly. I was overcome with sadness and grief and I didn't know what had hit me. It was like living under this dark cloud and everyone else was living in sunshine. It's really difficult to explain how it feels unless you've been there. I didn't think I had post-natal depression. I didn't know what was going on, but somehow I felt I needed to get back to my relationship with the Qur'an, which had slipped a bit.

I started doing something I had heard a revert brother had done: each day, he would write out one line of Qur'an and just sit and think about it. He would try to learn the meanings word for word. He ended up learning the whole Arabic vocabulary through doing that.

So I decided I was going to write down one line from the Qur'an every day. I started from Surah Mulk in Juz Tabarak. I found the words: TabarakaAlladhi bi yahdhil mulk, Blessed is Allah, in whose hand is the dominion. And suddenly I started crying – it was as if a dam had burst. Whenever things felt overwhelming for me, I would recite that verse. It helped me feel that everything would be okay because nothing is outside of His Power. Everything is part of His Plan.

I would talk to my heart and acknowledge: Right now, this is the worst thing ever. I feel like crap. It's horrible and it seems never-ending, but it's okay.

I was able to recognise that although the cloud was there, the sun was behind it. I couldn't see the sun, but it's definitely there. And one day I will see it, with Allah's Help. And eventually, I did.

Pause and Reflect

Living with the Qur'an is my third book, and this is the third time I am writing about this beautiful verse. It is one of my absolute favourites and provides me with so much comfort during the different seasons and experiences in my life.

This time, I want to draw your attention to how your seemingly small steps are always valued by Allah.

Sometimes life brings tests where you feel stuck, chained, imprisoned, crippled and all you can manage is to whisper 'Allah'. Or you lift your head up towards the sky, tears trickling from the corners of your eyes. It's okay. Allah knows.

That whisper, that small, seemingly insignificant step towards Allah is met by a Lord who has said that He is ‏قَرِيب‎, qarib, which means 'near'. He won't arrive after you fix up, after you muster up more energy, after your whisper turns to a 'proper' du'a or you wipe away your tears, sort yourself out and take real action. No, He 'azza wa jal tells you He is already near.

Romina took one step towards Allah and He pulled her out of the trenches. What does your one step towards Allah need to be when you face the most testing times of your life?

Live with His Words . . .

Here are three steps to live with this week's verse(s):

1. Start a journal noting all the ways Allah has responded to your du'a. Refer to it when you feel caught in a storm.

2. In your reading of the Qur'an this week, choose one action where you can respond to a call of Allah (a command, a reminder, or even a verse that moved you), and act on it this week.

3. Turn to the One who is near and tell Him: Al-Qarib, You have promised that when I call You, You respond. I am here, Rabbi, calling upon You as my imperfect self, with absolute need. Allah, draw me close. Guide me, respond to me, and make me of those who love to call upon You.

A Question for Your Heart

If you truly believe that Allah responds when you call upon Him, what do you need to stop carrying and instead start surrendering?

Fall in Love with The Author

Al-Qarib is The Lord Who is Ever Near. He never leaves your call unanswered. He is closer than you can imagine and is with you, observing you, listening to you and knows your call even if it is silent.

WEEK 26:

Turning Back

Verse(s) of the Week
Your Rabb's Words for Your Soul

وَبَلَوۡنَـٰهُم بِٱلۡحَسَنَـٰتِ وَٱلسَّيِّئَاتِ لَعَلَّهُمۡ يَرۡجِعُونَ ١٦٨

Wa balawnāhum bil-ḥasanāti wa as-sayyi'āti la'allahum yarji'ūn

'We tested them with prosperity and adversity, so perhaps they would return 'to the Right Path'.'

Surah Al-Araf 7:168

As I write this book, I find myself in the midst of a test that has lasted five years. It feels as though the weight of it is growing heavier, and it has been draining me both mentally and emotionally. Deep down, I know Allah is calling me to learn something through this trial. I can sense that the reason it has persisted is because I have yet to fully grasp the lesson He wants me to learn. Initially, I thought the lesson was in how I should respond, but I know the real lesson is what I must change within myself. Deep down I know and I'm nervous, because it requires me to address one of the deepest layers of myself and probably my most crucial lesson to date – the lesson of self-worth. I thought of this as I listened to the story of Ola Shoubaki of the Arabic Gems Institute, who was once my teacher of Arabic and then became my friend.

Ola's Story

I teach Qur'anic Arabic. And as I teach, there are some verses that just hit me at various times. Even a verse I know, at certain times, hits me differently.

For example, take the terrible suffering in Gaza right now, in 2025. My family is from Gaza. I've had to rely a lot on the Qur'an to try to make sense of it and not completely break down over what my family is going through.

There's a verse that has brought me much comfort:

ٱلَّذِينَ إِذَآ أَصَٰبَتْهُم مُّصِيبَةٌ قَالُوٓا۟ إِنَّا لِلَّهِ وَإِنَّآ إِلَيْهِ رَٰجِعُونَ ١٥٦

Alladhīna idhā aṣābat-hum muṣībatun qālū innā lillāhi wa innā ilayhi rāji'ūn.

. . . who say, when struck by a disaster, 'Surely to Allah we belong and to Him we will all return.'

Surah Al Baqarah 2:156

A museeba, مُصِيبَة, doesn't have to be a huge calamity. It can be anything that strikes you and causes discomfort. Those who are struck by a calamity and then turn to Allah and say innā lillāhi wa innā ilayhi rāji'ūn are the ones who will receive Allah's Blessings and Mercy.

Every single time you are struck by something difficult in your life, and then you say: I am turning back to Allah, I am reassessing and going back to the path that I should be on already; the one I turned from; the path where I should be walking towards Allah – the natural path of life – where every step I take turns me closer to Allah. That's when you will find His Blessings and Mercy even during the test. It's the act of turning back that matters. We are actively returning to Him as a state within ourselves. Those who do this are the ones for whom Allah 'azza wa jal has promised a reward.

I saw a video from Gaza where someone said: 'We have missiles, death, hunger, thirst. But we don't fear anything except the Lord of the Worlds. But we do fear the silence of the Ummah (Islamic community) – the state of the Muslims. What are they doing with their lives?!'

When you see the people of Gaza and you think, What on earth are you made of to be dealing with things in this way? It is because they are people of the Qur'an. There are more huffadh (memorisers of the entire Qur'an) in Gaza than the rest of the world. And they're constantly reciting amidst the bombings.

It's easy for us to say: 'Hope for your reward.' But could we, in our safe, warm homes, endure what the people of Gaza have been forced to today? These are people who exemplify innā lillāhi wa innā ilayhi rāji'ūn. They live by the Qur'an, as we all should.

Pause and Reflect

Allah 'azza wa jal says that it is a sunnah of life to be tested with alternating ease and hardship. Such alternations are to realign our souls to what is important, to truth and the straight path to Him.

Your tests are not random blessings or trials. Like an exam, they are prepared divinely in order for you to learn and grow.

Bil-ḥasanāti wa as-sayyi'āti means 'with good and bad'. You'll be tested with both. But look at the fact that hasanat (good) was placed before sayyi'at (bad). Your Lord does not wish to test you endlessly with difficulty. Allah often begins by testing you with blessings first to awaken your soul to who the blessings came from, so that you may be grateful, give thanks and remember who is nourishing you and providing for you. And when you don't take heed of your blessings, challenges may follow to wake you up.

The order of the words in this verse shows your Lord's Compassion. He gives ease before hardship. Why? Because La'allahum yarji'ūn, so that you may return to Him.

Allah uses la'alla (لَعَلَّ) to demonstrate that He gives you these tests only out of His Mercy. He hopes for your return. He is patient for this. He tests you with both blessings and hardship because He wants you close.

Live with His Words . . .

Here are three steps to live with this week's verse(s):

1. This week, when things go well, pause and say Alhamdulillah with presence. When things seem to go wrong, whisper innā lillāhi wa innā ilayhi rāji'ūn, and mean it. Train yourself to turn both ease and hardship into worship.

2. This week take yourself out to somewhere where you can reflect and journal: what has Allah been teaching me this week?

3. Turn to the One who always wants you to return and tell Him: O Allah, don't leave me to myself, not even for the blink of an eye. Be with me in every moment. Ya Rabb, my heart gets tired. I forget. I know I drift away. My Most Kind Lord, return me to You in a beautiful way. Let me come back to You not just in pain, but in every state.

A Question for Your Heart

In your current circumstances, what is your greatest blessing and what is your greatest trial? What are you meant to learn from both?

Fall in Love with The Author

Al-Haleem – The Most Forbearing – is a Lord who gives you time, signs, blessings and tests. Your tests are not to punish you, but as with the others, to turn your heart gently back to Him.

WEEK 27:

Repetition

Verse(s) of the Week
Your Rabb's Words for Your Soul

اللَّهُ نَزَّلَ أَحْسَنَ ٱلْحَدِيثِ كِتَـٰبًا مُّتَشَـٰبِهًا مَّثَانِىَ تَقْشَعِرُّ مِنْهُ جُلُودُ ٱلَّذِينَ يَخْشَوْنَ رَبَّهُمْ ثُمَّ تَلِينُ جُلُودُهُمْ وَقُلُوبُهُمْ إِلَىٰ ذِكْرِ ٱللَّهِ ۚ ذَٰلِكَ هُدَى ٱللَّهِ يَهْدِى بِهِۦ مَن يَشَآءُ ۚ وَمَن يُضْلِلِ ٱللَّهُ فَمَا لَهُۥ مِنْ هَادٍ ٢٣

*Allāhu nazzala aḥsana al-ḥadīthi kitāban mutashābihan
mathānī taqsha'irru min'hu julūdu alladhīna yakhshawna
rabbahum thumma talīnu julūduhum wa qulūbuhum ilā
dhikri Allāh; dhālika hudā Allāhi yahdī bihī man yashā', wa
man yuḍlili Allāhu fa-mā lahu min hād.*

*''It is` Allah `Who` has sent down the best message – a Book
of perfect consistency and repeated lessons – which causes
the skin `and hearts` of those who fear their Lord to tremble,
then their skin and hearts soften at the mention of `the mercy
of` Allah. That is the guidance of Allah, through which He
guides whoever He wills. But whoever Allah leaves to stray
will be left with no guide.'*

Surah Az-Zumar 39:23

I n one of the first lessons of my Qur'an course, my teacher shared a verse from Surah Yunus that perfectly mirrored the hopes I had for this course – that it would transform both me and my heart. The verse was:

يَـٰٓأَيُّهَا ٱلنَّاسُ قَدْ جَآءَتْكُم مَّوْعِظَةٌ مِّن رَّبِّكُمْ وَشِفَآءٌ لِّمَا فِى ٱلصُّدُورِ وَهُدًى وَرَحْمَةٌ لِّلْمُؤْمِنِينَ ٥٧

Yā ayyuhā al-nāsu qad jā'atkum maw'iẓatun min rabbikum wa shifā'un limā fī al-ṣudūri wa hudan wa raḥmatun lil-mu'minīn.

O humanity! Indeed, there has come to you a warning from your Lord, a cure for what is in the hearts, a guide, and a mercy for the believers.

Surah Yunus 10:57

I felt as though this verse was speaking directly to me. Here I was, with a soul parched from the wear of life, and Allah was reassuring me that the Qur'an would heal me, guide me and lead me to His Mercy. He knew exactly what I needed – to be filled, to be guided and to feel complete through it.

As Wasim's story continues, we see how the power of the Qur'an is such that sometimes all it takes is one verse to completely transform our mindset and heart for a specific moment in our lives.

Wasim's Story Continues

I was diagnosed with a cancerous tumour in my small intestine. I had an operation, but was told that the tumour might have spread. It was a very frightening time. I've never faced anything like that before. It literally might mean the end of my life. We all know we're going to die as Muslims. But hearing that it could be very soon – it's hard.

There was one ayah that I recited the most while I was waiting for news. It was the words of Ibrahim (alayhis-salam): 'And if I become ill, He is the One who cures.'

You read stories of the companions of the Prophet 鸞 who recite one verse repeatedly, over and over again in their salah. And you wonder, What is it about that verse? That one ayah must be so relevant to their situation. That was how it was for me. Besides salah, while doing anything, I didn't stop repeating Ibrahim's (alayhis-salam) words. I was calling upon Allah, using it as a du'a. As I recited the verse, I would place my hand just below my chest and I would almost feel the recitation of that specific verse was doing something. In my mind, as I recited it, I was visualising it killing any cancerous cells. Every time, I would imagine the Qur'an having that physical impact.

When the news came, it was good. The doctors had been worried about my cancer spreading, but that hadn't happened. I was okay for the moment, but they gave me all sorts of percentages about whether or not it might return. I had to be monitored for the next five years.

I talked to a brother about what I was going through, and he said to me: 'Don't work with percentages. You need to detach yourself from the chemo. The medicine can help you, but remember it is Allah who will cure you and help you, through the medicine, as a means.'

I only saw that brother once, but it is as though he was divinely sent to teach me a lesson in complete unwavering certainty. That's what got me through. Knowing that instead of constant fear and anxiety, and working out the chances of this or that happening, I could have peace and trust in Allah.

Pause and Reflect

Having covered the verse of Ibrahim (alayhis-salam) in a previous chapter, in Week 23, I wish to draw your heart's attention to something else in Wasim's story: the intimacy of holding on to one verse, believing in it, internalising it and repeating it with certainty and hope that it will open a way.

There are several narrations that describe the companions of the Prophet ﷺ repeating the same verse during their salah. Here is one such narration when the Prophet ﷺ himself did just that:

> Abu Dharr (radiAllahu anhu) who said: The Prophet ﷺ
> stood reciting a verse and repeating it until morning came.
> That verse was (interpretation of the meaning): 'If You punish
> them, they are Your slaves, and if You forgive them, verily,
> You, only You, are the All-Mighty, the All-Wise', Al-Ma'idah
> 5:118.
>
> *Sahih An-Nasa'i*

Like it was for Wasim, there are moments in life where you need Allah's Help, Mercy and Guidance so desperately that a single verse becomes almost a rope between you and your need, and the only One who can fulfil it.

This week's verse is a perfect description as to why the repetition of one verse – whether in salah or outside of it – is so deeply moving. It is because the Qur'an isn't just a book. It is Allah's Words that become alive in the hearts of those who live with them.

In the verse, Allah says that when مُتَشَابِهًا مَّثَانِيَ (mutashābihan mathānī), which means verses are repeated (mathānī) with layers of meaning, it deepens the heart's reaction. The lessons, stories and warnings in the Qur'an are repeated to drive truth, comfort and direction deeper into our hearts.

Dearest reader, I invite you to think about a current need or yearning that you have right now. Go to the Qur'an and choose a verse that aligns with that need. Memorise it, understand its meaning, use it in your salah and repeat it during the course of the day. And witness how this interaction with Allah's Words impacts your heart. It is incredibly powerful and soothing.

Live with His Words . . .

Here are three steps to live with this week's verse(s):

1. When you recite or hear a verse that moves you even slightly, stop and repeat it slowly. Don't rush to continue. Let the verse sink into your heart. Ask yourself after each repetition: What is Allah telling me through this right now?

2. After each sitting with the Qur'an, pick one verse that shook you or made you feel something. Write a short reflection: How did this verse move me? What part of my life does it touch?

3. Turn to the One whose Words are available to be absorbed, transforming your heart in the process and tell Him: Rabbi, make my heart illuminated by Your Verses, and grant me the ability to identify verses that will strengthen me, repeating them so that my soul is revived. Guide me to live with Your Words, finding in them peace and tranquillity.

A Question for Your Heart

What barriers within you prevent you from allowing the Qur'an to move you as it moved the companions and the Prophet ﷺ? How can you overcome them to truly feel its impact?

Fall in Love with The Author

Ar-Rahman – The Most Merciful – is a Lord who has blessed you with the Qur'an, a source of healing and guidance. He wants you to present yourself openly to its verses and reflect over them. When you do so, He will envelop your heart in mercy that moves your heart not only to survive your struggles, but find lessons and thrive through them.

PART 5:

Relationships

وَٱلْمُؤْمِنُونَ وَٱلْمُؤْمِنَـٰتُ بَعْضُهُمْ أَوْلِيَآءُ بَعْضٍ ۚ يَأْمُرُونَ بِٱلْمَعْرُوفِ وَيَنْهَوْنَ عَنِ ٱلْمُنكَرِ وَيُقِيمُونَ ٱلصَّلَوٰةَ وَيُؤْتُونَ ٱلزَّكَوٰةَ وَيُطِيعُونَ ٱللَّهَ وَرَسُولَهُۥٓ ۚ أُوْلَـٰٓئِكَ سَيَرْحَمُهُمُ ٱللَّهُ ۗ إِنَّ ٱللَّهَ عَزِيزٌ حَكِيمٌ ٧١

Wa al-mu'minūna wa al-mu'minātu ba'ḍuhum awl-
iyā'u ba'ḍin, ya'murūna bi-l-ma'rūfi wa yanhawna
'ani al-munkar, wa yuqīmūna al-ṣalāh, wa yu'tūna
al-zakāh, wa yuṭī'ūna Allāha wa rasūlah, ulā'ika saya
rḥamuhumu Allāh, inna Allāha 'azīzun ḥakīm

'The believers, both men and women, are guardians
of one another. They encourage good and forbid evil,
establish prayer and pay alms-tax, and obey Allah and
His Messenger. It is they who will be shown Allah's
Mercy. Surely Allah is Almighty, All-Wise.'

Surah At-Tawbah 9:71

169

WEEK 28:

Your Heart is Understood

Verse(s) of the Week
Your Rabb's Words for Your Soul

وَإِن تَجْهَرْ بِٱلْقَوْلِ فَإِنَّهُۥ يَعْلَمُ ٱلسِّرَّ وَأَخْفَى ٧

Wa in tajhar bil-qawli fa-innahu ya'lamu al-sirra wa akhfā

'Whether you speak openly 'or not', He certainly knows what is secret and what is even more hidden.'

Surah Taha 20:7

My greatest tests always seem to revolve around people. And I know I'm not the only one. Whether it's parents, siblings, a spouse or ex-spouse, children, friends, colleagues or extended family – relationships are complex. They can draw out your best qualities, and your deepest wounds. They can be a source of immense joy, and the reason your heart breaks.

171

At the core, I think we're all yearning for the same thing: to be seen by those closest to us, to be understood. Ahmed's story continues from Week 11 – from trying to establish himself as a young man to excelling in his career, he shared a reflection on a verse that took me by surprise. It offered me comfort and helped shift something deep within – a new perspective in my own pursuit to feel truly seen.

Ahmed's Story Continues

Alhamdulillah, after I received my medical licence and became established financially and career-wise, I became very involved and active in the Muslim community, which then led me to become the religious director of my local mosque. It was a very busy time and included a lot of work. And sometimes when you're in the position of helping others, whether it's community work or even with family and friends, you don't receive acknowledgement or appreciation from people. That can be difficult, because it's only human to want to be seen.

Surah Taha, verse 7, has really helped me with this feeling. A lot of people assume it has a negative connotation. They may think: I have so many bad secrets and I'm ashamed, and Allah knows about all of them.

But I look at this verse through a positive lens: I have so many good secrets that I don't share with others as I'm not seeking reward from people.

When I read it, I feel happy and content that Allah knows my good secrets and that He will reward me for them. It builds such a positive relationship with Allah. I have so many good things in my heart: the way I think about others in a positive way, the way I try to serve others in a positive way, the way I try to do things secretly.

This verse tells me that nothing I think, intend and do will ever be wasted. Allah knows everything that we're thinking about. And, insha'Allah, He will reward us for it. It gives you positive motivation and momentum to do the good things in life.

Also, sometimes you're misunderstood by others when you're trying to do something good. This verse tells you: don't worry. Allah knows what is in your heart.

Pause and Reflect

Ahmed was right in what he said; but still, we all have hidden yearnings of the heart. I wish to draw your attention to another verse, Surah Al-Baqarah 2:144:

قَدْ نَرَىٰ تَقَلُّبَ وَجْهِكَ فِى ٱلسَّمَآءِ ۖ فَلَنُوَلِّيَنَّكَ قِبْلَةً تَرْضَىٰهَا

Qad narā taqalluba wajhika fī al-samā' fa-lanuwalliyannaka qiblatan tarḍāhā

Indeed, We see you ʿO Prophetʾ turning your face towards heaven. Now We will make you turn towards a direction ʿof prayerʾ that will please you.

It was revealed when the Prophet ﷺ longed for the qiblah (direction of prayer) to be changed from Jerusalem to the Kabah in Makkah. Several of the mufasirun (scholars of tafseer) comment that the Prophet ﷺ used to look towards the sky at this time. He did not make du'a verbally, or say out loud what he longed for, but his heart made du'a. And this internal longing was seen by Allah.

My heart breaks at this verse. In fact, I'm trying not to cry as I type these words.

Sometimes, we can't quite bring ourselves to call upon Allah.

It could be that we just don't have the words, our voice feels tired because we've been making so much du'a or we are simply shy to ask.

This verse is deeply comforting. Allah sees you. He knows your struggle and He is fully aware and understanding of your situation.

Never think that you are alone. You have a Lord who not only sees the external manifestation of your fears, hopes and worries, but He 'azza wa jal sees the movements of your heart too. Whatever you don't voice, whatever you are unable to voice. He knows.

Look at how Allah consoled the Prophet ﷺ with فَلَنُوَلِّيَنَّكَ (fa-lanuwalliyannaka), meaning 'we will surely turn you'. Two forms of emphasis are used in the lam ل and nun نْ, stressing Allah's Absolute Divine Promise and Commitment that He will respond emphatically.

And not with an answer to the Prophet's yearning that Allah simply chooses, but with one that Allah chooses that he ﷺ will be pleased with. What love, what affection! We talk about seeking the pleasure of Allah but in this verse, Allah is pleased in pleasing His beloved. Allahu akbar! Never mind the eyes, it brings tears to the heart.

Go after that Love!

Live with His Words . . .

Here are three steps to live with this week's verse(s):

1. Whenever you feel someone hasn't seen you, acknowledged or understood you, just pause. Look towards the heavens and ask: How is Allah seeing me right now?

2. What good secrets do you have with Allah? What secrets can you cultivate for your Rabb? Make a list and sit back and smile, knowing that He sees them all.

3. Turn to the One who knows you deeply and intimately and tell Him: Al-Lateef, You are a Lord who hears the unspoken words of my heart. Turn me towards what pleases You. When I too look towards the heavens longing for Your Response, remind me that You will meet me with an intimate response that will soothe my aching soul.

A Question for Your Heart

How does your perception change, knowing that the quiet ache in your heart is being heard, right now, by the One who fashioned it? How do your feelings change, knowing His Response is unfolding as you read these words?

Fall in Love with The Author

Al-Lateef, the One who is subtle and kind, is a Lord who sees the yearnings of your soul and lovingly responds with the precise knowledge of when, where and how to complete you.

WEEK 29:

Bias

Verse(s) of the Week
Your Rabb's Words for Your Soul

يَـٰٓأَيُّهَا ٱلَّذِينَ ءَامَنُوا۟ كُونُوا۟ قَوَّٰمِينَ لِلَّهِ شُهَدَآءَ بِٱلْقِسْطِ ۖ وَلَا يَجْرِمَنَّكُمْ شَنَـَٔانُ قَوْمٍ عَلَىٰٓ أَلَّا تَعْدِلُوا۟ ۚ ٱعْدِلُوا۟ هُوَ أَقْرَبُ لِلتَّقْوَىٰ ۖ وَٱتَّقُوا۟ ٱللَّهَ ۚ إِنَّ ٱللَّهَ خَبِيرٌۢ بِمَا تَعْمَلُونَ ٨

*Yā ayyuhā alladhīna āmanū kūnū qawwāmīna lillāhi
shuhadā'a bil-qisṭ, wa lā yajrimannakum shana'ānu qawmin
'alā allā ta'dilū; i'dilū huwa aqrabu li-l-taqwā, wa-ttaqullāh,
inna Allāha khabīrun bimā ta'malūn*

*'O believers! Stand firm for Allah and bear true testimony.
Do not let the hatred of a people lead you to injustice. Be
just! That is closer to righteousness. And be mindful of Allah.
Surely Allah is All-Aware of what you do.'*

Surah Al-Maidah 5:8

There have been occasions during public events when someone has pointed out how 'unfair' it is that the charity I
founded, Solace, only supports women who have embraced

176

Islam, rather than all Muslim women. I try to explain that I created Solace based on my own lived experience as a revert, to fill a gap I personally knew existed: the lack of support tailored to the unique challenges faced by those who embrace Islam. Still, I've been accused of dividing the community.

I would love for Solace to one day offer services to all women, but I had to begin somewhere. And I began with what I knew. I began with pain. I began with a sincere desire that no other woman would have to go through what I did, alone, simply because she chose to embrace Islam.

I think it's natural to feel a strong sense of connection to those whose stories mirror our own – they see the world as we do. But I also recognise the danger in that: when we live and relate to others purely from our own subjective lens, we risk narrowing our sense of justice and compassion.

Ruzi, whose advice I shared back in Week 5, narrates an incident that reminded me of something powerful: the importance of regular interaction with the Qur'an, and the role Allah calls us to embody – of fairness and justice in all our dealings with everyone.

Ruzi's Story

When I was the lead for a women's masjid committee, there was a big dispute where I had to mediate between two people. This dispute was affecting the whole team. I had information and evidence which seemed to go more against one individual than the other. So I prepared myself to go into that meeting with what I knew.

That morning, I came across an ayah in my daily morning recitation:

يَـٰدَاوُدُ إِنَّا جَعَلْنَـٰكَ خَلِيفَةً فِى ٱلْأَرْضِ فَٱحْكُم بَيْنَ ٱلنَّاسِ بِٱلْحَقِّ وَلَا تَتَّبِعِ ٱلْهَوَىٰ
فَيُضِلَّكَ عَن سَبِيلِ ٱللَّهِ ۚ إِنَّ ٱلَّذِينَ يَضِلُّونَ عَن سَبِيلِ ٱللَّهِ لَهُمْ عَذَابٌ شَدِيدٌۢ بِمَا نَسُوا يَوْمَ
ٱلْحِسَابِ ٢٦

Yā Dāwūd, innā ja'alnāka khalīfatan fīl-arḍi faḥkum bayna
an-nāsi bil-ḥaqqi wa lā tattabi'il-hawā fa-yuḍillaka 'an
sabīlillāh; inna alladhīna yuḍillūna 'an sabīlillāh lahum
'adhābun shadīdun bimā nasū yawmal-ḥisāb.

'We instructed him:' 'O David! We have surely made you
an authority in the land, so judge between people with
truth. And do not follow your desires or they will lead you
astray from Allah's Way. Surely those who go astray from
Allah's Way will suffer a severe punishment for neglecting
the Day of Reckoning.'

Surah Sad 38:26

*I felt Allah was telling me: deal with people justly and don't
follow your own desires. I'd felt that this person was creating
havoc and I wanted to go in and tell them how it was. But
when I came across this verse, I realised I needed to be more
mellow and measured, calm myself down and deal with the
situation objectively. It really helped.*

*In the meeting, I actually started off by mentioning
that I had come across this ayah and invited everyone to
deal with things in an objective manner instead of getting
emotional.*

*I didn't let emotions get the better of me. So that situa-
tion was dealt with in an objective manner, rather than being
biased. Had Allah not guided me, I most likely would have
been heated and biased when I was meant to be there to
mediate.*

Pause and Reflect

Relationships are damn hard! Being in them can be tough. Being caught in the middle of two people in conflict is a serious challenge and responsibility.

There have been times where I have been judgemental, even if unintentionally, siding with someone who I love or who has shown me love, or simply siding with what I thought was right according to my own experience of the world. But age and experience are teaching me to step back, pause and emotionally detach myself as much as I can. Ruzi's story was a lesson in being objective and just towards others.

The hardest thing of all is to remain unbiased when you yourself are part of a disagreement. When every cell in your body goes into defence mode against the one you are disagreeing with, it is hard to step away from your feelings and focus on justice. But justice might mean accepting that you were the one in the wrong.

Allah tells us how this is possible. In this week's verse, He commands us اعْدِلُوا (i'dilū), be just, after prohibiting us from allowing our feelings to get in the way. What follows the prohibition is a command, for justice is a divine requirement. And even more than that, it is a spiritual act. As Allah tells us هُوَ أَقْرَبُ لِلتَّقْوَى (huwa aqrabu li-l-taqwā), it is closer to taqwa (God consciousness).

Dearest reader, memorise this week's verse. Internalise its meaning. In your own personal dealings with people, be aware that Allah is looking upon you. He knows the full truth of the situation. Do not be unjust to yourself for the sake of your own defensive aims. This verse teaches you that justice must be upheld even when you're hurt, even when the other party doesn't 'deserve' it by worldly standards. Because, as I said in one of my previous books, this life is never about them anyway.

Live with His Words . . .

Here are three steps to live with this week's verse(s):

1. Whenever you feel emotionally triggered, especially when hurt by someone, pause and ask: Am I responding fairly, or from a place of pain or pride?

2. Regularly ask yourself: Am I fair in how I speak about others, especially those I disagree with?

3. Turn to the One who is Most Just, who wants you to be balanced and fair, and tell Him: My Lord, You are a Lord who has never wronged my soul or any other soul. Teach me to be just in my heart so that it guides my words. Guide me to be just, even in my thoughts, to others. And when I'm not, humble me when I am called to account. Make me one who loves justice and lives by it, for no other reason than out of love for You and being conscious that Your Sight never leaves me.

A Question for Your Heart

Ask yourself: When was the last time I justified an action that deep down, I knew wasn't entirely fair, either to someone else or to myself? What would it look like to revisit that moment with Allah's Name, Al-Adl – The Most Just – in my heart?

Fall in Love with The Author

Al-Adl, The Most Just, is a Lord who never wrongs any of His Creation. His Justice is flawless and His Decree is always perfect. He wants you to align your character and approach with justice in how you deal with yourself and others, and the manner in which you respond to the tests He places before you.

WEEK 30:

Ihsaan

Verse(s) of the Week
Your Rabb's Words for Your Soul

قَوْلٌ مَّعْرُوفٌ وَمَغْفِرَةٌ خَيْرٌ مِّن صَدَقَةٍ يَتْبَعُهَآ أَذًى ۗ وَٱللَّهُ غَنِىٌّ حَلِيمٌ ٢٦٣

Qawlun ma'rūfun wa maghfiratun khayrun min ṣadaqatin
yatba'uhā athan; wallāhu ghanīyun ḥalīm

'Kind words and forgiveness are better than charity followed
by injury. And Allah is Self-Sufficient, Most Forbearing.'

Surah Al-Baqarah 2:263

One of my greatest challenges is being kind to those who have deeply hurt me. I really struggle with this. If someone hurts me badly enough, I cancel them (still giving them their Islamic rights) and move on without a second thought. I know this isn't particularly healthy. And I also know, deep down, it's not the way my Lord wants me to be. Allah knows how often I make du'a to be able to respond differently and better.

Romina's story touches on one of my favourite topics: ihsaan, striving for excellence. In her story, it is ihsaan with others. It has helped me to see things in a completely different light.

Romina's Story Continues

My daughter was getting married. Weddings can be difficult times. Everyone has such expectations – the bride, the in-laws, the extended family.

Unfortunately, there was a lot of tension. People weren't getting on, and the wedding became the focal point of their struggle. Relatives were saying: 'I'm not coming if this person is there', or, 'I'm not going to sit next to this person.' It was all very stressful and difficult to navigate. I was emotionally drained. I just remember asking Allah to help, and then I came to the Qur'an and read a small part in Surah Al-Baqarah, ayah 195:

وَأَنفِقُوا۟ فِى سَبِيلِ ٱللَّهِ وَلَا تُلْقُوا۟ بِأَيْدِيكُمْ إِلَى ٱلتَّهْلُكَةِ ۛ وَأَحْسِنُوٓا۟ ۛ إِنَّ ٱللَّهَ يُحِبُّ ٱلْمُحْسِنِينَ ١٩٥

Wa anfiqū fī sabīli Allāhi walā tulqū bi'aydīkum ilā al-tahlukati wa aḥsinū; inna Allāha yuḥibbu al-muḥsinīn

Spend in the cause of Allah and do not let your own hands throw you into destruction ʾby withholdingʿ. And do good, for Allah certainly loves the good-doers.

In this verse, Allah was telling me: Do ihsaan. Act with ihsaan. Act with your best for Allah. That's all you can do. Allah loves the muhsinun (the ones who excel). And He wants you to do ihsaan with your good deeds.

Up to then, I'd been thinking about all the people I had to please. With this verse, I realised, no, I've just got to do right by Allah ﷻ. I couldn't please all these people or give them *what they wanted. So I was going to do my best, be nice, invite everyone and do haqq (right) by everyone.*

I remember feeling free! So-and-so said she can't come, khalas – enough already! I can't change that or influence it. Whoever wants to come, come. Getting back to those simple principles really helped me.

Pause and Reflect

In my book *Ramadan Reflections*, I mentioned a dear friend of mine who was unable to give in monetary charity due to not having access to surplus income. She made up for it by coming close to Allah in other ways.

Life is fluid. It has seasons. There are moments when we're able to give generously in charity and there are tough times when we need to be careful with our expenses. But what I love about my friend's example is that we can always come close to Allah through actions that are unimpacted by external circumstances – ihsaan in worship and ihsaan in character.

The merits of giving in charity are numerous. But here, your Lord is saying that having ihsaan with others is even better. Forgiving them when you have every right not to do so, and offering the best of yourself in speech when they might have offered the worst of themselves is better for you.

Lord knows this is a struggle for me. Maybe it's a struggle for you too. If someone wrongs me, I have a hard time letting go. In my younger days, I would retaliate in the same or a worse way, may Allah forgive me. Now, I just go quiet and distance myself as far as possible. So to offer kindness and forgiveness really is another level – ihsaan (excellence). Everything is a divine training ground, subhanAllah.

What I love about this verse is how it ends. Allah ﷻ says that He is غَنِىٌّ (ghanīy), Free of Need and Self-sufficient, and حَلِيمٌ

(halīm), Forbearing and Patient. He doesn't need your charity or your wealth, whether you have good intention or not. Everything is for your own benefit. When you strive to have ihsaan with others, in doing so, you are prioritising your own soul.

Live with His Words . . .

Here are three steps to live with this week's verse(s):

1. Take a few seconds to pause before you speak and choose to speak with kind words and a kind tone.

2. When you give sadaqa or help someone, do it for Allah alone, and then, as the Arabic saying goes, throw it in the sea. Forget about it. If you ever find yourself mentioning your good deed to one you've helped or anyone else, for that matter, recite this week's verse and keep it moving.

3. Tell the One who always wants you to act from your higher self: O Allah, soften my heart and tongue. Let my words be healing, not harmful, even when I feel hurt. Ya Ghaniyy, You are Free of Need, but I am in constant need of You. Protect my good deeds from pride or expectation. Make all my interactions and my giving beautiful in Your Sight, even if it's unseen by others.

A Question for Your Heart

Ask yourself: In my interactions with others and my giving to others, am I more focused on how it makes me appear or how it will be received by Allah?

Fall in Love with The Author

Ash-Shakur – The Most Appreciative – is a Lord who appreciates when you have ihsaan with others. He sees every time you hold back when you could retaliate. He sees every small act of generosity done with sincerity and multiplies it beyond what you can imagine.

WEEK 31:

Trust

Verse(s) of the Week
Your Rabb's Words for Your Soul

فَإِذَا بَلَغْنَ أَجَلَهُنَّ فَأَمْسِكُوهُنَّ بِمَعْرُوفٍ أَوْ فَارِقُوهُنَّ بِمَعْرُوفٍ وَأَشْهِدُواْ ذَوَىْ عَدْلٍ مِّنكُمْ وَأَقِيمُواْ ٱلشَّهَـٰدَةَ لِلَّهِ ۚ ذَٰلِكُمْ يُوعَظُ بِهِۦ مَن كَانَ يُؤْمِنُ بِٱللَّهِ وَٱلْيَوْمِ ٱلْءَاخِرِ ۚ وَمَن يَتَّقِ ٱللَّهَ يَجْعَل لَّهُۥ مَخْرَجًا ٢ وَيَرْزُقْهُ مِنْ حَيْثُ لَا يَحْتَسِبُ ۚ وَمَن يَتَوَكَّلْ عَلَى ٱللَّهِ فَهُوَ حَسْبُهُۥ ۚ إِنَّ ٱللَّهَ بَـٰلِغُ أَمْرِهِۦ ۚ قَدْ جَعَلَ ٱللَّهُ لِكُلِّ شَىْءٍ قَدْرًا ٣

Fā-idhā balaghnā ajalahunna fa-amsikūhunna bimaʿrūfin aw fāriqūhunna bimaʿrūfin wa-ashhidū dhawā ʿadlin minkum wa-aqīmū al-shahāda lillāh; dhālikum yuʿazu bihī man kāna yuʾminu billāhi wal-yawmi al-ākhir; waman yattaqi llāha yajʿal lahu makhrajan wayarzuquhu min ḥaythu lā yaḥtasib; waman yatawakkal ʿalā llāhi fahuwa ḥasbuhu; inna llāha bālaghu amrihi qad jaʿala llāhu likulli shayin qadran

'Then when they have ˹almost˺ reached the end of their waiting period, either retain them honourably or separate from them honourably. And call two of your reliable men to witness ˹either

way` – and `let the witnesses` bear true testimony for `the sake
of` Allah. This is enjoined on whoever has faith in Allah and the
Last Day. And whoever is mindful of Allah, He will make a way
out for them, and provide for them from sources they could
never imagine. And whoever puts their trust in Allah, then He
`alone` is sufficient for them. Certainly Allah achieves His Will.
Allah has already set a destiny for everything.'

Surah At-Talaq 65:2–3

Hadiyah's story, which follows, is an example of a person
facing a moment of deep personal crisis in her marriage.
For many who face it, divorce can be the most terrible
crisis of their lives. I could see that it was difficult for her to relate
all that she'd been through that led to her marriage ending. Divorce
is never an easy choice, especially when children are involved. But
when a marriage negatively impacts the health of your soul – the
most precious thing you possess in this life, which will most certainly return to its Owner – then it is time to work with your spouse
to save the marriage and if that fails, to find a way to end this situation for the sake of the unseen, for the sake of what is eternal.

Even when this decision is made for the sake of Allah, we can
find ourselves holding very negative beliefs about divorce. Perhaps
these come from parents or from our upbringing, or from relatives
or friends. When voices around us are judgemental or critical, it
becomes even more crucial to replace them with the Words of
Allah. His Message is pure, perfect and true.

Hadiyah's Story

My marriage was very difficult and unhappy. This severely
affected my faith and deen. While I was married, I went from
doing a lot of memorisation of the Qur'an, reading a lot of

the Qur'an, to not being able to do any. I became a shadow of myself and felt so down and low because of the hardships I was suffering. I felt trapped, completely despondent and hopeless.

My husband was very manipulative, constantly putting me down. I was made to feel that all the problems in the marriage were my fault and that it would be bad for my deen if I left. The worst thing was the way he would use Islam to justify it all. This affected my relationship with the Qur'an, and there was no other voice to tell me differently. Eventually I was diagnosed with clinical depression.

A situation arose between us which forced me to remove the rose-coloured glasses that seemed to have found a home on my nose. And after removing them, I saw the marriage and his treatment of me for what they truly were. And when I was no longer under the spell of all the manipulated truths that I had been led to believe, I knew there was nothing left to stay for.

At that time, I did not feel that I had Allah supporting me. When I finally moved on and left the marriage, I understood that this was why I'd found it so hard to leave. I didn't have Him as my strength, and I couldn't do it by myself. But when I did turn to the Qur'an and turned to Allah, I had His Words. They became my guide.

When my husband said: 'You're going to taste the effects of poverty if you leave this relationship', now I could reply: 'Well, my rizq (provision) is from Allah.'

When he said: 'Your rizq is coming through me – so you're turning away from the messenger of your rizq', I could say quietly to myself: I don't think that's quite how it works!

After I left, what was a super-source of strength for me were verses 2 and 3 in Surah At-Talaq. I had nothing but kept holding on to Allah's Words – how Allah sent His Rizq from nowhere. My circumstances were a complete embodiment of that verse and I saw it in action. You need to have complete tawakkul (reliance) on Allah, not half, completely *trusting that He will give you your rizq and that it will certainly come.*

Pause and Reflect

I am sure you've been in a situation where you've been between a rock and a hard place, struggling with a complex dilemma. If there is khair (good) on both sides or sharh (bad) on both sides of a situation, how can we know which is the greater good or which is the lesser of two evils? And then there are decisions where it appears that one would lead to immediate difficulty in this life but then would be beneficial for your soul and most certainly lead to ease in the next.

Our human selves incline towards that which is tangible; what we can see, hear and feel. It's normal to lean towards that even if it's destroying us. It feels easier to choose it over that which requires belief in the unseen, the intangible. But we must always choose the latter – the intangible, our soul and its journey to its final resting place. In Paradise, there is no pain, no loss, no sorrow, just everlasting peace.

Here, I'm using divorce as an example of a very difficult decision, but it could be anything. It may be income that isn't halal. Its tangible benefits are many. But the impact on your akhirah is certain. The ones who are mindful will choose the unseen over the seen, akhirah over dunya, their soul before anything else, Allah before themselves. You can be that believer who is mindful, who possesses taqwa.

And you know what happens when you do this. Just as He did for Hadiyah, Allah reminds you of your worth. Your Rabb reminds you that you are not alone. Because of your heart's attachment to Him and His Akhirah, you will always be under His Protective Care.

Where your hardship makes you feel suffocated and trapped, where you feel unable to escape – taqwa leads to an exit. But you are never exiting alone. You are exiting with Allah by your side.

As if this isn't enough as a source of relief, release and ease, Allah 'azza wa jal tells us: Because you're worthy due to your taqwa, I will not only provide a way out, but I will increase your rizq in ways that you never imagined. Rizq is often thought of in the context of wealth and material possessions. But it is also peace of mind, love, health, guidance and barakah-filled blessings.

We should never choose fear over faith. Faith in Allah and belief that we came from Him and are surely returning to Him must always be our compass throughout all the difficult decisions in our life.

Live with His Words . . .

Here are three steps to live with this week's verse(s):

1. Every morning, say this du'a of reliance from the Prophet ﷺ, which is part of the daily morning and evening adhkaar:

حَسْبِيَ ٱللَّهُ لَا إِلَٰهَ إِلَّا هُوَ عَلَيْهِ تَوَكَّلْتُ وَهُوَ رَبُّ ٱلْعَرْشِ ٱلْعَظِيمِ ١٢٩

Hasbiya Allahu la ilaha illa Huwa, 'alayhi tawakkaltu, wa Huwa Rabbul 'Arshil 'Adheem.

Allah is sufficient for me. There is no God but Him. In Him, I put my trust, and He is the Lord of the Mighty Throne.

Surah At-Tawbah 9:129

2. Start an 'unexpected rizq' journal. Every time Allah provides for you in a way that you didn't expect, add it to your journal. Remember rizq isn't just monetary wealth. This will train your heart to recognise Allah's Hidden Blessings.

3. Turn to the One in whom you will find your worth and tell Him: My Lord, I trust You completely and place my full reliance upon You in every matter. Ar-Rahman, make me content with Your Decree, assured by Your Planning, and

confident that everything that comes from You is for my ultimate good.

A Question for Your Heart

When life feels uncertain and your heart is heavy with worry, do you gently remind yourself that Allah's Promise is for you too? Do you trust that if you turn to Him with sincerity, He will take care of you in ways more beautiful than you can imagine?

Fall in Love with The Author

Al-Muqeet – The One who Sustains – is a Lord who wants you to be certain that He is the One who holds all your affairs in His Hands. His Wisdom is boundless, and His Mercy knows no limits. As you face trials, your Rabb wants you to remember that your strength and sustenance comes only from Him and that He will guide you through periods of hardship.

WEEK 32:

The Relationship You've Been Waiting For

Verse(s) of the Week
Your Rabb's Words for Your Soul

مَّن ذَا ٱلَّذِى يُقْرِضُ ٱللَّهَ قَرْضًا حَسَنًا فَيُضَٰعِفَهُۥ لَهُۥٓ أَضْعَافًا كَثِيرَةً ۚ وَٱللَّهُ يَقْبِضُ وَيَبْۜصُطُ وَإِلَيْهِ تُرْجَعُونَ ٢٤٥

Man dhā alladhī yuqriḍu llāha qarḍan ḥasanan fayuḍāʿifahu lahu aḍʿāfan kathīrah; wa-llāhu yaqbiḍu wayabṣuṭu wa-ilayhi turjaʿūn

'Who will lend to Allah a good loan which Allah will multiply many times over? It is Allah ˹alone˺ who decreases and increases ˹wealth˺. And to Him you will ˹all˺ be returned.'

Surah Al-Baqarah 2:245

193

My Story

*I always find it interesting when people share their percep-
tions of me as someone confident, strong and successful. I
may have elements of such traits, but there is a backstory.
There always is. They don't know that I've, in fact, struggled
with confidence, that I've battled with self-acceptance and
that I've been my worst critic, mirroring the voice of my
father as I was growing up.*

*I believe the lack of that relationship and the little girl
within me who yearned to be held and loved by her father
has shaped many of my life's experiences – before embracing
Islam and certainly post-shahadah.*

*For the longest time, I didn't like myself. I felt I was lacking
in so many ways. I berated myself even at the smallest perceived 'failure'. The voice in my head was strong: you're not
enough; you need to do more, be more; you've made too
many mistakes and you'll never change.*

*It was no wonder why I felt the absence of love and
yearned for it: because it was missing within.*

*I remember my dear friend Sumayah once telling me that
the Qur'an would make me feel loved. As someone who
had believed for so long that that love would be found in
a romantic relationship, family ties or deep friendships, I
found it hard to fully believe her.*

*Through therapy, I realised that we can experience love
through such relationships, but the journey towards self-
love is one that helped to heal some of the deepest wounds
within me. My negative voice was quieter and didn't hold
as much influence as it once had.*

*But what really created a shift was experiencing the power
of the Qur'an – even just through daily recitation – and
most profoundly through studying its meanings and engaging in the art of tadabbur. Sumayah was right. I know with*

*certainty: the self-love journey is incomplete without the
soul-love journey.*

*And the soul-love journey is rooted in the Qur'an. A very
different voice began to take lead and it was healthy, caring,
loving and yet firm at the same time. It was the relationship I
didn't realise I very much needed. It was the best investment
I would make – one that brings ongoing endless returns.*

Pause and Reflect

Think about the things that we want most in life – love and good
relationships. Behind them are such basic human needs: to be
loved, to be seen, to be significant.

The Qur'an can give you all those things in greater measure than
any relationship. The Qur'an will see you, will counsel you, validate
you, love you, show you that you are worthy, illuminate your heart,
grant you contentment wherever in life you are and grant you the
ability to believe in yourself, to weather any storm and to feel content.

Living as a Muslim who is prioritising his or her own soul in this
world is really hard. I'm with you. I've been there and I'm wearing
the T-shirt! But you and I have a Lord who tells us in this week's verse
that everything done sincerely for His Sake is met by His Promise. He does not just return what we give; He multiplies it many
times over, a reward that is beyond any human or mathematical
calculation.

So keep going. Keep striving. Keep giving. And don't fear exhaus-
tion, or some kind of lack or poverty. Because it is only Allah who
withholds and expands provision. By Allah, everything you lend to
your Rabb now will be fully returned and multiplied, at that blessed
time when you meet Him. What a beautiful day it will be. I'm getting all emotional now.

Come to the Qur'an because it is for you, because it was revealed
for you and is a gift for you, and then you'll get everything.

The biggest investment you can ever make for your dunya and akhirah is investing in your relationship with the Qur'an. It's an investment no one can take away from you.

Can you imagine meeting your Lord with all of that, with all your fatigue and struggle, only to find Him smiling upon you, revealing reward beyond your wildest dreams? SubhanAllah, the smile of your Lord is enough. Ya Allah, The Most Loving, how we love You!

Live with His Words . . .

Here are three steps to live with this week's verse(s):

1. Make sure all that you do is for Allah's Pleasure alone. Before doing any good deed, remind yourself that you are doing it for Allah's Sake, not for recognition or reward from people.

2. Keep a diary this week where you intentionally engage in good deeds and notice the returns that you receive. Remember true worship is never for the returns. Any return is a bountiful blessing that should make you a more grateful servant of Allah, wanting to do more good.

3. Turn to the One who always responds to everything you intend and everything you do with beautiful returns and tell Him: Rabbi, how do I express my gratitude to You for what You give from Your Grace and Generosity? Ya Arham ar-Rahimeen, You are a Lord who never sends me away disappointed. Make every step I take towards You a path to Your Pleasure, and bless every moment I live in grateful obedience to You.

A Question for Your Heart

When was the last time you paused to reflect on the small acts of worship you do for Allah, and the immense blessings Allah has returned to you? How can you incorporate more gratitude and mindfulness into your daily actions to truly appreciate His Generosity?

Fall in Love with The Author

Al Jabbar – The Compeller and Restorer – is a Lord who shows you His Perfect Generosity by multiplying even the smallest of your efforts, turning them into blessings beyond measure. He wants you to turn to Him with humility and gratitude because you have experienced Him as an Appreciative Lord – evident in His Returns for your small efforts.

PART 6:

A Journey for Life

وَقُرْءَانًا فَرَقْنَٰهُ لِتَقْرَأَهُ عَلَى ٱلنَّاسِ عَلَىٰ مُكْثٍ وَنَزَّلْنَٰهُ تَنزِيلًا ١٠٦

Wa Qur'ānan faraqnāhu li-taqrā'ahu 'alā al-nāsi 'alā muk-
thin wa nazzalnāhu tanzīlā

''It is' a Quran We have revealed in stages so that you may
recite it to people at a deliberate pace. And We have sent
it down in successive revelations.'

Surah Al-Isra 17:106

The Training You Need

Verse(s) of the Week
Your Rabb's Words for Your Soul

وَمَنْ أَحْسَنُ قَوْلًا مِّمَّن دَعَآ إِلَى ٱللَّهِ وَعَمِلَ صَـٰلِحًا وَقَالَ إِنَّنِى مِنَ ٱلْمُسْلِمِينَ ٣٣

*Wa man aḥsanu qawlan mimman da'ā ilā llāhi wa 'amila ṣāliḥ
an wa qāla innanī mina al-muslimīn*

*'And whose words are better than someone who calls ˈothersˈ
to Allah, does good, and says, "I am truly one of those who
submit"?'*

Surah Fussilat 41:33

One of my favourite supplications to make is 'O Allah, use me for Your deen.' But get ready for how Allah 'azza wa jal answers such a du'a. He will move people out of your life, bring new ones in and push you to heal and grow – all part of the preparation for how He has planned to use you. It will be challenging. Most likely, it won't be comfortable. It might be really tough, like a spiritual boot camp.

'Use me for your deen' is a powerful du'a and I still make it today, bracing myself for the changes that must happen within me before I can truly serve Him.

So it was refreshing to hear that Shaykha Saleha, who once struggled to recite the Qur'an, whose story continues here from Week 17, experienced the same. If you want to be the best with Allah, ask Him for it, and be prepared to go through the boot camp of life to become it.

Saleha's Story Continues

I wanted to challenge myself to memorise Surah Al-Baqarah, but I had doubts that I could do it. It was tough. I memorised some on my own, but then decided that I needed a teacher. I found one and our lessons began.

When I reached a verse about talaq (divorce), I struggled to retain my memory of it. Sometimes, in that situation, it helps to look into the tafseer and the meanings of the verses and that's exactly what I did.

The verse was:

ٱلطَّلَٰقُ مَرَّتَانِ فَإِمْسَاكٌ بِمَعْرُوفٍ أَوْ تَسْرِيحٌ بِإِحْسَٰنٍ وَلَا يَحِلُّ لَكُمْ أَن تَأْخُذُوا مِمَّا ءَاتَيْتُمُوهُنَّ شَيْئًا إِلَّا أَن يَخَافَا أَلَّا يُقِيمَا حُدُودَ ٱللَّهِ فَإِنْ خِفْتُمْ أَلَّا يُقِيمَا حُدُودَ ٱللَّهِ فَلَا جُنَاحَ عَلَيْهِمَا فِيمَا ٱفْتَدَتْ بِهِ تِلْكَ حُدُودُ ٱللَّهِ فَلَا تَعْتَدُوهَا وَمَن يَتَعَدَّ حُدُودَ ٱللَّهِ فَأُو۟لَٰٓئِكَ هُمُ ٱلظَّٰلِمُونَ ٢٢٩

At-talāqu marratāni fa-imsākun bima'rūfin aw tasrīḥ
un bi-iḥsānin walā yaḥillu lakum an ta'khudhū
mimmā ātaytumūhunna shay'an illā an yakhafā allā
yuqīmā ḥudūda llāhi fa-in khiftum allā yuqīmā ḥudūda llāhi
falā junāḥa 'alayhimā fīmā iftadat bihi tilka ḥudūdu llāhi falā

202

ta'tadūhā waman yata'adda ḥudūda llāhi fa-ulā'ika humu
aẓ-ẓālimūn

Divorce may be retracted twice, then the husband must
retain ʿhis wifeʾ with honour or separate ʿfrom herʾ with
grace. It is not lawful for husbands to take back anything
of the dowry given to their wives, unless the couple fears
not being able to keep within the limits of Allah. So if you
fear they will not be able to keep within the limits of Allah,
there is no blame if the wife compensates the husband to
obtain divorce. These are the limits set by Allah, so do not
transgress them. And whoever transgresses the limits of
Allah, they are the ʿtrueʾ wrongdoers.

Surah Al-Baqarah 2:229

*As I struggled with this verse, my teacher remarked that talaq is
one of the most difficult tests, and the most disliked of the things
that are permissible to Allah, as per the hadith of the Prophet
ﷺ – and yet it still happens. That reflection really struck me.*

*Growing up, I had seen women suffer in marriages, not
just Muslim women but many others. I remember saying to
myself: One day I'm going to help women know the truth
and spread the truth so that they know they don't have to
suffer in silence.*

*I wanted to help Muslim women who were going through
difficult divorces, especially in helping them understand how
divorce works. It isn't a battle against each other. It is there
to allow separation in an Islamic manner where no harm
comes to either party or to children – and that's the point we
miss. Yes, it's difficult, and so it needs to be done according
to Islam.*

*I kept reading this verse. In my heart, I said to Allah: Show
me how I can help women. Shortly after that, I received an
offer from a shariah (Islamic law) council. They were looking
for more female scholars, and asked if I could join the board.*

I was the only female among a board of male scholars. That was the beginning of me working with shariah councils, mainly around divorce and marriage. Alhamdulillah. Allah guided me through His Book, while I was memorising, to a childhood yearning to make a difference within the community.

Pause and Reflect

This new part of the book takes you through the many beautiful ways in which Allah develops you to fulfil your full potential and become a benefit for yourself, your family and others.

Allah 'azza wa jal is always developing you and preparing you to live out your individual purpose. This week's verse is an invitation to become curious as to what that purpose might be. You could be an incredible artist, deeply empathetic, physically strong, an academic or incredibly helpful towards others. Whatever your skills and characteristics are, I want you to identify them. If you're unable to identify them, ask your three closest family members or friends to tell you what they are.

Once you have identified them, consider them in light of this week's verse, where Allah ﷻ clearly states, there is no one better than those who دَعَا إِلَى اللَّهِ (da'ā ilā llāhi), call to Allah, and do وَعَمِلَ صَالِحًا (wa 'amila ṣāliḥan), righteous deeds. The 'وَ' (and) shows that calling to Allah is incomplete without righteous action. You must walk your talk. Your life must embody your words. And then you must say: وَقَالَ إِنَّنِي مِنَ الْمُسْلِمِينَ (wa qāla innanī mina al-muslimīn), 'Indeed, I am among the Muslims', a public declaration of firmness in identity, confidence in being Muslim, a commitment to journey with submission to Allah in humility, because it is all for Him.

Be energetic, be creative, rise to the challenge and enjoy!

Live with His Words . . .

Here are three steps to live with this week's verse(s):

1. Complete the steps in this week's chapter.

2. Take yourself down memory lane and look at the last six months. What might Allah be preparing you for? Get curious.

3. Turn to the One who is ready to support you in your dreams and goals for His Sake and tell Him: Ya Allah, make me among those who sincerely call others to You, live by what I preach, and rejoice in being of the Muslims.

A Question for Your Heart

Ask yourself: If Allah chose me today to be a means of guidance for someone, would my heart, words and actions be ready to carry that trust? If not, what needs to change?

Fall in Love with The Author

Al-Kareem – The Most Generous – is a Lord who, when He chooses you to deliver goodness to others, wants you to know it is a sign that He has poured His Generosity upon you, allowing you to be a means through which His Mercy and blessings reach the hearts of those in need.

WEEK 34:

Ilm

Verse(s) of the Week
Your Rabb's Words for Your Soul

وَٱتَّقُواْ ٱللَّهَ ۖ وَيُعَلِّمُكُمُ ٱللَّهُ ۗ

Wa-ttaqū llāha wa-yuʻallimukumullāh

'Be mindful of Allah, for Allah is the One Who teaches you.'

Surah Al-Baqarah 2:282

I have noticed there are students in my Qur'an class who are taking instructions from the same teacher, listening to the same lessons, reading the same course notes. Yet the different ways some of them absorb the information, understand it and, most importantly, live it is extraordinary, subhanAllah.

This happens because Islamic knowledge isn't something you just learn – it's something you're gifted by The Most High. May Allah bless them and increase them all. Ameen.

It is also a humbling reminder that while we can take a step towards knowledge, it is Allah who cracks open the heart and allows it to penetrate deep within. Without His Permission, knowledge remains on the tongue or in the mind; but with His Mercy, it takes root in the soul.

Saleha's Story Continues

From the moment I started learning how to read the Qur'an, there was a deep passion within me to further my studies. It took me a couple of years to read fluently and a further couple of years to remove old mistakes in pronunciation. But with that journey, came so much blessing and barakah. I felt like there were signs that Allah was accepting me and it encouraged me to go further.

After I finished the tajweed course, and then took steps towards memorisation, Allah opened the door for a sheikh who had taught in Madinah for nearly 70 years to come to the UK to give ijazat (authorised licence). I remember thinking, If only I could just sit in his company, I would learn from him and his relationship with the Qur'an. It was a dream to be his student; it would have been enough to just be in his company. I spoke to Allah: I know I'm not worthy of this, but I really want to have a strong relationship with the Qur'an. If being in his company would give me that, then please make this possible.

Alhamdulillah, I was offered the opportunity to become his student. But I hesitated. I wanted to, but I was still second-guessing myself and questioning: was I really capable enough?

I finally realised that when Allah presents you with opportunities, you shouldn't question them. Don't ask yourself if you're worthy. Let Him decide that. Accept the opportunities. Take the challenge. That was Allah's Guidance. When He offers you something and you have the capacity to take it on, if you reject it out of fear, you're actually rejecting a blessing.

That was the beginning of me starting my journey with the 10 qiraat (ways of recitation). I'm still studying with the sheikh. I've received ijazah from him in Hafs and Asim (two ways of reciting the Qur'an). Insha'Allah, hoping to complete the rest with him. May Allah grant him a long life. Ameen.

During one of my first lessons with him, he mentioned verse 46 in Surah Al-Kahf:

ٱلْمَالُ وَٱلْبَنُونَ زِينَةُ ٱلْحَيَوٰةِ ٱلدُّنْيَا ۖ وَٱلْبَٰقِيَٰتُ ٱلصَّٰلِحَٰتُ خَيْرٌ عِندَ رَبِّكَ ثَوَابًا وَخَيْرٌ أَمَلًا ٤٦

Al-mālu wal-banūna zīnatul-ḥayātid-dunyā wal-bāqiyātu ṣ-ṣāliḥātu khayrun 'inda rabbika thawāban wa khayrun amalā'

Wealth and children are the adornment of this worldly life, but the everlasting good deeds are far better with your Lord in reward and in hope.

He explained: salihaat are the females of our ummah, our sisters. There are many instances where sisters are left in the background in the name of hijab and niqab (face veil or face cover). But he had decided to take on female students because they are a blessing who have a ripple effect of good in this world. It makes me resolute in teaching our sisters, because a woman is always the first teacher of any child.

Pause and Reflect

The Prophet ﷺ said:

Whoever travels a path in search of knowledge, Allah will make easy for him a path to Paradise . . .

Sahih Muslim

Notice how Allah guides you to opportunities to learn or invites you to check in on yourself to determine what – namely your sins – may be preventing you from such gifts.

In verse 282 of Surah Al-Baqarah, He invites you to be mindful of Him, to have taqwa اتقوا, which comes from وَقَايَة, wiqayah, meaning to shield or protect oneself. Linguistically, taqwa means to place a shield between yourself and anything that displeases Allah. This part of the verse is delivered to you in the form of a command to live in a state of God-consciousness for your own benefit. And when you live such a life, Allah tells you He will وَيُعَلِّمُكُمُ اللَّهُ (wa-yuʿallimukumullāh), teach you.

But now here's the beauty: يُعَلِّمُكُمُ (yuʿallimukum) is from the root ع-ل-م (ilm), knowledge, and the verb is in the present tense, which indicates not a one-off lesson, but that the Lord of the Worlds will be your teacher continuously through life.

Taqwa leads to ilm. Living life as though you see Him, and knowing He certainly sees you, is the very means of being taught by the Teacher of teachers. You will receive divine instruction, both in Islamic knowledge and in wisdom.

Various tafseer scholars like Al-Qurtubi and At-Tabari have explained that this divine teaching can manifest in many ways: a light in one's heart by which the person gains insight without even realising it. Or even the ability to perceive deeply what is required of your relationship with Allah and the ability to act upon it.

Social media is full of posts and videos where people share their personal insight on various matters, and we watch them hoping to glean something that will shift our perception and add value to our lives.

My dearest reader, the Creator of the heavens and the earth tells you that the key to unlocking the accurate perception of your heart, which will bring about premium value, is found through taqwa, where knowledge penetrates your heart, changes your behaviour and transforms you completely.

Allah is the Ultimate Teacher. When you focus on filling your heart with taqwa and guarding your actions, Allah ʿazza wa jal will teach you through life events, reflections, people you meet, beautiful ways of knowing Him and special interaction with His Perfect Words.

Live with His Words . . .

Here are three steps to live with this week's verse(s):

1. Before every decision, big or small, stop and reflect on how it aligns with Allah's Teachings. Ask yourself: Is this pleasing to my Lord?

2. When you seek knowledge, whether religious or worldly, do so with the intention that Allah will grant you understanding.

3. Turn to the One who possesses all knowledge and wants you to know Him and live as deeply aware of Him, and tell Him: Rabbi, make me among those who are mindful of You in every matter of my life. Teach me what benefits me, open the doors of understanding and awareness for me and grant me deep insight and patience in the days of my life. Open up my heart to the understanding of the Qur'an. Guide me with Your Wisdom through every step.

A Question for Your Heart

How can you cultivate a deeper sense of taqwa in your life, knowing that through it, true knowledge is granted?

Fall in Love with The Author

Al-Hakim – The All Wise – is a Lord who imparts wisdom to you when you are mindful of Him. He rewards you with guidance as you pursue knowledge because your goal was not knowledge itself, but to be close to Him. His Wisdom extends to when and how He gifts you with the ability to learn that which He knows you need.

WEEK 35:

Guidance

Verse(s) of the Week
Your Rabb's Words for Your Soul

وَمَن يَهْدِ ٱللَّهُ فَهُوَ ٱلْمُهْتَدِ

Wa man yahdillāhu fahuwa al-muhtadī

'Whoever Allah guides is truly guided.'

Surah Al-Isra 17:97

Every Muslim loves a shahadah story. Even though I have my own, I still love hearing how others have been guided to Islam. There's something especially special about them for me now, particularly when their journeys are connected to the Qur'an.

When I reflect on my own story, I'm always struck by how, despite the negative portrayal of Islam in the media, I was still drawn to the Qur'an and found its beauty. A true gift from Allah 'azza wa jal.

But guidance doesn't end when someone embraces Islam or begins to practise it. Guidance is something we must all keep seeking – we need it like we need water to survive. Without it, we are lost.

Aminah, from Week 9, who used to make excuses for her lack of relationship with the Qur'an, continues in this week's story, taking us back to the night she decided – or rather, was guided – to start looking into Islam.

Aminah's Story Continues

In the month of Ramadan, just before I accepted Islam, I was reading the Qur'an cover to cover.

I was deeply struck by the verse:

إِذْ يُغَشِّيكُمُ ٱلنُّعَاسَ أَمَنَةً مِّنْهُ وَيُنَزِّلُ عَلَيْكُم مِّنَ ٱلسَّمَآءِ مَآءً لِّيُطَهِّرَكُم بِهِۦ وَيُذْهِبَ عَنكُمْ رِجْزَ ٱلشَّيْطَـٰنِ وَلِيَرْبِطَ عَلَىٰ قُلُوبِكُمْ وَيُثَبِّتَ بِهِ ٱلْأَقْدَامَ ١١

Idh yughashshīkumun nu'āsa amanan minhu wa yunazzilu
'alaykum minas-samā'i mā'an liyutahhirakum bihi wa
yudhhiba 'ankum rijza ash-shayṭān wa liyarbiṭa 'alā
qulūbikum wa yuthabbita bihi al-aqdām

'Remember' when He caused drowsiness to overcome you,
giving you serenity. And He sent down rain from the sky to
purify you, free you from shaytaan's whispers, strengthen
your hearts, and make 'your' steps firm.

Surah Anfaal 8:11

At the very beginning of my journey to Islam, I found myself in a situation where I felt helpless and afraid. I did not think I was going to be able to sleep due to fear. I prayed and said: 'O Allah, if you exist, help me. Save me.' As soon as I got into bed, I immediately fell asleep, which isn't usual for me. That night, it poured with rain.

When I woke up, I felt like the earth around me had been purified.

The verse transported me back to that moment, I felt this instant connection in my heart to Allah's Words. Everyone finds a verse in the Qur'an they feel was written for them and written to impact them. That was mine. Though it was revealed for another time and another situation, it was valid for me many, many years later.

Pause and Reflect

I really don't like the term 'practising' in the context 'he's practising Islam' or 'she's practising Islam'. What does it even mean? Judgements about who is choosing Allah and who isn't choosing Allah are too often based on outward appearance alone. But are we flies on the walls of each other's homes to label who is and isn't practising Islam? It really irks me.

Are we all not both striving and sinful? Practising and forgetful? Deeply conscious of Allah and at other times, heedless? We are – all of us! I'd rather say we are all blessed and are all in need of being guided by Allah, and that we should all be begging the One who guides to continue to receive His Guidance!

When you seek Allah, you will find Him. He is not a Lord that turns away from the seeker of truth. Ever. Whenever I have sat with a non-Muslim who has been looking into Islam and asks me 'how will I know Islam is the truth?' or 'how will I know when it's time to take the step and become Muslim?', I have always given them the same piece of advice: pray to God and ask Him to guide you to the truth. And He will. That's it.

After embracing Islam or returning to Allah, guidance is still needed continuously – through prayer, du'a, good deeds and gratitude. When was the last time you thanked Allah for the fact that you still acknowledge Him, are able to still worship Him and are still being guided by Him? By Allah, guidance is the greatest blessing you will ever experience in the life of this world. It is the greatest mercy from Him that requires endless praise of Him 'azza wa jal. Consider where you would be and what your life would be like without it.

Pause your reading for a moment and please go thank Allah for moving you forward to who you are right now – one with a believing heart that is alive with faith and with eyes fixed on the ultimate destination.

Live with His Words . . .

Here are three steps to live with this week's verse(s):

1. Start your day with du'a, asking Allah to guide your actions, decisions and interactions throughout the day. Ask for His Help in making choices that align with His Will and your spiritual growth.

2. Set aside a few minutes at the end of each day to reflect on your actions and ask yourself whether you are living in accordance with what Allah wants from you. Note down any necessary changes based on your reflections and ask Allah for help in rectifying your shortcomings.

3. Turn to the One whose guidance is always available to those who seek it and tell Him: My Lord, when I lose my way, guide me towards what is best for me. Show me the truth in all aspects of my life. Open the eyes of my heart to recognise Your Signs and give me the humility to embrace Your Guidance. Make me of those who are grateful and steadfast in their faith.

A Question for Your Heart

Are there parts of your life where you are happy to receive Allah's Guidance, and other parts where you allow your own desires to blind you to His Signs and Wisdom?

Fall in Love with The Author

Ar-Razzaq – The Provider – is a Lord who ensures that you are guided to everything you need, whether material or spiritual, and it is granted to you in the best way and at the perfect time.

WEEK 36:

Leave Your Comfort Zone

Verse(s) of the Week
Your Rabb's Words for Your Soul

وَعَسَىٰٓ أَن تَكْرَهُواْ شَيْـًٔا وَهُوَ خَيْرٌ لَّكُمْ ۖ وَعَسَىٰٓ أَن تُحِبُّواْ شَيْـًٔا وَهُوَ شَرٌّ لَّكُمْ ۗ وَٱللَّهُ يَعْلَمُ
وَأَنتُمْ لَا تَعْلَمُونَ ٢١٦

*Wa 'asā an takrahū shay'an wa huwa khayrun lakum, wa 'asā
an tuḥibbū shay'an wa huwa sharrun lakum; wallāhu ya'lamu
wa antum lā ta'lamūn*

*'Perhaps you dislike something which is good for you and like
something which is bad for you. Allah knows and you do not
know.'*

Surah Al-Baqarah 2:216

217

A most important lesson I have learned is how Allah may completely turn your path around, and I mean by 180 degrees! He might steer you towards what you once resisted, only for it to become the very thing that propels you forward in life.

SubhanAllah, He has taught me that what I think is good for me might actually turn out to be harmful, and what I once thought was bad for me can end up being the best thing that ever happened to me. I have no idea how. None of us knows. All I can do is leave enough space in my heart to trust.

Your Rabb wants you to succeed in the next life. So He will always bring you exactly what you need, even if you don't realise it at the time.

Nadia's story now goes on as she shares how something she was once averse to became one of the greatest blessings of her life.

Nadia's Story Continues

I knew I needed to change a few things in my life, especially my relationship with the Qur'an. Reciting Surah Al-Kahf on a Friday was a regular thing, and I would mostly read a set portion daily – but it was a tick-box exercise. I didn't understand what I was reading or reflect on it.

Alhamdulillah, I was then invited to perform Hajj (pilgrimage to Makkah). After that, I knew I had to do something about the Qur'an. I began to attend a lecture at a sister's home. It was once a week. Sometimes I would attend a couple times a month, but I still wasn't a regular there.

A friend suggested a Qur'anic course. It ran for two years and I immediately thought, No, I don't have time. Two years is too intense. She persuaded me to just come along to the course orientation. I still wasn't keen on the idea – I was planning to take a quick look around then slip away.

I had loads of misconceptions. I thought that studying the Qur'an was a secondary thing, that you could leave it to the later stages of life. Or that it made you really rigid and serious. I certainly wasn't like that; I love to joke around. I didn't want to become that strict person.

When I walked into the orientation, what greeted me was a five-star reception. I thought I must be in the wrong place. I was expecting a dim room with a circle of sisters studying, but instead there was a fancy table with notepads, pens, drinks – like a corporate conference!

The teacher of the course walked onto the stage. She was hilarious and educated in computer science, not just the Qur'an. Immediately I could relate to her. She spoke about how we need the Qur'an in our lives, no matter what we're doing. Without the Qur'an, she said, you're unable to focus on other areas. The Qur'an will complete you.

All my prejudices were dispelled that night. I decided I wanted this course, but it would go on being a struggle until my heart was cracked open – and that could only be done by Allah ﷻ.

Pause and Reflect

This week's verse refers to a time when some of the early Muslims were hesitant to engage in battle for the sake of Islam. They feared the hardship and loss that always comes with war. Allah revealed this verse to remind them that even though what they faced was hard, it was part of His Divine Plan and good would come from it, even if they could not see that immediately.

Allah's Plan is always greater than your immediate perception. It is from your Lord's Infinite Wisdom that what you may dislike might lead to something far better than you could have ever imagined.

In this verse, Allah acknowledges that this life isn't easy. But He is an understanding Creator who knows that your human self is naturally averse to stepping outside of your comfort zone. Your Rabb validates your human experience and feelings.

And He also wants you to grow. He wants you to learn an important lesson: that perseverance, as you step outside your comfort zone, has a great reward.

He ﷻ says وَعَسَىٰ أَن تَكْرَهُواْ شَيْئًا وَهُوَ خَيْرٌ لَّكُمْ (Wa 'asā an takrahū shay'an wa huwa khayrun lakum), perhaps you dislike something, and Allah makes therein much good.

This part of the verse is essential for your soul. Allah wants you to know that your limited human understanding will never be able to see the divine good within your challenges. What you may hate in the short term might be beautiful for you in the long term – both in this life and the next.

Nadia had to step outside her comfort zone and face the challenge of her prejudices head on. And there were hidden blessings, as we will come to discover in the next chapter. This is the case for you too. Whenever you need to step outside your comfort zone, turn to Allah and ask Him to settle your heart upon that which will lead you to what is absolutely best for you, even if you don't initially like it.

It is time to sign up for acceptance. You do not know. But Al-Aleem – The All Knowing – does. Turn to Him and trust Him to lead the way.

Live with His Words . . .

Here are three steps to live with this week's verse(s):

1. As you go about your everyday life, make du'a asking Allah to grant you the strength to see the hidden good within your challenges, and patience and trust in His Wisdom.

2. During moments that challenge you, write down your feelings of discomfort and shift your focus towards how this situation could be part of Allah's Greater Plan for your growth and ultimate success.

3. Turn to the One who stretches you, only to develop you with His Love and Mercy, and tell Him: Ya Allah, I want to feel secure and safe and so sometimes the unfamiliar scares me. I know You are a Lord who cares deeply, and I trust in Your Wisdom and Plan for me. Allow me to see the hidden blessings within the struggles I endure.

A Question for Your Heart

Are you willing to place your full trust in Allah's Plan, even when your heart desires something you cannot have, knowing that your limited understanding cannot fathom the wisdom behind what He has ordained for you?

Fall in Love with The Author

Al-Hakim (The All-Wise) is a Lord who wants you to know that He knows what is best for you because He sees and knows your past, present and future. His Wisdom is that He guides you towards what will bring you the greatest benefit, even if it is hidden from your immediate perception.

WEEK 37:

Submission

Verse(s) of the Week
Your Rabb's Words for Your Soul

وَمَا كَانَ لِمُؤْمِنٍ وَلَا مُؤْمِنَةٍ إِذَا قَضَى ٱللَّهُ وَرَسُولُهُ أَمْرًا أَن يَكُونَ لَهُمُ ٱلْخِيَرَةُ مِنْ أَمْرِهِمْ ۗ وَمَن يَعْصِ ٱللَّهَ وَرَسُولَهُ فَقَدْ ضَلَّ ضَلَٰلًا مُّبِينًا ٣٦

Wa mā kāna li-mu'minin wa lā mu'minatin idhā qaḍā Allāhu wa Rasūluhu amran an yakūna lahumu al-khiyaratu min amrihim, wa man ya'ṣi Allāha wa Rasūlahu faqad ḍalla ḍalālan mubīnān

'It is not for a believing man or woman – when Allah and His Messenger decree a matter – to have any other choice in that matter. Indeed, whoever disobeys Allah and His Messenger has clearly gone 'far' astray.'

Surah Al-Ahzab 33:36

've always been a rebel, from a young age. I wanted to do things differently, to stand against the crowd. And I definitely carried that into adulthood. I've never feared speaking up or standing up. Has it got me into trouble? Absolutely. Because strong stances require wisdom, and that's something I didn't always have.

When I look at my life now, I can see how Allah has taken this fearless rebel and is taming her – teaching me lessons that force me to balance courage with clarity and fearlessness with objectivity.

This next part of Nadia's story made me smile. She's like me: always rebelling against systems, wanting to be her own person, not realising that the true path to being your own person is actually about liberating yourself by letting go fully and entirely becoming Muslim – one who wholeheartedly submits.

Nadia's Story Continues

Though I'd decided to sign up to the Qur'anic course, I was still critical and sceptical. We began, and I was making demands, trying to change things. I became a troublemaker.

Then, six or seven months in, I started to notice the change it was making to me. The system was working – even though I'd been resisting it – and I could feel its effects. So I ended up adopting not only the course, but also the philosophy of the course and everything it came with. Because it was clear something amazing was taking place.

Everything I did during that time was connected to the Qur'an. The course involved a lot of preparation before lessons. We met once a week, and there were constant questions and provocative thinking before each ayah. I wasn't like other students in the class who had a BA in Shariah or understood the Qur'an because this was their third time going through it. I was the new kid on the block.

I was spending every single free minute with the Qur'an or researching something for it. If I was waiting at a doctor's appointment or picking up my kids from school, I was reading tafseer (exegesis) or seerah (the life of the Prophet ﷺ) connected to the ayat (verses). The constant immersion in the science of the Qur'an changed me as a person.

As we were learning about the munafiqeen (hypocrites), who used to show Islam to the people but in their hearts were not really accepting it, it hit me. I was one of them. I was living my life thinking I was submitting, but I wasn't. My heart hadn't fully surrendered to all that Allah wanted from me and my actions were proof of it. I realised that the munafiqoon are definitely not just a group in Madinah at the time of the Prophet ﷺ.

I needed to address my walaa al baraa – the love for what Allah loves and complete dislike of all that does not please Him. And then live by it – not just some of it, not just what suits me, but all of it. That's when my entire practice of Islam changed.

Pause and Reflect

What I'm about to write in this chapter requires me to swallow my ego. It's uncomfortable and it may be uncomfortable for you to read too. Let's both breathe and take this in together.

I love Allah. I love my deen. I am actively working towards making the journey of my soul the best it can be, with the aim to please Allah. But – and it's a big but – subhanAllah, I do struggle with some of the commands of Allah ﷻ. I honestly feel my soul resists certain verses, certain hadith and certain requirements of me as a Muslim. I know I'm not alone and maybe you're reading this saying: Alhamdulillah, finally someone has said it!

According to Qurtubi and others, this week's verse was revealed when the Prophet ﷺ chose Zainab bint Jahsh (radiAllahu anha) as a wife for his adopted son Zayd ibn Harithah (radiAllahu anhu). As Zayd was a freed slave and was still stuck with that label, Zainab and her brother Abdullah Ibn Jahsh rejected the proposal on the basis they were nobler than him in family and lineage. This week's verse was then revealed, giving instruction that when Allah and His Prophet order something, it becomes an obligation. When Zainab (radiAllahu anha) and her brother heard this verse, they retracted their rejection and agreed to the proposal.

Allah is reminding believers that when a divine command comes, personal preference must be set aside.

The reality is this deen is easy. It's our nafs, desires, environment or pre-Islamic mindset (whether that's before shahadah or before the decision to practise Islam) that makes the deen feel difficult.

If you, at times, feel like me, let me tell you, we are not alone. The blessed companions of the Prophet ﷺ also experienced this. It's normal. It's human.

There's this internal battle between your thoughts and opinions about certain matters and then the truth of what Allah ﷻ and His Messenger have said. I think this is the ultimate test of submission. You may not say aloud: 'I don't quite like that ruling.' 'That doesn't resonate with me.' Or even, well, 'I'll just live my life pretending this or that ruling doesn't exist.' But your actions will reveal these thoughts.

Real submission is when your heart aligns with Allah's Decisions. It is feeling content even when it is hard. That is the jihad. This is the struggle. Modern life trains us to value autonomy and choice. And while you certainly have both, your Lord is realigning your heart to true freedom, which is to submit wholeheartedly to Him. Often, you'll only understand the wisdom behind Allah's Commands much later.

This verse invites you to trust His Wisdom even when you can't see it. I'll let you sit with that and reflect, just as I am. Ya Allah – help us all. Ameen.

Live with His Words . . .

Here are three steps to live with this week's verse(s):

1. Train yourself to surrender decisions to Allah's Guidance first, not last. Use salatul istikharaa for small decisions to build the muscles of your heart for a life that requires full submission.

2. Practise joyful submission, not reluctant submission. True submission isn't dragging your feet towards Allah's Command; it's running towards it with trust and joy. Wholehearted believers obey even when it's hard, trusting that unseen blessings are hidden inside obedience. Each time you obey Allah in something challenging, write down one hidden blessing or personal growth you experienced afterwards. This will build positive emotional memory around submission.

3. Turn to the One who created you, who you came from and will return to and tell Him: Ya Allah, help me to submit to You. Mould my heart until it beats only with Your Commands. Teach my soul to trust that whatever You decree is better for me than what I desire.

A Question for Your Heart

Ask yourself: What areas of my life am I still holding on to, resisting full submission to Allah's Will? How can I release them and trust completely in my Lord's Plan, knowing that His Wisdom is beyond my limited understanding?

Fall in Love with The Author

Al-Wali – The One who Protects – is a Lord who not only guides, but shields you through every moment, even when you feel uncertain. He wants you to lean on Him in full submission, trusting that He is always looking after your best interests.

WEEK 38:

Barakah

Verse(s) of the Week
Your Rabb's Words for Your Soul

وَلَوْ أَنَّ أَهْلَ ٱلْقُرَىٰٓ ءَامَنُوا وَٱتَّقَوْا لَفَتَحْنَا عَلَيْهِم بَرَكَٰتٍ مِّنَ ٱلسَّمَآءِ وَٱلْأَرْضِ وَلَٰكِن كَذَّبُوا فَأَخَذْنَٰهُم بِمَا كَانُوا يَكْسِبُونَ٩٦

*Walaw anna ahla al-qurā amanū wa-ttaqaw la-fataḥnā
'alayhim barakātin mina as-samā'i wa-al-arḍ, walākin
kadhdhabū fa-akhadhnāhum bimā kānū yaksibūn*

*'Had the people of those societies been faithful and mindful
of Allah`, We would have overwhelmed them with blessings
from heaven and earth. But they disbelieved, so We seized
them for what they used to commit.'*

Surah Al-Araf: 7:96

The topic of barakah (divine blessings) is a joy to write and
speak about. Using barakah feels like tapping into an unseen
realm, defying the usual laws of nature and instead calling

upon Allah's Abundance. That's the beauty of divine blessings from Al-Kareem, The Most Generous.

As I continued my interview with Ola, I was reminded that Allah moves us forward in life, sometimes through grand, unmistakable moments, and sometimes through quiet, subtle shifts.

I have seen first-hand in my own life and in the lives of those I love that a true relationship with the Qur'an is the greatest source of barakah there is. It's something extraordinary to witness. And Ola's story about her mother is a beautiful testament to that.

Ola's Story Continues

There was a period when I had started Arabic Gems (an institute teaching Qur'anic Arabic) and then stopped due to having children and homeschooling. After that, I wasn't interacting with the Qur'an as much. When I started it up again, it was a much more intimate part of my life – every day I was interacting with Allah's Book and seeing the amount of barakah and blessings that fell into my lap without me doing anything. This reminded me of the power of the Qur'an. Sometimes I would think I should make du'a for such and such thing, and suddenly Allah would give it before I even made du'a for it. I hadn't put my hands out and made du'a in the formal wording, but He had heard the words of my heart and granted me my request. That's when I saw the blessings of having the Qur'an as a central priority in my life.

My mother was always a woman of the Qur'an. I have memories of her writing out the verses she was memorising, which she would then paste onto the wall. As she was committing them to memory, she would glance over to the relevant place. The borders of our wallpaper were pages of the Qur'an, written out by her.

She recently developed Alzheimer's and was diagnosed with cancer. But, still, she recites the Qur'an. Apart from the Alzheimer's, she doesn't have any physical pain and she's still very positive, joking and laughing. I put it down to the Qur'an and her deep relationship with it. Despite forgetting so many things in her life, she still remembers what she has memorised. Seeing the blessings in her life has made me realise how important it is to do the same for my children, demonstrating to them what she has always demonstrated to me.

Pause and Reflect

The Qur'an is the strongest means that leads to barakah. Everything Allah's Words touch is blessed. In my book *The Power of Du'a*, I shared a quote from Sheikh Wahaj Tarin:

Whatever the Qur'an touches, Allah blesses and honours. The night on which the Qur'an was revealed became the best of nights. The month on which the Qur'an was revealed became the best of months. The Prophet to whom the Qur'an was revealed became the best of Prophets. The angel through whom the Qur'an was revealed became the best of angels. The nation to which the Qur'an was revealed became the best of nations.

And when you come to the Qur'an, it touches you too, as the Most High leads you to become the best version of yourself.

There are a few things I want to draw your attention to in this week's verse. The first is لَفَتَحْنَا عَلَيْهِم (la-fataḥnā 'alayhim), meaning we would have opened upon them. The word fataḥnā (opened) is beautifully descriptive, as though you can see in your mind's eye an image of a door wide open, granting you unlimited access to ease and abundance. All without struggle, it's open and available to you.

Now look at how the verse begins. If the people had ءَامَنُواْ وَٱتَّقَوْاْ (āmanū wa-ttaqaw), believed and had taqwa, they would have found abundant, consistent, multiplied blessings. This is an invitation to up your game. How long have you been a believer without taqwa? What needs to change? These are questions I ask myself and must regularly reflect upon.

Live with His Words . . .

Here are three steps to live with this week's verse(s):

1. Before starting any task, whether small or large, make the intention to do it for the sake of Allah, asking for His Blessing in it. Be sincere and mindful in the process.

2. Set up five standing orders of donating £1 or $1 or your own local currency per month to five different charities. Have the intention that you are setting this up for life purely for His Sake.

3. Turn to the One whose divine blessings are readily available for you and tell Him: Allah, I thank You for every blessing You have bestowed upon me. Ya Allah, bless my life, my family and my work. Bless every step I take, and make all that I do be crowned with Your Barakah and Mercy. I am a soul in need of Your Blessings. Grant me barakah in my sustenance, in my actions, and in my health. O Allah, make me one of the grateful, and help me always remain thankful for Your Infinite Generosity and Mercy. Ameen.

A Question for Your Heart

Ask yourself: In seeking Allah's Barakah, how often do I pause to truly reflect on the small blessings He has already granted me, and am I showing enough gratitude for them, or am I waiting for something bigger to recognise His Generosity?

Fall in Love with The Author

Al-Muhsi – The One Who Takes Account of All Things – is a Lord who knows every single blessing, no matter how small, that He has granted you. It is in His Infinite Knowledge that He provides barakah in ways you may not even notice. He will continue to give and continue to bless you even when you are ungrateful. But when you are thankful, He increases you extraordinarily.

Go with His Flow

Verse(s) of the Week
Your Rabb's Words for Your Soul

وَعْدَ ٱللَّهِ ۖ لَا يُخْلِفُ ٱللَّهُ وَعْدَهُ وَلَكِنَّ أَكْثَرَ ٱلنَّاسِ لَا يَعْلَمُونَ ٦

Wa'da Allāh, lā yukhlifu Allāhu wa'dah, wa lākinna akthara an-nāsi lā ya'lamūn

''This is` the promise of Allah. `And` Allah never fails in His promise. But most people do not know.'

Surah Ar-Rum 30:6

There was an incident in the life of the companion of the Prophet ﷺ Umar ibn al-Khattab (radiAllahu anhu) that I absolutely love. Before he embraced Islam, he once snuck up quietly to observe the Prophet ﷺ while he was praying at night in front of the Kabah. Umar (radiAllahu anhu) was deeply hostile towards Islam at the time but found himself drawn to this moment out of curiosity. As he listened secretly, the Prophet ﷺ was reciting the Qur'an aloud. The verses he was reciting moved Umar's heart.

The Prophet ﷺ was reciting verses from Surah Al-Haqqah (69: 38–52). These are powerful ayat about the Day of Judgment and the truthfulness of the Qur'an. In the darkness of the night, Umar thought to himself, *This is poetry, as the Quraysh say*. And then the Prophet ﷺ recited:

وَمَا هُوَ بِقَوْلِ شَاعِرٍ ۚ قَلِيلًا مَّا تُؤْمِنُونَ ٤١

Wa mā huwa bi-qawli shā'ir; qalīlan mā tu'minūn

And it is not the word of a poet; little do you believe.

Surah Al-Haqqah, 69:41

Umar's next thought was, *It must be the word of a soothsayer*. And the Prophet ﷺ continued his recitation:

وَلَا بِقَوْلِ كَاهِنٍ ۚ قَلِيلًا مَّا تَذَكَّرُونَ ٤٢

Wa lā bi-qawli kāhin; qalīlan mā tadhakkarūn

Nor is it the word of a soothsayer; little do you remember.

Surah Al-Haqqah, 69:42

Umar was stunned. It was as if the Prophet ﷺ was responding to his very thoughts though he hadn't uttered a word! His heart began to soften towards Islam from that point, although his acceptance of the faith would come later.

The reason why I love this story is that Allah's Timing is absolutely perfect. What is meant for you will never miss you. What is meant to miss you will never reach you. Allah's Timing is precise.

My Story

I often wonder why it is only after more than 25 years of being a Muslim that I am now embarking upon an intense journey with the Qur'an. Why not back when I had more time and fewer responsibilities? Because Allah has deemed this the right time.

I have to be honest with you: when I was gifted the place on the Qur'an course, I had a 'subhanAllah moment' because I already knew that Book 3 was going to be this one. And I thought, Wow, guided to embark upon a Qur'an course just before I start writing a book about living with the Qur'an! This couldn't have been a coincidence.

This is the beauty about divine timing. There's a special reason why, and even if you may not know it, just knowing that Allah 'azza wa jal is interacting with you and your life, intervening when necessary, at exactly the right time, is deeply comforting.

Pause and Reflect

I work well under pressure. It doesn't matter how much time I am given beforehand, I only get the job done when I have to. I remember discussing this with a few sisters on a WhatsApp group I'm on where one sister shared that she was the same. When she came to study for her master's, she decided she would do things differently with her first assignment. She planned ahead, giving herself more than enough time to work on her essay. The result? The lowest grade she'd ever received.

She quickly returned to her usual way of working on her assignments – at the last minute, under pressure. Her grades rocketed.

I'm certainly not telling you to leave everything to the last minute.

Do what works for you. But Allah knows how you work best. And His Method of helping you and His Timing in helping you are perfect.

Remember Wasim's story from week 3, where we learned he was a student at Madinah university and didn't know how to read the Qur'an. He knew that if he didn't memorise the surahs or learn to read, he was going to get kicked off the course. That urgency, that pressure was divinely orchestrated and became the very means to the continuation of his studies and him becoming a sheikh.

Some people need that level of urgency too. Only a deadline will make them buckle down and do it.

I made du'a to write and publish a book before I leave this world. Allah 'azza wa jal did not fail in His Promise to be Al Mujeeb – the One who responds to du'a – to me. But He also knew that, left to my own devices, I would never get it done. He knew sending the largest publisher my way, with a publishing contract and a tight deadline, is what it would take to push me to finish writing.

In this week's verse, Allah speaks of وَعْدَ ٱللَّهِ (Wa'da Allāh), the Promise of Allah, using the word Wa'd, which linguistically means an absolutely certain commitment or guarantee. He لَا يُخْلِفُ ٱللَّهُ وَعْدَهُ (lā yukhlifu Allāhu wa'dah), never fails in His Promise. Yukhlifu (يُخْلِفُ) is linked to khalf (خلف), which means 'to go back on something'. Your Lord never retracts or neglects His Promises to you. His Timing, Fulfilment and Delivery are flawless. His Promises operate on His Scale, never on yours. So go with His Flow.

Live with His Words . . .

Here are three steps to live with this week's verse(s):

1. Take time to look back at instances in your life where things worked out in ways you never expected, at exactly the right time. Reflecting on these moments helps reinforce

your belief that Allah's Timing is always perfect, even when we can't see it in the moment.

2. When making du'a, be confident in the knowledge that Allah will answer in the best possible way and at the best time. You may not always receive what you want, but you will always get what you need, at the time that's best for your spiritual and dunya growth.

3. Turn to the One whose timing is absolutely perfect and tell Him: You, my Lord, are the Best of Planners, and I place my trust in Your Divine Timing. Grant me the patience to wait for Your Plan to unfold. Ya Allah, grant me the strength to accept Your Timing with peace and contentment.

A Question for Your Heart

How can you embrace Allah's Perfect Timing, trusting that His Plan is unfolding in the best way, even when it doesn't align with your own expectations?

Fall in Love with The Author

Al-Muqaddim – The Expediter – is a Lord who brings forward that which is best for you at exactly the right time. He arranges everything for the perfect moment. His Timing is never early, never late, and always precisely as it should be.

WEEK 40:

Salah

Verse(s) of the Week
Your Rabb's Words for Your Soul

إِنَّ ٱلْإِنسَـٰنَ خُلِقَ هَلُوعًا ١٩ إِذَا مَسَّهُ ٱلشَّرُّ جَزُوعًا ٢٠ وَإِذَا مَسَّهُ ٱلْخَيْرُ مَنُوعًا ٢١ إِلَّا ٱلْمُصَلِّينَ ٢٢ ٱلَّذِينَ هُمْ عَلَىٰ صَلَاتِهِمْ دَآئِمُونَ ٢٣ وَٱلَّذِينَ فِىٓ أَمْوَٰلِهِمْ حَقٌّ مَّعْلُومٌ ٢٤ لِّلسَّآئِلِ وَٱلْمَحْرُومِ ٢٥ وَٱلَّذِينَ يُصَدِّقُونَ بِيَوْمِ ٱلدِّينِ ٢٦ وَٱلَّذِينَ هُم مِّنْ عَذَابِ رَبِّهِم مُّشْفِقُونَ ٢٧ إِنَّ عَذَابَ رَبِّهِمْ غَيْرُ مَأْمُونٍ ٢٨ وَٱلَّذِينَ هُمْ لِفُرُوجِهِمْ حَـٰفِظُونَ ٢٩ إِلَّا عَلَىٰٓ أَزْوَٰجِهِمْ أَوْ مَا مَلَكَتْ أَيْمَـٰنُهُمْ فَإِنَّهُمْ غَيْرُ مَلُومِينَ ٣٠ فَمَنِ ٱبْتَغَىٰ وَرَآءَ ذَٰلِكَ فَأُوْلَـٰٓئِكَ هُمُ ٱلْعَادُونَ ٣١ وَٱلَّذِينَ هُمْ لِأَمَـٰنَـٰتِهِمْ وَعَهْدِهِمْ رَٰعُونَ ٣٢ وَٱلَّذِينَ هُم بِشَهَـٰدَٰتِهِمْ قَآئِمُونَ ٣٣ وَٱلَّذِينَ هُمْ عَلَىٰ صَلَاتِهِمْ يُحَافِظُونَ ٣٤

Inna al-insāna khuliqa halū'ā idhā massahu al-sharru jazū'ā
wa idhā massahu al-khayru manū'ā illā al-muṣallīn alladhīna
hum 'alā ṣalātihim dā'imūn wa alladhīna fī amwālihim
ḥaqqun ma'lūm lilssā'ili wa al-maḥrūm wa alladhīna yuṣ
addiqūna biyawmi al-dīn wa alladhīna hum min 'adhābi
rabbihim mushfiqūn inna 'adhāba rabbihim ghayru ma'mūn
wa alladhīna hum lifurūjihim ḥāfiẓūn illā 'alā azwājihim aw
mā malakat aymānuhum fa-innahum ghayru malūmīn famani
ibtaghā warā'a dhālika fa-ulā'ika humu al-'ādūn wa alladhīna

238

*hum li-amānātihim wa ʿahdihim rāʿūn wa alladhīna hum
bishahādātihim qāʾimūn wa alladhīna hum ʿalā ṣalātihim yuḥ
āfithūn*

*'Indeed, humankind was created impatient: distressed when
touched with evil, and withholding when touched with
good – except those who pray, consistently performing their
prayers; and who give the rightful share of their wealth to the
beggar and the poor; and who 'firmly' believe in the Day of
Judgment; and those who fear the punishment of their Lord –
'knowing that' none should feel secure from their Lord's
punishment—and those who guard their chastity except with
their wives or those 'bondwomen' in their possession, for
then they are free from blame, but whoever seeks beyond
that are the transgressors. 'The faithful are' also those who are
true to their trusts and covenants; and who are honest in their
testimony; and who are 'properly' observant of their prayers.'*

Surah Al-Maarij 70:19–34

When I look back, some of the sweetest moments in salah (prayer)
were when I was first learning how to pray as a new Muslim. Tears
would hit the prayer mat as I begged for relief during a test. When
I reflect on why those moments were so powerful, I realise it was
because I was approaching salah with true purpose. As a new
Muslim, I was deeply focused – carefully pronouncing each word,
trying to perform each action correctly, fully aware that this was my
direct line to Allah ﷻ.

Salah becomes sweet when you seek connection to Allah through
it. But it becomes monotonous when life becomes disconnected
from the Qur'an, as we come to see through the next part of Nadia's
story.

Nadia's Story Continues

As you know, my life completely changed after Allah brought the intensive Qur'an course my way. That intense exposure to the Qur'an led to a sweetness I have never experienced in my life. It completely changed my practice of Islam. I was spending every minute with the Qur'an and I was looking forward to finishing the course so that I could memorise and be with the Qur'an at a slower pace.

Then the course ended. I was working several jobs. It was non-stop and I wasn't able to read the Qur'an except during my salah. So now I wasn't reading the Qur'an. I wasn't interacting with the Qur'an. I was just repeating the same surahs and my salah became automatic.

During this period, I felt my soul was leaving me. I stopped enjoying salah. I was doing it just because I had to pray five times per day. I wasn't enjoying my life in general. It wasn't just the stress of work, because you can have that going on and still enjoy your time with Allah. It was like there was no soul in me. Even my compass for right and wrong was off. I would say things then think, Why did I say that? That's old me. That's not Nadia now.

Then I had a lightbulb moment: it was because I had lost that connection with the Qur'an. And because I was away from the Qur'an, my salah was affected. There wasn't much khushoo (focus in prayer) in the salah. Now I understand there is a connection between the Qur'an and salah – if I lose it with the Qur'an, my salah and everything else is impacted.

What I learned is: if you allow life to take over again, you will drift. It's as simple as that. You will no longer enjoy your ibadah (worship). You won't enjoy your life, and you won't find purpose in what you're doing.

Pause and Reflect

This week's verses make us feel naked and exposed. He 'azza wa jal describes our raw, unrefined human condition: when we're tested, we become restless and in need of Him. Then, when He relieves us, we forget and become selfish with the blessings He has gifted us. Allah forgive us. Ameen.

If you find yourself falling into the above description, know that Allah will guide you to purify you. Your tests will be hand-picked until you become refined, trusting Him when in need and grateful when blessed – a true believer.

Allah mentions prayer at the beginning of the verse *and* at the end. Salah is what will save you from all the instability that comes with your human experience. It will anchor you, change you and stabilise you emotionally and spiritually.

Pray and strengthen your connection to the Qur'an, and allow the Qur'an to strengthen your attachment to prayer.

Live with His Words . . .

Here are three steps to live with this week's verse(s):

1. Choose short meaningful Qur'anic verses that deeply resonate with your current life circumstances and use them in your salah.

2. Spend two to three minutes before each salah reading or thinking about one Qur'anic verse – its meaning and how it applies to your life. Go into salah with that reflection.

3. Turn to the One who will look at the condition of your salah before any other good deed and tell Him: O Allah, fill my heart with the light of Your Qur'an so that every word I recite in salah is filled with meaning and connection. My Beloved, make the Qur'an the soul of my salah, and my salah the nourishment of my soul.

A Question for Your Heart

What is the honest state of your salah? If it feels empty or you find yourself distracted, could it be because you have neglected to fill your heart with the Words Allah 'azza wa jal sent to bring it to life?

Fall in Love with The Author

Al-Haleem – The Most Forbearing – is a Lord who patiently guides your heart back to Him through every recitation and every prostration, even when you intentionally or unintentionally drift away.

WEEK 41:

Vigilance

Verse(s) of the Week
Your Rabb's Words for Your Soul

وَٱتْلُ مَآ أُوحِىَ إِلَيْكَ مِن كِتَابِ رَبِّكَ ۖ لَا مُبَدِّلَ لِكَلِمَـٰتِهِۦ وَلَن تَجِدَ مِن دُونِهِۦ مُلْتَحَدًا ٢٧

*Wa-utlu mā ūḥiya ilayka min kitābi rabbika; lā mubaddila
likalimātihi wa lan tajida min dūnihi multaḥadā*

'Recite what has been revealed to you from the Book of your
Lord. None can change His Words, nor can you find any
refuge besides Him.'

Surah Al-Kahf 18:27

To me, the charity I founded, Solace, is like my baby. I'm deeply protective of it, having worked so hard to establish it and grow it to where it is today – and all praise is due to Allah alone, for His Help and Permission. As the founder, I remain vigilant in protecting it so that it continues to serve its purpose.

We return to Maryam's story from Week 4, when she lost her relationship with the Qur'an. As her story continues, it makes me pause and ask myself: how vigilant am I in protecting the most precious part of my existence – my relationship with the One who caused me to exist?

I invite you to look inward at your decisions and actions – those subtle choices that could, without you realising, either nourish or unconsciously erode the most vital part of your life: living with Him and His Words.

Maryam's Story

I've experienced polar opposites: living immersed in the Qur'an and being completely distant from it. Over ten years ago, I felt really close to Allah's Book. I began memorisation again. I was attending a halaqa (circle of knowledge). I felt like my heart was really switched on. I was fully present. Then I lost this, through my own desires and mistakes. And, in the absence of the Qur'an, I realised how exposed and unprotected I felt.

Now, if I just look back a little, I feel my connection with the Qur'an is different. I don't wake up for qiyam (night prayer). I'll go back to sleep after my alarm stops ringing and wake up with less time to pray. Those mistakes make me lose out, and the impact happens immediately. There's no delay.

My relationship with the Qur'an is affected by what I do. It's like a gauge – it shows me immediately what's going on. All acts of worship, particularly with the Qur'an, are gifts. So, if I don't act right, they're taken away or decreased. I can see this because I'm tracking myself.

There's a verse that motivates me to strive for Allah. It is:

وَٱلسَّٰبِقُونَ ٱلسَّٰبِقُونَ ١٠ أُوْلَٰٓئِكَ ٱلْمُقَرَّبُونَ ١١ فِى جَنَّٰتِ ٱلنَّعِيمِ ١٢ ثُلَّةٌ مِّنَ ٱلْأَوَّلِينَ ١٣ وَقَلِيلٌ مِّنَ ٱلْٰٔاخِرِينَ ١٤

Wa as-sābiqūna as-sābiqūn ula'ika al-muqarrabūn fī jannāti
an-na'īm thullatun mina al-awwalīn wa qalīlun mina
al-ākhirīn

And the foremost ʾin faithʾ will be the foremost ʾin Paradiseʾ.
They are the ones nearest ʾto Allahʾ, in the Gardens of Bliss.
ʾThey will beʾ a multitude from earlier generations and a
few from later generations.

Surah Al-Waqiah 56:10–14

*As-saabiqoon are the early believers and a few of the later
ones. As-saabiqoon are a special and rare breed: they race
to do good deeds. The fact that only a few are from the end
of time (which we are moving towards), shows how rare this
group is. You can't be part of it when you're half-stepping.
You have to be on point. So I try to catch myself when I get
lazy or start losing steam or sliding backwards. I can't afford
to. I have to pick myself up and try to move forward and
push up the hill again. This is what our journey with faith is
going to be like until we die. This is who as-saabiqoon are –
and I want to be one of the few.*

Pause and Reflect

In this beautiful verse of the week, Allah 'azza wa jal is commanding
the Prophet ﷺ to hold on to the Qur'an. And in your life, particularly
in times of distress, you must also hold on to the blueprint for the
relief of your distress and the map forward. Allah's Words are perfect and timeless. There is no refuge except with Him – through His

Book. Maintaining your relationship with Allah, primarily through His Book, is what will get you through this rollercoaster called life.

Right at the beginning of the verse, the verb وَاتُلُ (wa-utlu) from تلا يتلو (talā yatlū) means to recite, follow closely, with reflection. Your Lord is telling you clearly, turn to His Book, not casually, but with attention. It is this deeper level of reading that will support you. Why?

Because مِن كِتَابِ رَبِّكَ (min kitābi rabbik), it is a book from your Rabb. Allah ﷻ could have said that it is a book from Ar-Rahman, Al-Lateef or Al-Hakim. But He says this is the Book from your Rabb, your Lord who is your nurturer, is looking after you with deep care.

If this is how Allah is the Most Loving towards You, then it is incumbent upon You to also approach your relationship with the Qur'an with micro vigilance of anything that may interfere with it or, Allah forbid, take you away from it.

Hold on to the Qur'an, live with it, protect it – through all the seasons of life.

Live with His Words . . .

Here are three steps to live with this week's verse(s):

1. Link your daily interaction to the Qur'an to an existing habit. Perhaps it could follow fajr prayer or take place on a regular commute, so that it becomes a protected, non-negotiable part of your day.

2. Replace mindless scrolling or background noise with Qur'an recitation and tafseer lectures.

3. Turn to the One who is vigilant with you and tell Him: Rabbi, protect my heart from drifting away from Your Book. Make me vigilant in upholding Your Words, living by Your Guidance and loving the recitation of Your Words. Let the

Qur'an be my closest companion in life, my light in the grave and my proof on the Day I meet You.

A Question for Your Heart

Reflect: what daily decisions are you making that unconsciously and consistently weaken your bond with the Qur'an? What can you change today to protect it with everything that you are and have?

Fall in Love with The Author

Al-Hafidh – The Ever-Protecting Guardian – is a Lord who watches over your heart through His Protection, safeguarding your connection with His Perfect Words. Be vigilant as to what distances your soul from Him, for He is a Lord who is vigilant with you and draws you near.

WEEK 42:

Joy

Verse(s) of the Week
Your Rabb's Words for Your Soul

مَنْ عَمِلَ صَـٰلِحًا مِّن ذَكَرٍ أَوْ أُنثَىٰ وَهُوَ مُؤْمِنٌ فَلَنُحْيِيَنَّهُ حَيَوٰةً طَيِّبَةًۖ وَلَنَجْزِيَنَّهُمْ أَجْرَهُم بِأَحْسَنِ مَا كَانُوا۟ يَعْمَلُونَ ٩٧

*Man 'amila ṣāliḥan min dhakarin aw unthā wa huwa
mu'minun falanuḥyiyannahu ḥayātam ṭayyibatan
walnajjziyannahum ajrahum bi'ahsan mā kānū ya'malūn*

'*Whoever does good, whether male or female, and is a believer,
We will surely bless them with a good life, and We will
certainly reward them according to the best of their deeds.*'

Surah An-Nahl 16:97

I came across an Instagram post by the lovely Asmaa Hussein. She spoke about allowing ourselves to experience joy fully. I cried buckets reading it.
The reason it touched me so deeply is that as a child, I watched

my mother sit in her pain, as if she believed she had to live there. Alhamdulillah, I haven't gone to that extreme, but I've always limited my joy, capping it as though too much happiness wasn't allowed.

It wasn't until I brought this to therapy that the walls finally crumbled. I gave myself permission to feel joy.

It began with the smallest of things: agreeing to do a phone survey because I knew it would bring the operator joy. Sitting on the grass playing Uno with my youngest. Looking up at the sky and taking in just how blue it was. Savouring my chai latte. And in all these moments, quietly thanking Allah for these glimpses of joy.

But joy doesn't end there.

There's also the joy of being Muslim: the joy of worship, of reciting the Qur'an, of being in intimate conversation with Allah. I've realised I wasn't truly living until I stepped into that joy. And even more than that, I didn't know the depth of life until I allowed myself to find joy through His Words – just like Nadia, whose story goes on with that very realisation.

Nadia's Story Continues

Whether your life seems amazing right now or you're miserable, without the Book of Allah, you are on autopilot. You're just passing the days – happy then sad then happy then sad – until your time is up. Someone shared with me: people are heedless, but when they die, they wake up. And I was like – whoa! That might seem morbid, but it's true. We need to start living now before it's too late, and we're not living until we experience the Words of Allah.

This dunya is full of trials. There are celebrities who we imagine have everything – money and fame – and then we're shocked when they end their own lives. Something is always missing. Everyone's always looking for something more – we're all looking to fill this void within us. This cannot be filled except by the remembrance of Allah. There is nothing better than the Words of Allah.

I have spent my life looking for happiness. And I received many things that should have made me happy, but they didn't. The only time I felt truly happy was when I started to understand what Allah said in the Qur'an. It was then that I started living.

Pause and Reflect

I'd like you to remember the last Islamic reminder you heard, whether in person or online, that really touched your heart. It may have assisted you in moving to a more motivated position, where you set intentions and acted towards pleasing Allah. Maybe it just melted your heart for your Rabb. How did it feel? I'm sure it was something you wish you could bottle up and drink anytime you felt parched. Such instances are sips of emaan – the only constant drink that will continuously quench your thirst is the Qur'an.

In this week's verse, Allah 'azza wa jal has made a promise: whoever does good deeds and are believers, He will guide them to the good life. This doesn't mean no trials. You will always be tested with something, but the good life is being divinely equipped with all that He knows you need to react to those tests, and manage them and how you feel during them.

Have you ever found yourself at peace during a trial, or ever observed someone who was being tested but just seemed so content, even in difficulty? That right there is also part of Allah's Promise of what the good life can really mean.

Live with His Words . . .

Here are three steps to live with this week's verse(s):

1. Pick something small yet impactful each morning: texting a loved one a du'a, preparing a meal for your family with love or giving a little money in charity. Tell yourself: 'This is for Allah alone.' Let this be your daily act of quiet righteousness. Absorb its joy.

2. Choose one action to strengthen your emaan, perhaps reciting one page of the Qur'an with reflection, listening to a short lecture about one of your favourite verses or journalling your gratitude to Allah. Make it doable and meaningful so it becomes a source of daily nourishment.

3. Turn to the One who gives true life and tell Al-Hayy, Al-Qayyum: Let me live a life that is rich in meaning and full of joy in pleasing You. Plant sincerity in my intentions, sweetness in my worship and softness in my heart for You. Grant me contentment in every act I do for You. Let my life be good with You and for You, and my end be even better.

A Question for Your Heart

What would your day look like if you approached every quiet act of goodness feesabilillah, for the sake of Allah, knowing that these are already bringing you a beautiful life and an even more beautiful eternity?

Fall in Love with The Author

Al-Barr is the One who is the source of everything that is pure and kind. He is a Lord who brings true goodness into your life. When you do good sincerely for His Sake, He responds with a life full to the brim with joy and barakah and an akhirah that has even more than that!

WEEK 43:

Learning Arabic

Verse(s) of the Week
Your Rabb's Words for Your Soul

ٱلَّذِينَ قَالَ لَهُمُ ٱلنَّاسُ إِنَّ ٱلنَّاسَ قَدْ جَمَعُواْ لَكُمْ فَٱخْشَوْهُمْ فَزَادَهُمْ إِيمَـٰنًا وَقَالُواْ حَسْبُنَا ٱللَّهُ
وَنِعْمَ ٱلْوَكِيلُ ١٧٣

*Alladhīna qāla lahumu alnnāsu inna alnnāsa qad jama'ū
lakum fa-ikhshawhum fazādahum īmānā waqālū ḥasbunā
llāhu wanī'ma alwakīl*

*'Those who were warned, "Your enemies have mobilised
their forces against you, so fear them," the warning only made
them grow stronger in faith and they replied, "Allah 'alone' is
sufficient 'as an aid' for us and 'He' is the best Protector."'*

Surah Ali-Imran 3:173

When my youngest was just six weeks old, I enrolled in
a course called 'Arabic Through the Qur'an', taught
by Ola, who we met in Week 26. The course guided

us through the study of Qur'anic Arabic, and I can only describe the experience as intensely beautiful.

Although I couldn't dedicate myself to it as fully as I wanted – my baby being so young at the time – it still left a deep impact on me. I took away so much and, insha'Allah, I look forward to signing up again once my current Qur'an course finishes. I believe that we all need to learn the language in which The Most Wise chose to reveal His Final Message.

Ola's Story Concludes

Trying to understand the Qur'an through the original language it was revealed in is important. That's because the depth of meaning found in the Arabic is incomparable to what can be found in the translations. There is so much that is lost in translation. You can only translate the surface-level meaning of one language to another. You can't translate the deeper-level meanings.

Learning the language of the Qur'an is completely life-changing. You read with mindfulness. You become curious and ask: What's going on with the language here? You're not just pondering the meaning of the verse; you end up pondering the way that the language has been used. And you don't have to be a pro at the language – every little bit helps.

Let me give you an example from Surah Ash-Sharh 94, verse 5:

فَإِنَّ مَعَ ٱلْعُسْرِ يُسْرًا ٥

Fa-inna ma'a al-'usri yusran

So, surely with hardship comes ease.

ٱلْعُسْر , the hardship – the ٱل Al before the word usra indicates a specific hardship, like you would say 'the book', which refers to a specific book rather than 'a book'. And the tanween (the two horizontal lines on top of the last letter) in the word يُسْرًا (ease), which indicates unspecific and unlimited ease. Allah has used the mention of specific hardship and unlimited ease side by side in the same ayah.

You can start thinking to yourself, Why has this happened? What is Allah conveying here?

Al-usri, hardship, is something limited and known. Yusra (ease) is unlimited and unknown. So in the grammar of the Arabic language, one of the deeper-level meanings of this verse is: with a limited, defined amount of hardship comes an unlimited amount of ease. That's one example of depth found in the Qur'an when you embark upon the study of the Arabic language.

Pause and Reflect

Here's one more example of what we gain when we understand the Qur'an in its own, original language. Allah describes the believers as those who, when struck with a blow, put their complete trust in Him, and say حَسْبُنَا ٱللَّهُ وَنِعْمَ ٱلْوَكِيلُ (Hasbuna Allahu wa ni'mal wakeel). This is translated roughly as: 'Allah is All-sufficient for me, and the best one to trust in.' The word حَسْبُنَا (Hasbuna) comes from the root ح س ب (ha-sa-ba).

But when we get into the grammar, there's more going on. ح س ب is a complex root. It doesn't only mean 'being enough'. It covers calculation and estimation, sufficiency, consideration and accountability. It's an acknowledgment that this sufficiency is truly comprehensive. It's not limited to material needs, but extends to spiritual, emotional and psychological aspects as well.

Just as in a financial context where one would reckon with or account for funds, in a spiritual context, this means entrusting one's affairs fully to Allah, believing that He will account for them in the best way.

So when we say hasbunnAllah, what we're really saying is: having considered all the factors, we have concluded that relying on Allah is enough for us in that the assistance, guidance and provision that He gives us will entirely cover our needs, be they spiritual, emotional, physical or psychological, and that we entrust all of our affairs to Him because He will look after them in the best way.

By understanding the nuances of the term, it becomes easier to understand how people can find solace, and spiritual and moral growth through applying حَسْبُنَا in their lives.

Live with His Words . . .

Here are three steps to live with this week's verse(s):

1. As you continue to live with the Qur'an, if and when fear, anxiety or overwhelm creeps in, making you feel inadequate, time-pressured or making you doubt your ability, pause and say, 'HasbunAllahu wa ni'mal-wakeel', sufficient for us is Allah, and He is The Best Disposer of our Affairs. Reset and keep the Qur'an journey moving.

2. Make living with the Qur'an your goal, and anchor that goal to your tawakkul in Allah that He will support you fully.

3. Turn to the One who you can rely on with a true unshakeable reliance and tell Him: My Lord, sometimes

I feel completely overwhelmed. I want to live with Your Book and remain connected to Your Words for life, but there are moments when fear, self-doubt and distractions cloud my heart. Carry me through such moments. Increase me in faith and full trust in You. You are enough for me and on You, in faith and trust, I fully rely.

A Question for Your Heart

If and when you feel afraid to take the initial or next step in your journey with the Qur'an, after saying 'HasbunAllahu wa ni'mal wakeel', what must your immediate tangible step be to prove that you said this with absolute certainty?

Fall in Love with The Author

Al-Wakeel is The Ultimate Guardian who revealed the Qur'an to the Prophet ﷺ when he was afraid and overwhelmed. Your Lord is more than capable of anchoring His Words to your heart too. Trust Him and keep journeying with and for Him.

WEEK 44:

Losing the Qur'an

Verse(s) of the Week
Your Rabb's Words for Your Soul

أَفَمَن شَرَحَ ٱللَّهُ صَدْرَهُ لِلْإِسْلَٰمِ فَهُوَ عَلَىٰ نُورٍ مِّن رَّبِّهِ ۚ فَوَيْلٌ لِّلْقَٰسِيَةِ قُلُوبُهُم مِّن ذِكْرِ ٱللَّهِ ۚ أُوْلَٰٓئِكَ فِى ضَلَٰلٍ مُّبِينٍ ٢٢ ٱللَّهُ نَزَّلَ أَحْسَنَ ٱلْحَدِيثِ كِتَٰبًا مُّتَشَٰبِهًا مَّثَانِىَ تَقْشَعِرُّ مِنْهُ جُلُودُ ٱلَّذِينَ يَخْشَوْنَ رَبَّهُمْ ثُمَّ تَلِينُ جُلُودُهُمْ وَقُلُوبُهُمْ إِلَىٰ ذِكْرِ ٱللَّهِ ۚ ذَٰلِكَ هُدَى ٱللَّهِ يَهْدِى بِهِ مَن يَشَآءُ ۚ وَمَن يُضْلِلِ ٱللَّهُ فَمَا لَهُ مِنْ هَادٍ ٢٣

Afaman sharaḥa Allahu ṣadrahul lil-islāmi fahuwa ʿalā nūrin
min rabbihī fawaylun lil-qāsiyati qulūbuhum min dhikril-lāh,
ūlāʾika fī ḍalālin mubīn.

Allāhu nazzala aḥsanal-ḥadīthi kitāban mutashābihan mathāniya
taqshaʿirru minhu julūdu alladhīna yakhshawna rabbahum
thumma talīnu julūduhum wa qulūbuhum ilā dhikril-lāh,
dhālika hudā Allah yahdī bihi man yashāʾ, wa man yuḍlilillāh
famā lahu min hādin

'Can the misguided be like those whose hearts Allah has
opened to Islam, so they are enlightened by their Lord? So
woe to those whose hearts are hardened at the remembrance

258

of Allah! It is they who are clearly astray. 'It is `Allah `Who` has sent down the best message – a Book of perfect consistency and repeated lessons – which causes the skin `and hearts `of those who fear their Lord to tremble, then their skin and hearts` soften at the mention of the mercy of` Allah. That is the guidance of Allah, through which He guides whoever He wills. But whoever Allah leaves to stray will be left with no guide.'

Surah Az-Zumar 39:22–23

I feel that my heart has grown even more attached to the Qur'an since I first began writing this book. I can sense that my relationship with Allah's Book has changed, and I pray it continues to deepen.

This part of the book is about continuing the journey onward. My hope, and my du'a, is that by the time you reach the end of this section, you will have experienced a shift – in both mindset and heartset – and gained tools to help you stay connected to the Qur'an for life.

Because you don't know the value of something unless it's taken away from you. One of the signs of the Day of Judgment is that the Qur'an will be taken away from the people – it will be lifted from the earth. Some scholars say it doesn't mean the physical copy will disappear. It means that the people who have memorised the Qur'an will die. There won't be anyone around who has memorised the Qur'an. Having tasted the sweet comfort that the Qur'an brings and having tasted life without the Qur'an, I fully understand the saying 'absence makes the heart grow fonder'.

As the story of Ahmed, the mosque director from Weeks 7, 11 and 28, concludes, he shares a hard-hitting reflection to ponder upon.

Ahmed's Story Concludes

One day I lost my smartphone. I felt so lost without it. I was delivering an Islamic circle to a group of youths and asked

*them the following question: What would happen if tomor-
row you woke up and there were no smartphones left in the
world? Some of them said, 'I'd feel lost', 'I'd feel bored', 'I'd
feel scared', 'I'd feel empty'.*

*As they shared their answers and as I took my own feelings
into account, a thought came to my mind:* What if tomorrow
I wake up and there's no Qur'an or I can't have access to the
Qur'an? What if I can't find a mushaf on the shelf, or there's
no app or website to open it online? What if I don't have
access to the Qur'an at all? *I knew I would be lost, scared
and have this feeling of emptiness. If we don't have the same
feeling at the thought of not having access to the Qur'an as
we have at the thought of losing our phones, then this is a
clear sign to revise our relationship with the Qur'an.*

Pause and Reflect

This week's verses are powerful. Its opening describes those whose
hearts are hardened to the Words of Allah. As we read it, we can find
ourselves thinking only of others – the disbelievers and hypocrites
whose hearts may be completely hardened to Allah's Words. But the
truth of the matter is that it applies to those who believe in la ilaha
illAllah too. And of course, the next verse is a loving invitation to
all hearts.

Allah 'azza wa jal presents a clear contrast between those who
do not prioritise the Words of Allah and those who do. He clearly
sets out the effects of both on the soul. It is an invitation for you to
ascertain where you're at: to which camp do you currently belong?

The following verse, verse 23, describes the Qur'an in an exqui-
sitely beautiful way. The description of the effects of the Qur'an on
the heart is just simply irresistible.

شَرَحَ اللَّهُ صَدْرَهُ لِلْإِسْلَامِ (sharaḥa Allahu ṣadrahul lil-islāmi), whose chest
(heart) Allah has opened to Islam, *Sharh al-sadr* means expanding or

opening the chest. Your Rabb takes your heart, opens it up with the Qur'an and fills it with inner acceptance, peace and readiness for submission. But this isn't all. He says: نُورٌ مِّن رَّبِّهِ (nūrin min rabbihī), which means light from his Lord. Inner peace isn't all you're provided. You are provided with light, a gift from An-Nur – the One who is light – and your soul's journey is one guided with clarity, faith and deep tranquillity. Isn't that inner peace and clarity through life something we're all searching for?

Allah ﷻ continues: تَقْشَعِرُّ مِنْهُ جُلُودُ ٱلَّذِينَ يَخْشَوْنَ رَبَّهُمْ, taqsha'irru minhu julūdu alladhīna yakhshawna rabbahum. The skins of those who fear their Lord shiver from it – a physical trembling out of awe. ثُمَّ تَلِينُ جُلُودُهُمْ وَقُلُوبُهُمْ, thumma talīnu julūduhum wa qulūbuhum, then their skins and hearts soften towards Allah's Remembrance; the awe creates a tender affection and deep attachment to Rabbul Alameen.

Believe me when I say: you can certainly experience this meaningful relationship with the Book of Allah too. If you haven't already, it may be because you haven't given yourself to it fully yet. But when you do, you will experience the way it adds value to you and your life like nothing else.

Live with His Words . . .

Here are three steps to live with this week's verse(s):

1. Create a du'a habit before recitation: ask for inner opening (sharh al-sadr).

2. Every week, ask yourself: How and why has my heart become spiritually hard this week? How can I soften again?

3. Turn to the One who cracks open the heart and fills it with the nourishment of the Qur'an and say to Him: Let Your Qur'an be my light in this life, my companion in the grave, and my intercessor on the day I meet You.

A Question for Your Heart

When was the last time you truly allowed the Qur'an to move you, not just through recitation but by letting it change the way you feel, think and live?

Fall in Love with The Author

Al-Wahhab – The One Who Gives Endlessly – has given you the Qur'an as His Greatest Gift. It is a timeless treasure for hearts that are willing to be opened. And when your heart opens, it will experience His Endless Generosity.

WEEK 45:

Two Pages Daily

Verse(s) of the Week
Your Rabb's Words for Your Soul

قُلْ كُلٌّ يَعْمَلُ عَلَىٰ شَاكِلَتِهِ فَرَبُّكُمْ أَعْلَمُ بِمَنْ هُوَ أَهْدَىٰ سَبِيلًا٨٤

Qul kullun ya'malu 'ala shākilatihi fa rabbukum a'lamu biman
huwa ahda sabeelan

'Say, 'O Prophet,' "Everyone acts in their own way. But your
Lord knows best whose way is rightly guided."'

Surah Al-Isra 17:84

This week, I want to bring out some practical ways you can
continue your Qur'an journey.

As I mentioned back in Week 2, there is no one-size-fits-
all path to the Qur'an – only your own. That path is shaped by your
personal circumstances, intentions and sincere effort.

Nadia's Story Concludes

My Hajj was a training ground for me. It was intensive, with continuous dhikr (remembrances of Allah) and ibadah (worship). When we were finishing Hajj and people were getting ready to go home, one of the two dai'yat (female Islamic lecturers) who had been giving us lectures during Hajj gave her final talk. She told us how we could maintain our connection with Allah after we returned to our normal daily lives.

She began with an example: 'If you received a letter from a king but it wasn't in your language, what would you do? How would you deal with this message? What would you do with this letter? Will you just frame it and hang it on the wall?'

Sisters began to respond. We concluded that the first step would be to go to people who know the language and translate it, so we could understand the message and act upon it. After all, it was a very important message from a king.

She then asked, 'What about the message from the King of Kings? The Qur'an is Allah's Message to you.'

She pointed to every single one of us, saying, 'To you, to you, to you. Allah 'azza wa jal has given you His Message and it is the Qur'an. So how are you responding? Putting it on your bookshelf? Reading it during Ramadan? But not really interacting with it? Not actually implementing what's in it?'

Then she shared the following project for us to do for after we got back home:

1. Take a notebook. Set down a target for yourself that you are going to read two pages per day (you'll finish the Qur'an in less than a year).
2. Every day read two pages.
3. Go to your choice of tafseer and understand what the two pages are talking about.

4. *In your notebook, write down the takeaways for those two pages for you, asking yourself:* What does my Lord want from me in these pages?

5. *By the end of the year, you have a notebook of all of what Allah wants from you. You keep implementing it. You have your manual for life. This is your crash course to understanding the Qur'an.*

Afterwards you can build on this. You can take tafseer classes and engage in tadabbur, hifdh and tajweed – it's a continuous project.

But first, just read it. It's a personal message from Allah to you.

Pause and Reflect

The great companion of the Prophet ﷺ Abu Bakr (radiAllahu anhu) was asked: which is the most positive verse of the Qur'an? And he replied with this week's verse.

It is saying that everyone acts according to their nature. Abu Bakr (radiAllahu anhu) was asked: 'How do you see positivity in it?' He said, 'If Allah says everyone acts according to their own nature, and I know that Allah's Nature is Mercy, then He will act with me based on that Mercy.'

Dig deep into the Words of Allah. Don't just take them at face value. Don't let the treasures of the Qur'an pass you by without paying attention to them. Look for the treasures and the positivity found within the verses that will bring life to the heart and joy to life.

Dig deep by sitting with each verse and asking yourself:

1. What is Allah's Message for me?

2. Is there something He wants me to follow?

3. Is there a character quality of a believer which I should seek to embody?

4. What are the character traits of hypocrites and unbelievers that I should avoid?

5. What are the overarching lessons from the stories in the Qur'an?

6. Is Allah calling me to repent? Let me repent.

7. Is Allah reminding me to be grateful? Let me show gratitude.

8. Has Jannah been mentioned? Let me make du'a for it.

9. Has Jahannam been mentioned? Let me make du'a for protection from it.

Keep a notebook next to you as you interact with the Qur'an; journal your thoughts and then take action! This is how you can live with the Qur'an.

And finally, here is the beautiful advice from our pious predecessors. The companion of the Prophet ﷺ Abdullah bin Mas'ud (radiAllahu anhu) said:

> When a man amongst us learned ten verses [of the Qur'an], he would not move on [to the next verses] until he had understood their meanings and how to act by them.
>
> *Al Tabari*

Abu AbdulRahman Al Sulami (rahimuAllah) said:

> Those who used to teach us the Qur'an (the Companions) told us that they used to learn the Qur'an from the Prophet ﷺ.When they had learned ten verses they would not move on until they put into practice what was in them. So we learned knowledge and deeds (implementation) together.
>
> Musnad Ahmad

Dearest reader, I hope you're excited! Go get yourself a new journal (yes, any excuse to buy stationery!). Make du'a for guidance, ease, openings and blessings with the Words of Allah and say Bismillah. A lifelong journey with the Qur'an awaits you. Enjoy!

Live with His Words . . .

Here are three steps to live with this week's verse(s):

1. Identify what connects you strongly to Allah. Are you someone who finds connection through du'a, khidmah (service), writing, contemplation in nature or seeking knowledge? Live with the Qur'an according to your spiritual disposition.

2. Add a reminder to your phone so that every day of Jumuah between Asr and Maghrib you ask Allah to bless your lifelong commitment to live with the Qur'an.

3. Turn to the One who knows you so well and guides you accordingly and tell Him: Rabbi, You know me better than I know myself. Let my unique self take personal, deep messages from Your Words and draw near to You.

A Question for Your Heart

What is one consistent habit you can commit to (it doesn't matter how small it is) that will keep you connected to the Qur'an even during busy or challenging periods of your life?

Fall in Love with The Author

Ar-Rabb – The One Who Nurtures and Sustains – knows your heart and will guide you to Him in a manner that aligns with your nature.

WEEK 46:

Find Your LWQ Tribe

Verse(s) of the Week
Your Rabb's Words for Your Soul

وَأَقِيمُواْ ٱلصَّلَوٰةَ وَءَاتُواْ ٱلزَّكَوٰةَ وَٱرْكَعُواْ مَعَ ٱلرَّٰكِعِينَ ٤٣

Wa aqeemoo al-salata wa aatoo al-zakata wa arka'oo ma'a al-rāki'īn

'Establish prayer, pay zakat and bow down with those who bow down.'

Surah Al-Baqarah 2:43

My Story
〰〰〰〰〰

When my co-hosts, LaYinka and Sumayah, and I filmed the final episode of the final season of our YouTube series Honest

269

Tea Talk (HTT), there was a mixure of sadness and celebration. We had accomplished what we set out to do: to bring raw, unspoken topics within the Muslim community to the forefront, with the hope that others would begin having those conversations too. And they did.

Many people called us trailblazers. And it's true that when we began, Muslim women, especially Muslim women of colour, speaking so openly and candidly on YouTube was something unheard of. Since then, alhamdulillah, countless podcasts and shows have emerged, some of which have grown even larger than HTT, doing incredible work in the community. May Allah bless them all. Ameen.

We felt content closing the chapter on HTT because it had become a growing, vibrant community dialogue. Though I was the one who first came up with the idea for the show, it would never have been what it was without my beautiful co-hosts and without viewers who took those conversations into their homes, families and online spaces.

You need your people to make moves, and that's why this chapter is coming now.

My dream and my du'a is that this book becomes the seed of something far greater: a movement. I've called it the Living With Qur'an movement (LWQ).

Every day, at least 17 times in our 5 daily prayers, we say: 'Guide us to the straight path.' This journey through dunya to Allah was never meant to be walked alone. And that applies to the journey with the Qur'an too. There's a collective dimension. We are a jama'ah (ummah) and we are stronger together.

Pause and Reflect

Although this week's verse was addressed to the Children of Israel, it is still applicable to us, especially knowing the Prophet ﷺ said:

> The parable of the believers in their affection, mercy and compassion for each other is that of a body. When any limb aches, the whole body reacts with sleeplessness and fever.

Sahih Bukhari

Here the Prophet ﷺ is speaking of the Muslim ummah as a body, reacting with sleeplessness and fever when just one person aches. That ache can also be the spiritual emptiness that comes with a life without the Qur'an. You want Jannah? Want that for your brothers and sisters too! You want a close relationship with Allah? Want that for your brothers and sisters too! You want to live beautifully with the Qur'an? Want that for your brothers and sisters too! And prove that you want it for them through action! This week's verse encourages togetherness in spiritual practice and the importance of being part of a worshipping community.

So I invite you to do something I pray will be incredibly beneficial for you, insha'Allah.

1. Establish your LWQ tribe! Your tribe can be you and just one other person. It can be a small group or a large group. The size is irrelevant. But your intentions are everything.

2. Choose a tribe in which your hearts are filled with love for the sake of Allah for each other. Choose a tribe in which you're close enough to give each other a dose of tough love when needed. Choose a tribe in which you really are genuinely concerned for the journey of each other's soul.

3. Sit down together and establish your own individual goals with the Qur'an. They can be long-term goals broken down into annual, monthly, weekly and daily goals. Your goals do not need to be the same as each other's. But make your goals known to each other. Then, agree to regular check-ins with one another. Maybe you'll have a daily check-in but will also meet once a week to share your

reflections. Talk about the verses that hit your heart, those that comforted you and strengthened you. Support each other through life with the Qur'an. When one of you is going through something heavy, let the others rally round and carry that person with the Beautiful and Perfect Words of Allah.

4. Celebrate each other as you meet your goals. When larger goals are met, go all out in your celebrations. When some of the tribe fall short of reaching their goals, support one another. Sometimes that will look like gentle loving encouragement and sometimes it will need to be a firm push. And of course, make du'a for each other. If you've read my second book, you'll know du'a has to be a consistent feature of this tribe. And remember, as you make du'a for each other, you'll be blessed with the angels saying, 'Ameen, for you too.'

Live with His Words . . .

Here are three steps to live with this week's verse(s):

1. Make du'a. Ask Allah to guide you to those He knows would be the best members for your LWQ tribe.

2. In your first meeting, set the initial format of how the tribe will work. Be fluid. You may wish to start reading this book together, completing the weekly activities from this book, daily check-ins for your individual goals, times when you'll meet once a week online or in person – sharing tadabbur reflections, how you're going to give thanks to Allah collectively and how you'll celebrate each other's milestones.

3. Turn to the One who loves a strong ummah and tell Him: Ya Allah, make our LWQ tribe one that supports one another to live with the Qur'an with sincerity. Fill our hearts with love for each other, help us uplift one another as we embark upon this journey together.

A Question for Your Heart

During your time with your LWQ tribe, regularly take yourself to account by asking yourself: Who am I becoming through this tribe, and am I helping others grow closer to the Qur'an through me?

Fall in Love with The Author

Al-Wadood is The Most Loving, who places love and mercy between the hearts of His servants. As you walk the path of Qur'an together, remember to ask Him constantly for His Blessings: to be a tribe that is rooted in love for His Words and one that is united with a common goal; to fall in love with the Qur'an and to become His beloved.

WEEK 47:

Gratitude

Verse(s) of the Week
Your Rabb's Words for Your Soul

وَإِذْ تَأَذَّنَ رَبُّكُمْ لَئِن شَكَرْتُمْ لَأَزِيدَنَّكُمْ

Wa-idh ta'adhdhana rabbukum la'in shakartum la'azeedannakum

'And ʳrememberˀ when your Lord proclaimed, "If you are grateful, I will certainly give you more."'

Surah Ibrahim 14:7

My Story

One Friday morning, I was sitting at my desk, which is situated in the corner of my bedroom, chipping away at a work deadline. My youngest child, who was 10 years old at the time, was sitting on my bed reciting Surah

Al-Kahf as part of her Friday routine, as per the sunnah of the Prophet ﷺ.

Suddenly her recitation stopped, and she interrupted my thoughts with a question: 'Ummi, Allah is an author, right?'

I turned in my chair towards her and looked at her big brown innocent eyes staring back at me, waiting for an answer.

I smiled at her and said: 'Yup, Allah is the Best Author. The Author of authors!'

She paused, her eyes staring into space as she processed my answer before snapping out of her momentary trance to return to her recitation of the 19th chapter of the Qur'an.

I turned back to my laptop, smiling at her innocent question. My thoughts were interrupted again with a second query.

'So, I'm reciting the Words of Allah?'

Turning around again, I could see her eyes had widened in amazement.

'Yeah, that's right,' I confirmed.

'Cool!' she exclaimed with excitement, returning once again to her recitation.

This time, I didn't turn back to my desk. I looked at her, legs crossed, shoulders hunched over the Qur'an as it rested on her lap. I paused and took in the lesson my 10-year-old daughter had taught me. Through the fitrah of her soul, that natural inclination we are all born with, she taught me something profound: within the walls of my home, I am honoured – privileged – to possess multiple copies of the perfect, unchanged and preserved Words of the Creator of the Heavens and Earth. Allahu akbar!

Pause and Reflect

We do not consider how remarkable it is, as my daughter realised, that we can speak the language of our Creator, with the exact words that He has chosen to give us.

We're people of weakness and faults and mistakes. We can say ugly things with our tongues. And yet Allah allows us to be honoured enough to recite His Words. As if that isn't enough of an honour in itself, through reciting them, we purify our hearts. We purify our souls. Through reciting them, we find lessons in how to navigate the difficulties and opportunities Allah gives us, so that we can live through life drawing close to Him, 'azza wa jal, through His Words.

As you continue your journey of living with the Qur'an, ensure you thank your Rabb at each juncture of your journey. Thank Him in your du'a. Thank Him by giving sadaqa. Thank Him by inviting others to embark upon this journey with the Qur'an too. But ultimately, show Him gratitude by practically living with His Book through all the seasons of your life – regularly and consistently.

And when you show Him gratitude, He will increase you as He beautifully says in this week's verse. Note that in this part of the verse لَئِن شَكَرْتُمْ لَأَزِيدَنَّكُمْ (la'in shakartum la'azeedannakum) the lam of emphasis (لَ) and the verbal noun with nun of emphasis (نَّ) are used. Double emphasis is used by your Lord to tell you that your gratitude is incredibly special to Him. The double emphasis literally means: 'If you are grateful, I will most certainly, most definitely increase you.' The increase is open-ended: it may be in wealth, health, guidance, patience, contentment or connection to the Qur'an. SubhanAllah, blessings upon blessings, increase upon increase. A Lord who gives and leads us to be grateful to Him and rewards us for being grateful to Him and increases us further the more grateful we are! I don't know about you, but I feel shy and humbled in front of my Generous Lord.

Live with His Words . . .

Here are three steps to live with this week's verse(s):

1. Shukr (gratitude) is recognising your blessing, attributing it to Allah and taking action as a form of worship. What is the one way you can show Allah gratitude this week?

2. Set a time this week to look back over the ways you have lived with the Qur'an and the blessings you have accordingly received from your Lord. Spend time thanking Him specifically for each one. Allow your heart to feel humble as you thank and praise Him.

3. Turn to the One who is ever so Generous and Kind and tell Him: Ya Rabbi, You are the One who rewards even the smallest of deeds. I fall short in recognising Your Endless Blessings. Plant deep within me a heart that sees, names and acts upon Your Favours – especially that relate to my relationship with You and Your Book. Let my gratitude become a path to closeness with You.

A Question for Your Heart

When was the last time you just paused and lived in a moment of gratitude, allowing it to move you to change something, give thanks or give something purely for the sake of Allah?

Fall in Love with The Author

Ash-Shakur – The One who Appreciates Deeply – is a Lord who will never let your good deeds and your sincere forms of gratitude go unnoticed. He appreciates you and promises you increase every time your heart acknowledges all your blessings are gifts from Him.

PART 7:

Akhirah

وَسِيقَ ٱلَّذِينَ ٱتَّقَوۡاْ رَبَّهُمۡ إِلَى ٱلۡجَنَّةِ زُمَرًا ۖ حَتَّىٰٓ إِذَا جَآءُوهَا وَفُتِحَتۡ أَبۡوَٰبُهَا وَقَالَ لَهُمۡ خَزَنَتُهَا سَلَٰمٌ عَلَيۡكُمۡ طِبۡتُمۡ فَٱدۡخُلُوهَا خَٰلِدِينَ ٧٣

Wa sīqal-ladhīna ittaqaw rabbahum ilā al-jannah zuma-ran ḥattā idhā jā'ūhā wa futiḥat abwābuhā wa qāla lahum khazanatuhā salāmun 'alaykum ṭibtum fadkhulūhā khālidīn

'And those who were mindful of their Lord will be led to Paradise in ˹successive˺ groups. When they arrive at its ˹already˺ open gates, its keepers will say, 'Peace be upon you! You have done well, so come in, to stay forever.''

Surah Az-Zumar 39:73

WEEK 48:

The Grave

Verse(s) of the Week
Your Rabb's Words for Your Soul

يَوْمَ تَرَى ٱلْمُؤْمِنِينَ وَٱلْمُؤْمِنَٰتِ يَسْعَىٰ نُورُهُم بَيْنَ أَيْدِيهِمْ وَبِأَيْمَٰنِهِم بُشْرَىٰكُمُ ٱلْيَوْمَ جَنَّٰتٌ تَجْرِى مِن تَحْتِهَا ٱلْأَنْهَٰرُ خَٰلِدِينَ فِيهَا ۚ ذَٰلِكَ هُوَ ٱلْفَوْزُ ٱلْعَظِيمُ ١٢

Yawma taral-mu'minīna wal-mu'mināti yas'ā nūruhum bayna aydīhim wa bi-aymānihim bushrākumu al-yawma jannātun tajrī min taḥtihā al-anhāru khālidīna fīhā dhālika huwa al-fawzul 'athīm

'On that Day you will see believing men and women with their light shining ahead of them and on their right. ' They will be told,` "Today you have good news of Gardens, under which rivers flow, 'for you` to stay in forever. This is 'truly` the ultimate triumph."'

Surah Al-Hadid 57:12

once heard a sheikh share a deeply moving practice he uses to keep his soul in check – to hold himself to account before he's held to account. It's radical: he closes the curtains, switches off all the lights, lies down in the middle of an empty room, closes his eyes and imagines himself in the grave.

No, I haven't lost my mind sharing this with you. If anything, what's truly irrational is how much we give to this dunya, this illusion. In reality, it's all so fleeting.

After listening to that lecture, I tried it myself. And subhanAllah, it changed something within me. Whatever was weighing on me no longer mattered. Life became clearer, simpler. I'm here to worship Allah. And I don't have much time left.

Khadija, the beautiful soul behind the *Women of Quran* podcast, has dedicated her efforts to sharing the stories of women who are living with the Qur'an. What she shared with me felt so fitting for this part of the book. Because to truly live with the Qur'an is to dare to reflect deeply, to do things that feel radical in a world that's asleep, to awaken to the truth that we only have one life to prepare for the eternal one.

Khadija's Story

Imagine yourself in your grave.

It's a long period of time – longer than you'll ever live. The companion of the Prophet ﷺ Uthman ibn Affan (radiAllahu anhu) lived for 80 years or so, and subhanAllah he has spent more than 1,300 years in the grave. He had an exceptional relationship with the Qur'an, so he has lived the best 1,300 years.

Life expectancy is roughly 80, although it could be far less. You only have to live those few years with the Qur'an and, in return, will have thousands of years with the protection, company and light of the Qur'an in your grave.

Even after the barzakh (the period between death and res-urrection), when we're resurrected, the only thing that will stay with us is the Qur'an. It is said that all the good deeds you have done will take you to the doors of heaven and leave you there – except the Qur'an, because inside heaven it will take you to the different levels of Jannah.

The Prophet ﷺ said:

It will be said to the companion of the Qur'an: Recite and ascend as you recited in the world! Verily, your rank is determined by the last verse you recite.

Sunan Tirmidhi

You'll be elevated according to the last ayah you recite. It makes you realise this is a race. If I'm not working for the Qur'an now, am I saying that I don't want to be with the Prophet ﷺ? Do I not want to be able to look at the face of Allah? Do I not want to be in the highest part of Jannah? We all need to think about what we want our akhirah to look like and work for it.

When I'm in my grave, I'll have no wealth and no family to take with me. I will hear the footsteps of my loved ones walking away from my new home. The one thing that will accompany us, along with our good deeds, is the Qur'an.

The grave is a very dark and difficult place. But the Qur'an is described as Nur-ul qabr, the light of the grave. You go to the cemetery and you see everyone has their own place. Can you imagine not being alone but having it as your compan-ion there?

Imagine yourself in your grave. There's nothing more you can do. Have you treated the Qur'an as a friend and com-panion? Or is it completely unknown to you? The more you give to it, the more it will give you – in both lives.

Pause and Reflect

Whenever I walk down a street lined with large, beautiful homes, I want one. So I ask Allah for one – both in this life and the next.

There will always be people more successful than you. Perhaps they have what you dream of – a top education, a great career, a spouse, children, a beautiful home, an expensive car, holidays, wisdom, insight, a noble character, wonderful friends. And the list goes on.

One of my daughters very honestly said: 'Hijab is hard, especially when you see everyone around you dressing so freely.' I agreed. It's true.

I love my hijab. My daughter loves her hijab. But there are times when it can feel like those upon paths other than Islam are living easier lives. And in many ways, it does appear easier. You can eat any type of meat you want. You have the 'freedom' to dress as you please outside.

However, true freedom isn't simply choice. All that really does is enslave you to your own desires, which are shaped by your environment and change with the wind. I'd rather be enslaved to what my Lord – the Creator I came from and the One to whom I'm returning – wants from me.

This week's verse is simply beautiful. After death, light is given to those who chose Allah in the dunya and lived for Him. The light will illuminate the way for them as they cross the siraat (bridge) to Paradise. Where once you looked at other people and what was missing – what you sacrificed for the sake of Allah and the akhirah – that day you will be the object of attention and others will yearn to be like you. They will hope for your light. That light is a consequence of many things, but one of them is most certainly the Qur'an, because the Qur'an is light.

Live with His Words . . .

Here are three steps to live with this week's verse(s):

1. Each evening, ask yourself: What did I do today that would contribute to light in my grave?

2. One day this week, complete the exercise that I mentioned right at the beginning of this chapter. Thereafter, journal how you would like to furnish your grave.

3. Turn to the One who is light and grants light to whomever He wills and tell Him: Rabbi, grant me a light that guides me through this life, that is carried into the grave and I find myself encompassed on the Day of Judgment. Illuminate my path through my relationship with You and Your Book.

A Question for Your Heart

What are you doing today to nurture the light of faith within you, so that it will become a companion of light for you in your grave and light up the way before you on the Day when all other lights are extinguished?

Fall in Love with The Author

An-Nur is a Lord who grants light in the darkest of places. Use this life to walk with the light of His Words, so that everything in the next life is illuminated by the Mercy He presented to your human efforts.

WEEK 49:

The Throne Verse

Verse(s) of the Week
Your Rabb's Words for Your Soul

ٱللَّهُ لَآ إِلَٰهَ إِلَّا هُوَ ٱلْحَىُّ ٱلْقَيُّومُ ۚ لَا تَأْخُذُهُۥ سِنَةٌ وَلَا نَوْمٌ ۚ لَّهُۥ مَا فِى ٱلسَّمَٰوَٰتِ وَمَا فِى ٱلْأَرْضِ ۗ مَن ذَا ٱلَّذِى يَشْفَعُ عِندَهُۥٓ إِلَّا بِإِذْنِهِۦ ۚ يَعْلَمُ مَا بَيْنَ أَيْدِيهِمْ وَمَا خَلْفَهُمْ ۖ وَلَا يُحِيطُونَ بِشَىْءٍ مِّنْ عِلْمِهِۦٓ إِلَّا بِمَا شَآءَ ۚ وَسِعَ كُرْسِيُّهُ ٱلسَّمَٰوَٰتِ وَٱلْأَرْضَ ۖ وَلَا يَـُٔودُهُۥ حِفْظُهُمَا ۚ وَهُوَ ٱلْعَلِىُّ ٱلْعَظِيمُ ٢٥٥

Allāhu lā ilāha illā huwa al-ḥayyul-qayyūm lā ta'khudhuhu sinatun walā nawm lahu mā fī as-samāwāti wamā fī al-arḍ man dhā alladhī yashfa'u 'indahu illā bi'idhnihi ya'lamu mā bayna aydīhim wamā khalfahum walā yuḥīṭūna bishay'in min 'ilmihi illā bimā shā'a wasi'a kursiyyuhu as-samāwāti wal-arḍ walā ya'ūdhu hifẓuhumā wa huwa al-'aliyyu al-'athīm

'Allah! There is no god 'worthy of worship' except Him, the Ever-Living, All-Sustaining. Neither drowsiness nor sleep overtakes Him. To Him belongs whatever is in the heavens and whatever is on the earth. Who could possibly intercede with Him without His Permission? He fully knows what is ahead of them and what is behind them, but no one can

grasp any of His Knowledge—except what He wills to reveal. His Seat encompasses the heavens and the earth, and the preservation of both does not tire Him. For He is The Most High, The Greatest.'

Surah Al-Baqarah 2:255

This week's verse is the peak of Surah Al-Baqarah, the surah that the Prophet ﷺ speaks of in this way:

Do not turn your houses into graveyards. Verily, Satan flees from the house in which Surah Al-Baqarah is recited.

Sahih Muslim

It's the 255th verse and is known as the Throne Verse, Ayat Al-Kursi. It's a complete description of Allah's Oneness, Majesty and Authority, unmatched in any other place within the Qur'an. It is known for its power in protection, healing and so much more.

My Story

My dear friend, Sumayah, whose story I included in Week 18 of when she became severely ill and used the Qur'an as ruqya to get better, is probably the biggest proponent of the daily recitation of Surah Al-Baqarah of whom I know. I listened to her story. I admired her relationship with the Qur'an and I was so happy for her. But it wasn't until I needed clarity for a new direction in my life that I actually started doing the same. And when I did, I was shocked at how quickly I began to experience its power and effects.

I didn't start sooner because I was extremely busy – CEO of a charity, author, speaker, Qur'an student, mum, home-educator – and I was afraid of starting because I didn't believe I would be able to keep it up. Reciting Surah Al-Baqarah every day seemed unachievable. So, I decided to start small. Surah Al-Baqarah has 286 verses. I split the verses into four, reciting 71–72 verses per day, completing the recitation of Surah Al-Baqarah once every four days.

Before I began, I made du'a:

'Rabbi, I'm turning to You. Make this easy for me. As I recite this powerful surah, cleanse me, make things clear for me, guide me, soothe me, comfort me, heal me and open up doors that You know I need. Ameen.' And then, I said, 'Bismillah' (In the Name of Allah), and I began.

I cannot tell you how calm I felt just on the first day. The second day, I found myself feeling happy as I recited. The third day, I finished reciting my portion for that day, feeling like I was hungry for more. The fourth day, the solution to a personal worry that had been bothering me for years became crystal clear after my recitation and the completion of Surah Al-Baqarah.

My feeling of looking forward to my time with Surah Al-Baqarah became more intense. I'd never felt such a pull towards recitation before this.

When I told Sumayah what was happening, she laughed and said: 'Girl, get ready! It is going to clean you up. Surah Al-Baqarah is going to cut out anything inside you or in your life that isn't going to help you on your path to Allah.' And then she added: 'Oh, and you're going to be tested.'

'Nooo!' I replied. It was the last thing I wanted.

But she told me that she's often seen this. Someone suddenly finds themselves faced with two paths (often this is not about something major in life – it could just be an everyday situation) and the test is: will they choose the higher path?

That same night the most bizarre situation occurred. My two sons left to go pray salatul maghrib in the local masjid. Some time passed, and I wondered where they were, as they normally returned quite quickly. Then one of them rang me and told me they'd found a baby fox wandering the streets. It had tried to venture onto a busy road. My children are all animal lovers, so of course they tried to help the baby fox.

My instant reaction was: 'Don't even think of bringing that fox here!'

It was quite a long time before we heard a knock at the door. And then, there were the boys with the cutest, tiniest baby fox. He wasn't even ginger yet, he was so small.

We put him in our cat carrier and went back to where he was found to see if we could find the mother. We waited for ages – no sign at all. By this time, it was past 9pm. I was calling the RSPCA animal rescue shelters and couldn't get through to anyone. Then came the test. I really did not want a fox in my home! But here he was, and he was such a vulnerable little thing, and cute at that, and he was a creation of Allah. The Lord of the Worlds pays attention to everything that lives, however small and fragile. What was the higher thing to do in this moment? What would my Rabb want from me?

Even though my own inclination was to just put the fox in a corner of a park somewhere and hope for the best, we took him back home and fed him. He was going to stay the night!

Then Alhamdulillah, my last attempt at contacting a rescue centre was successful. They were near closing time, but they said they would wait for us to bring him along; so we jumped into the car with the fox.

I got back around midnight, completely shattered. Before I lay down to sleep, I whispered to my Rabb: 'Accept this from me and grant me ease, for bringing ease to Your Creation.' I felt that I had chosen what was most pleasing to Allah and maybe, just maybe, had passed my first 'Surah Al-Baqarah test'.

Pause and Reflect

Surah Al-Baqarah is powerful. Speak to anyone who recites it regularly, and you will hear about the impact of it on them and their lives.

In Ayat Al-Kursi, the Throne Verse, which is the greatest verse in Surah Al-Baqarah, Allah 'azza wa jal is mentioned 17 times! And His Names, Allah, Al-Hayy, Al-Qayyum are mentioned. Some scholars say that Allah's Greatest Name is Allah. Others say it is Al-Hayy, or Al-Qayyum.

Al-Hayy or Al-Qayyum is a Lord who is Everlasting, who gives and sustains life. Both names point to His Greatness and Perfection. Many classical scholars say these two names are the heart of the verse, encapsulating the essence of who Allah is.

This verse is for you and for every striving believer. It is reassuring that Allah's Control over you, your life, your family, your affairs and, in fact, the whole universe, is easy and effortless for Him. Nothing is beyond Him, and His Knowledge and Will are absolutely complete.

Surah Al-Baqarah will open you up to salawaat, istighfaar and du'a, and a heart that is alive with the Lord of the Universe. It will draw you in to where you need to be – close to Him in this life with the aim to be close to Him in the next.

Live with His Words . . .

Here are three steps to live with this week's verse(s):

1. Take the 286 verses of Surah Al-Baqarah and make an intention to recite it regularly in your life. If you can recite it all in one day, then do that. If you can't, consider completing it once a week.

2. Make it a daily habit to recite Ayat Al-Kursi after each obligatory prayer and before sleeping. Do so with presence.

3. Turn to the One who never slumbers or sleeps and tell Him: Rabbi, Your Kursi extends over the heavens and the earth. Nothing is outside of Your Knowledge and Control – not my tests, my future or my healing. You never sleep. You never forget. You will never leave me unprotected. My heart rests knowing that You are watching over me. Help me to live with unwavering trust in Your Care, and protect me from the thought that I am ever alone.

A Question for Your Heart

Allah is looking at you attentively right now. Ask yourself: What would change about how I live, think and feel if I reminded myself that my Lord is constantly guarding me – never absent from my life, not even for a single second?

Fall in Love with The Author

Al-Hayy is The One who is Ever-living. He never dies and He Sustains all that exists. Relying upon Him and trusting in Him is your safe sanctuary and a place your heart can truly rest.

WEEK 50:

Roadmap

Verse(s) of the Week
Your Rabb's Words for Your Soul

وَنَزَّلْنَا عَلَيْكَ ٱلْكِتَـٰبَ تِبْيَـٰنًا لِّكُلِّ شَىْءٍ وَهُدًى وَرَحْمَةً وَبُشْرَىٰ لِلْمُسْلِمِينَ ٨٩

Wa nazzalnā 'alayka al-kitāba tibyānan likulli shay'in wa hudan wa raḥmatan wa bushrā lil-muslimīn

'We have revealed to you the Book as an explanation of all things, a guide, a mercy, and good news for those who fully submit.'

Surah An-Nahl 16:89

What message do I most want to leave you with as this book draws to a close? It's this: like this book, everything comes to an end. But what I truly hope lingers long after you turn the final page is a deep and lasting connection with the Qur'an.

I recently watched an Instagram reel by the Australian 'Muslim undertaker' @aussiemammoth, in which he spoke about the passing of his beloved father. He described how he washed his father's body just as his father had once bathed him as a child. How he wrapped him gently in a shroud, just as his father had wrapped him in a blanket when he was little. That moment deeply moved me.

Between birth and death lies a life filled with decisions, events, storms, beauty, heartbreak, healing, joy, trauma and triumph. Through it all, you need direction. You need divine clarity. You need an anchor. That anchor is the Qur'an. And as Sheikh Wasim so beautifully describes below, it is the Qur'an that will help you live and die well.

Sheikh Wasim described to me how Allah ﷻ tells us that the Qur'an is a clarification for everything. For everything that you will ever face in your life, there will be an answer, or a guidance or a piece of advice connected to it, in the Qur'an.

He said that as long as you can hold the Qur'an close to you and have some knowledge of it, it will stop you from doing things that will take you away from Allah. No matter what the situation, Allah's Book will tell you how you need to be, or how you need to understand the situation.

The Qur'an helps us navigate high highs and low lows. It shows you how to remain on the middle path, centred, where you then find peace and contentment.

Zainab's Story Continues

After reading verse 10 from Surah Ar-Rad, and verses 1–11 of Surah Al-Mu'minun and verses 63–74 of Surah Furqan, I wanted to be the type of believer of Allah that was described in those verses.

I didn't want fame. I wanted a hidden strong tie to Allah. I wanted a personal connection with Him. These verses described the type of servant I wanted to be. And so, that's when I decided I wanted to read the Qur'an, but not just like a book. I wanted to reflect and really understand. And so I spent a year where I read one verse at a time and spent a significant amount of time reflecting on it.

It was a long journey, but by the end, I had gone through a complete transformation in my study of the Qur'an from my own bedroom. The Qur'an became special. I wasn't the same person after that. My Qur'an was tabbed and full of notes. It set everything off. It was a gateway to learning Arabic and years later completing my hifdh.

Pause and Reflect

You've spent more than 50 weeks learning from the personal experiences of those who are living with the Qur'an, taking their recommendations and discovering the depth and beauty of Allah's Verses. And now, living with the Qur'an means continuing this journey for life.

That means approaching the Qur'an as a map. It will show you how to remain on the siraat ul mustaqeem. It will bring you back if you take a wrong turn. If you find yourself lost, it will guide you back. If you find yourself confused, it will provide you with clarity. If you feel lonely, it will become your companion. It will strengthen you, comfort you, teach you, remind you of your worth and show you all that you need to be and do to live as His beloved.

In this verse, Allah 'azza wa jal says لِّكُلِّ شَىْءٍ (li-kulli shay'in) – for all things – which is everything necessary for your guidance, including belief and creed, law, morality, character, purpose and spirituality. It is for everything. I invite you to make the Qur'an your everything.

I'm going to invite you to do something right now. Not later. Now. Go get your physical copy of the Qur'an and then come back to this page. (Go on – this book isn't going anywhere.) Now hold it in your hands. This is your map for life. This is your manual of how to do this thing called being human.

I want you to place the Qur'an in the most important room in your home, the room where you spend most of your time. I want you to choose the shelf, table or place that is significant for you such that, every time you see the Qur'an there, you're drawn to pick it up, read it and engage with it. Go and place it there right now.

My dearest reader, by Allah, you don't know how many days you have left in this world. Do not die before your death. Live – live beautifully – which I pray to Allah you know is only truly possible by making the Qur'an the most precious thing in your life. Live with it as the divine clarification for absolutely everything about you and your life.

Live with His Words . . .

Here are three steps to live with this week's verse(s):

1. Use the Qur'an as your first reference, not your last resort. When you're confused about anything in life, even your own feelings, pause and ask: What does my Lord want me to know through His Qur'an? Open it regularly to seek real-time direction, even before asking others.

2. After reading a verse that hits your heart, pause and make a du'a, then plan one step to implement its message that day. Transform your life one verse at a time, one day at a time.

3. Turn to the One who has made life clear for you through His Book and tell Him: Ya Allah, remove all shadows of doubt from my mind and heart. Allow me to turn to Your Book through all the seasons of my life. Let me live by Your Words until the day I die.

A Question for Your Heart

What recent situation left you feeling confused? How different might your response have been had you turned to the Qur'an and asked Allah for clarity first?

Fall in Love with The Author

Al-Mubeen – The One Who Makes Everything Clear – is a Lord who has given you His Book to live by and with, not just to read. He wants you to know that there is no confusion for the heart that is attached to it and connects with its meanings.

WEEK 51:

Endless Devotion

Verse(s) of the Week
Your Rabb's Words for Your Soul

فَإِذَا فَرَغْتَ فَانصَبْ ٧ وَإِلَىٰ رَبِّكَ فَارْغَب ٨

Fa-itha faraghta fansab wa-ila rabbika fargab

*'So once you have fulfilled ˹your duty˺, strive ˹in devotion˺,
turning to your Lord ˹alone˺ with hope.'*

Surah Ash-Sharh 94:7–8

My Story

▰▰▰▰▰▰▰

*I want to take you back to a moment I experienced in East
London Mosque. It was early on a Saturday morning when I
took myself there, seeking some quiet time to write this book.
I found a spot in the corner of one of the side rooms, where*

a few sisters were already seated, reciting the Qur'an softly to themselves.

Before long, the room began to fill with Somali women who gradually formed a circle. One by one, more sisters entered and joined the gathering, until the space was almost full. Then, an elderly white Arab woman entered the room. She asked if she could join, and they warmly made space for her.

I found this sight so striking: a circle of Somali women, all dressed in black hijab, and among them, this elderly Arab woman, wearing a white satin scarf.

The recitation began. One of the Somali sisters led with a beautiful, melodious voice, and the others followed along with their own copies of the Qur'an, taking turns reading verses. When it was the elderly Arab lady's turn, she recited the closing verses of the surah with emotion, then gently closed her mushaf. With her voice trembling and eyes welling with tears, she shared the following hadith with the group:

Allah's Messenger ﷺ said: 'Allah has some angels who roam about the streets in search of people mentioning Allah's Names. When they find such a gathering, they call one another saying: Come to the object of your pursuit.' The Prophet ﷺ added: 'The angels surround them with their wings up to the lowest heaven (sky of the world).' He further added: '(When the people in the gathering disperse, the angels ascend to the heaven).' Their Lord, who knows best about the people, then asks them: 'What do My slaves say?'

The angels reply: 'They were glorifying You (by repeating the words "Allah is the All-Glorified", exalting You (by repeating the words "Allah is All-Great", praising You (by repeating the words "All praise be to Allah"), and dignifying You.'

He asks them: 'Have they seen Me?' The angels reply: 'No, O Lord! They haven't seen You (at all).'

He asks: 'How would it be if they saw Me?' The angels reply: 'If they saw You, they would worship You more devotedly, dignify You more fervently and exalt You more sincerely.'

Then Allah asks them: 'What do they ask Me?' The angels reply: 'They ask You for Paradise.' He asks them: 'Have they seen it?' The angels reply: 'No, by Allah, they have not seen it.' He asks: 'How would it be, if they saw it?' The angels reply: 'If they saw it, they would crave for it eagerly, seek after it vigorously and desire it ardently.'

He asks: 'From what do they seek My protection?' The angels reply: 'They seek your protection from Hell.' He asks: 'Have they seen it?' The angels reply: 'No, by Allah, O Lord! They haven't seen it.'

He asks: 'How would it be, if they saw it?' The angels reply: 'If they saw it, they would fear it extremely and flee from it hastily.'

Then Allah says (to the angels): 'I make you witness that I have forgiven them.'

One of the angels then added: 'O Lord! among them was so-and-so (a much sinning slave) who was not actually included in the gathering. He happened to come there for some need and sat down with them.'

Allah replied: 'Well, they were all sitting together, so their companion will not be reduced to misery. He will receive forgiveness also as a reward for his or her association with the people remembering Allah.'

Sahih Bukhari

When she reached the end of the hadith, her voice broke completely. She buried her face in her hands, sobbing. Among the group was a very elderly Somali woman – she looked like she could have been in her early nineties. As the Arab sister finished speaking, this elderly woman clasped her hands together, slowly waddled over, bent down and gently kissed the top of her head. Then she wrapped her arms around her and held her close.

The Arab sister disappeared into the folds of the big black Somali hijab as she was pulled into the embrace. When she finally emerged, her face was red and soaked with tears. The old Somali woman returned to her spot, tears now streaming down her own cheeks, yet she had the widest smile.

I sat there, laptop open on my lap, silently fighting back my own tears as I smiled at the scene before me: the love for the Qur'an, and the love between the lovers of the Qur'an. It was deeply, profoundly beautiful.

Pause and Reflect

The courage of the Arab woman was inspiring. She most likely came to the masjid for another reason, found this group of sisters, joined them and then shared her heart with them.

This life is so short. But you are still alive. You still have life to exert full effort on this path back to Allah. He is telling you: Don't waste time; keep going. Keep striving with full hope, love and yearning for Me alone.

There's no time to be idle. Rest, by all means, but with the intention that it is refuelling you so that you can keep going and do more. Opportunities must always be seized. In this week's verse, Allah instructs the Prophet ﷺ, and by extension all believers, that once we complete our daily responsibilities and daily worship, we should move on to another act of devotion. Just because duty is done does not mean the end of action.

The scholar Imam Al-Razi said these verses describe a spiritually productive life – moving from duty to devotion, never wasting a single moment and grabbing hold of every moment as an opportunity for nearness to Allah ﷻ.

Dearest reader, never ever let opportunities with the Qur'an pass you by. You don't know which opportunity may be your very last.

Live with His Words . . .

Here are three steps to live with this week's verse(s):

1. Use moments between tasks – like after finishing school or work, after a commute or having completed chores – as prompts to connect with Allah, even for just a few minutes. Recite a verse and make a du'a.

2. Instead of waiting for the perfect time for the Qur'an, begin each day or each task block with the Qur'an, whether that's by reading, listening or reflecting on one verse. Build the habit of making the Qur'an your starting point for everything.

3. Turn to the One who lovingly presents you with daily opportunities to draw close to Him and tell Him: Ya Allah, Al-Fattah, open for me doors of goodness that bring me closer to You. Help me seize small pockets of time and transform them into moments of deep connection with Your Book. Don't let me be among those who delay or neglect the opportunities You so generously present to me.

A Question for Your Heart

Ask yourself: How many moments do I let pass by, telling myself 'later'? How long will I keep approaching time in this way? And how is this affecting my dunya and my akhirah?

Fall in Love with The Author

Ar-Raqib – The Ever Watchful – is a Lord who sees the moments you waste and the chances you ignore; yet He 'azza wa jal still grants you more. To live with the Qur'an is to honour His Watchful Gaze by responding with sincere action.

WEEK 52:

Arriving Home

Verse(s) of the Week
Your Rabb's Words for Your Soul

جَزَآؤُهُمْ عِندَ رَبِّهِمْ جَنَّـٰتُ عَدْنٍ تَجْرِى مِن تَحْتِهَا ٱلْأَنْهَـٰرُ خَـٰلِدِينَ فِيهَا أَبَدًا ۖ رَّضِىَ ٱللَّهُ
عَنْهُمْ وَرَضُواْ عَنْهُ ۚ ذَٰلِكَ لِمَنْ خَشِىَ رَبَّهُ ٨

Jazā'uhum 'inda rabbihim jannātu 'adnin tajrī min taḥtihā al-anhāru khālidīna fīhā abadan raḍiya Allāhu 'anhum wa raḍū 'anhu dhālika liman khashiya rabbah'

'Their reward with their Lord will be Gardens of Eternity, under which rivers flow, to stay there for ever and ever. Allah is pleased with them and they are pleased with Him. This is ˹only˺ for those in awe of their Lord.'

Surah Al Bayyinah 98:8

My youngest daughter once randomly said: 'Ummi, you know, no one alive knows what it feels like to die.' She was right. We cannot know.
Picture yourself shrouded in your grave. If you have performed

303

ghusl (ritual washing for purification) for a deceased person, remind yourself that one day your body will be turned over and washed too. Take yourself to this moment in your imagination now. Because your story will not end there.

Your Story

It is the day of your death. The angels from heaven descend with bright faces like the sun. They carry your shroud that is fragranced with the perfume of Jannah. The angel of death sits by your head and says: O pure soul, come out to the forgiveness of Allah and His Pleasure. You take your final breath and your soul is wrapped in the shroud of Paradise. As your soul begins to ascend through the heavens, a trail of perfume – more pleasant than any musk on earth – is left behind. You are no longer required to strive in the dunya. Your soul passes gatherings of angels who are gentle and radiant, greeting you with mercy, exclaiming, 'What a pure soul!' and calling you by the best of names. Your soul ascends until it reaches the seventh heaven where Allah 'azza wa jal says: 'Write the record of My servant in the righteous register and return him to the earth, for from it I created them, to it I return them, and from it I will take them out once again.'

The grave you feared is now a resting place – full of light, not from the sun, but from the Qur'an you clung to in the silence of your nights and the chaos of your days. You are not alone there – the verses become your beautiful companions in your new home. Your time in the grave is the sweetest siesta as though you rested only between dhur and asr.

Then, the Trumpet is blown. The sky splits and the mountains scatter like dust. And you rise, naked and barefoot, exposed to the sun that has been brought close. But there is shade given to a select few and you are beneath it. You look around and see others you knew from the dunya, those who loved the Qur'an, who wept at its verses, who paused at its commands and followed through, who found themselves in its pages.

The scales are brought out and your deeds are placed upon them. You tremble until you hear your recitation of the Qur'an, the familiar rhythm of the ayat you whispered in salah, the verses you lived by. They intercede for you and lift the scale. You're handed your book in your right hand as you smile with relief, gratitude and full joy.

You cross the siraat, the bridge over Hell, with a light paving a way before you because of the light that was nurtured in your heart each time you acted upon the Qur'an. Some stumble. Some fall. But you? You walk with ease, light guiding your every step.

Then comes the moment – the moment your longing heart yearned for. The gates of Jannah open and you are greeted with a fragrance that is unlike anything your senses ever knew. Your home is ready. Your name is on the door. The gardens are alive with colour, the rivers flow beneath without end and your loved ones await you with joy that knows no bounds.

And then, the meeting with The Author of the Qur'an, Allah, The Most High, you did your best to live for. You stand in humility, overwhelmed by sheer awe and love. You don't know what to say except utter abundant praises of Him. Your Lord looks upon you. He knows you. He was observing you all along – when you chose a verse over your own desires, when you sat with the Qur'an even through your pain, when you returned to Him, again and again.

He 'azza wa jal smiles upon you. You are Home.

And you realise: this is what you were created for. To live with His Words. To meet Him, the Author of your favourite book, The Glorious Qur'an.

Pause and Reflect

This is it: Week 52. The final chapter.

What a journey it has been. But let me be clear: it doesn't end here. This week's story is my deepest hope that I carry for every single one of you. I pray that every stage of your dunya, and more importantly, every stage of your akhirah, is laced with ease, barakah, openings, peace and light. I ask Allah 'azza wa jal to grant you the honour of being from Ahlul-Qur'an – the people of the Qur'an.

Know this: the story above is not just possible for you; it is what you were created for. This is your purpose.

This week's verse is your Lord speaking of the highest reward: His Rida – His Pleasure. Not only will you, bi'idhnillah, enter jannah, but you will do so with the full approval of the Lord of the Worlds. You will arrive with every trial behind you and every promise fulfilled. You'll realise it was all worth it: the decision to surrender, the courage to submit, the moments you lived with His Qur'an when no one else was watching.

There is no feeling greater than knowing your Creator is proud of you – proud of the way you held on to His Rope through the Qur'an.

For now, your story continues. Keep going. Keep holding on. Keep living with the Qur'an.

Live with His Words . . .

Here are three steps to live with this week's verse(s):

1. Make the Qur'an your daily companion. Recite it. Reflect on it. Let it question you, guide you and comfort you. Choose one verse each week to live by, and watch your heart soften and strengthen at the same time.

2. This week, take yourself out for a walk. Put your phone away, and just imagine walking through Jannah, enjoying its wonders with your loved ones and meeting Allah, The Most Merciful.

3. This one is a bit different. This is my du'a for you: My Perfect Lord, my Beloved, I turn to You – my Rabb who has gifted us with His Qur'an; my Creator that I have come from and the Especially Merciful who I am returning to. Rabbi, I have written this book to draw others to Your Book. Accept this humble effort of mine. Ya Allah, whichever hands You place this book into, allow it to be a means of transforming their journey in living with Your Qur'an. O Allah, take my dearest reader and fill their heart with what You know is needed so that they become beloved to You. Grant me that too.

My Lord, do not allow this to be the end of Your servant's journey with the Qur'an. Let it be a beautiful beginning of a life where the Qur'an becomes their closest companion, a mirror for all You want them to see and their strongest anchor through this turbulent dunya. O Allah, let us not leave this world, having not tasted the best part of it – Your Qur'an. Rabbi, grant us the blessing of living for Your Pleasure and allow us to enter Jannah by Your Pleasure. Be pleased with us. We are pleased with You.

A Question for Your Heart

If today were the final page of your story, have you lived in a way that would earn the pleasure of The Author of your life?

Fall in Love with The Author

Al-Wadood – The Most Loving – is a Lord who wants you to know there is no journey more worthy, no companion more loyal and supportive, no pursuit more powerful than living your life wrapped in the Qur'an. Live with it and die with it in the deepest place of your heart.

Conclusion

Dearest reader, as you close this book, I want to leave you with a story that's stayed with me ever since I heard it in the early years of my life as a Muslim.

A sheikh once told a story about an American guy who was using drugs. One day he was smoking a spliff and a Moroccan guy joined him to smoke. As they were getting high, they started talking about life and Islam. Their conversation continued for hours and hours. The American guy later embraced Islam, never to meet this Moroccan brother ever again. The American brother changed his life and went on to do so much good for the sake of Allah. As the sheikh recounted the story, he said something which I'll never forget.

He said, 'That Moroccan brother may arrive on the Day of Judgment with a mountain of sins and then find beside it a mountain of good deeds. And he may wonder: *Where did this come from?*'

SubhanAllah. One moment. One conversation. One seed planted. And the fruits multiplied by the One who sees all.

You may never know how your living with the Qur'an might affect someone else's life. How your transformation, your sincerity, your quiet striving might one day reach someone's heart. That's the beauty of this journey – it is for you but it never ends with you. The Qur'an is the Perfect Unchanged Words of Allah 'azza wa jal, which was passed to the Angel Jibreel (alayhis-salam), which then arrived upon the heart of the Prophet (ﷺ) and has been passed onto us for our own lives, but it must also pass through to others – one verse at a time, one reflection at a time, to one heart at a time.

Always remember that the Qur'an was always meant for you. So, take what you've gained from this journey. Let the Qur'an live in your heart and live through your actions. Let Allah's Words guide your life. And, when the time is right, let it overflow to someone else.

كِتَٰبٌ أَنزَلْنَٰهُ إِلَيْكَ مُبَٰرَكٌ لِّيَدَّبَّرُوٓاْ ءَايَٰتِهِۦ وَلِيَتَذَكَّرَ أُوْلُواْ ٱلْأَلْبَٰبِ ٢٩

Kitābun anzalnāhu ilayka mubārakun liyaddabbarū āyātihi waliyatazakkara ūlu al-albāb

'This is' a blessed Book which We have revealed to you 'O Prophet' so that they may contemplate its verses, and people of reason may be mindful.

Surah Sad 38:29

May we all live with the Qur'an until our final breath. Ameen.

Glossary

Adhkaar: morning and evening prayer and remembrance
Ahadith: narration
ajzaa: parts
akhirah: eternal life
Al Fattah: the One who opens a way/the Supreme Opener
Al Haqq: the Lord who is the Truth
Al Kareem: the Most Generous
Al Khabeer: a Lord who alone is worthy of exaltation
Al Lateef: the One who is subtle and kind
Al Mubeen: the One who makes everything clear
Al Muqeet: the One who sustains
Al Mujeeb: the One who responds to du'a
Al Mutakabbir: the Supremely Great
Al Qarib: a Lord who is ever near
Al Quddus: the Holy One
Al Razzaq: the Provider
Al Wafiyy: the Most Faithful
Al Wahhab: the One who gives endlessly
Al Wali: the One who protects
Al Wasi': the All-Encompassing
Al-Adl: the Most Just/the Absolutely Just
Al-Alim: the All-Knowing
Al-Barr: the One who is the source of everything pure and kind
Al-Fattah: the Supreme Opener
Al-Ghafur: the Most Forgiving
Al-Hafidh: the Ever-Protecting Guardian
Al-Hakim: the All-Wise
Al-Haleem: the Most Forbearing
Al-Hayy: the Ever-Living
Al Jabbar: the Compeller and Restorer

Al-Lateef: the One who is subtle and kind

Al-Mubeen: the One who makes everything clear

Al-Muqaddim: the Expediter

Al-Mushi: the One who takes account of all things

Al Mutakabbir: the Supremely Great

Al-Quddus: the Holy One

Al Razzaq: the Provider

Al Shafi: the One who heals

Al Wadood: the Most Loving

Al Wakeel: the Most Trustworthy Disposer of Affairs/the Ultimate
    Guide/One who protects

Al-Wadud: the Most Loving

Al-Wakil: the Ultimate Guide/Protector

Al-Wasi': the All-Encompassing

Alhamdulillah: all praise and thanks are due to Allah

Allah: God who has no partners

Ameen: Amen

An-Nur: the One who is light

Ansar: the supporters from Madinah who took the Prophet ﷺ and
    his followers into their homes

anzala: sent down

Ar Rahman: the Most Merciful

Ar-Rabb: the One who nurtures and sustains

Ar-Raheem: the Especially Merciful

Ar-Raqib: the Ever Watchful

Ar-Rashid: the Perfectly Wise Guide

Ar-Rahman: the Most Compassionate

As-saabiqoon: the early believers

Asr: the third daily prayer

Ash-Shakur: the Most Appreciative

AstaghfiruAllah: I seek forgiveness from Allah

Ayn: evil eye

Ayah: verse

Ayat: verses

Banu Israel: the people of Moses

baligh: denotes something that reaches full extent
Barakah: blessings
Barzakh: barrier/realm between this world and the next
Basirah: deep perception
Batlah: magicians
Biidhnillah: by the permission of Allah
Bismillah: in the name of Allah
Dai'yat: female caller to Islam
Dars: religious class
Dawah: calling people to Islam/invitation to Islam
deen: religion
Deen: way of life
dhikr: remembrances of Allah
Dhu'l Rahma: Possessor of Mercy
Du'a: personal supplication
Duha: forenoon prayer/chapter in Qur'an
dunya: life of this world
emaan: faith
Esha: fifth night prayer
Fitrah: innate disposition/the natural state in which we were created,
    uncorrupted
ghusl: ritual washing for purification
Hadith qudsi: revelation of Allah to the Prophet ﷺ, narrated in the
    Prophet's own words/divine narration
Hajj: pilgrimage to Makkah
Hafs: one out of ten ways of reciting the Qur'an
Halaqa: circle of knowledge/religious study circle
Halal: permissible
haram: impermissible
hasanat: good deeds
haqq: absolute truth
Hifdh: memorisation
hijab: covering for Muslim women
hisab: calculation
Huffadh: memorizers of the Qur'an

Ibadah: worship
ihsaan: striving for excellence
Ijazat: authorised licence
ilm: knowledge
InshaAllah: God willing
insaan: human beings
Istikharaa: prayer of seeking guidance
Istiğfaar: the act of seeking forgiveness from Allah
jama'ah: ummah/congregation
Jannah: Paradise
Jahannam: Hellfire
Jumu'ah: Friday prayer
Juz 'Amma: the 30th part of the Qur'an
Khair: goodness
khāshi'īn: a deep humility with fear and presence
Khidmah: service
Khushoo: tranquillity/humility in prayer
La ilaha illAllah: there is no god but Allah
mashaAllah: as Allah willed
Muqarabeen: those drawn near (to Allah)
mufasirun: scholars of tafseer
Mufasirun: exegetes
muhsinun: the ones who excel in doing good
Mumin: strong believer/believer
munafiqeen: hypocrites
Munafiqoon: hypocrites
Mushaf: written version of the Qur'an in Arabic
nafs: lower self
niqab: face veil
nunnazil: implies continuous revelation and relevance throughout
    time
qadr: Divine Decree
Qiblah: direction of prayer (towards Makkah)
qiyam: night prayer
Rabbuka: Your Lord

radiAllahu anhu: may Allah be pleased with him

radiAllahu anha: may Allah be pleased with her

Raghaba: hope, longing, a deep desire for reward and closeness to Allah

Rahaba: fear, awe, dread of His displeasure and punishment

rahimuAllah: may the mercy of Allah be upon the person who has died

Rahmah: mercy

Rahman: The Most Compassionate

Rakat: prayer unit

Rizq: provision

Ruh: soul/spirit

Ruku: bowing in prayer

Ruqya: recitation for delivery from ailments/spiritual healing

saabiqoon: the forerunners in doing good deeds

saabiroon: the ones who are patient

sabab: cause/means

Sabr: patience

sadaqa: charity

sadaqa jariah: ongoing charity that you are rewarded for beyond death

Sahabah: companions of the Prophet ﷺ

salah: ritual daily prayers

salatul istikharaa: the prayer of seeking guidance

Salawaat: peace and blessings/prayers

salihaat: females of ummah

Sanad: chain of narration

sara'a: to race or compete

Sayyi'at: bad deeds

seerah: life of the Prophet ﷺ

shahadah: declaration of faith

Shariah: Islamic law

Shifaa: healing

sihr: black magic

Siraat: bridge/path

Siraat-ul-mustaqeem: the straight path
sujood: prostration
Sukoon: tranquillity
Sunnah: established way/prophetic tradition
surah: chapter
Tadabbur: contemplation of the Qur'an
Tafseer: exegesis or interpretation of text/Qur'an
Tajweed: science of reciting the Qur'an correctly
Taqwa: consciousness of Allah/God-consciousness
tawakkul: reliance upon Allah
Tawbah: repentance
ummah: the collective believers of Islam
Umrah: minor pilgrimage
walaa al baraa: love for what Allah loves
waqa: to shield and protect
wird: regular portion
Wudu: ablution
wudu: ablution before prayer
Yusra: eas

Bibliography

Where publication or edition details have not been listed, the English translations in the text have been provided by independent translators.

Al-Nawawi, *al-Tibyan*
Ibn al-Jawzi, *Sayd al-Khater*
Translations from Quran.com
Various books of Tafseer

Gratitude

In my previous books, the Gratitude section stretched over many pages. This time, it is much shorter. Not because there aren't people to thank, but because I carry a deeper realisation within me: every single person who has supported me in writing this book is, in truth, a gift from my Lord, The Most High.

Every person who has walked with me on this journey – my beloved children, dear friends, the dedicated team at Penguin Random House, my agent, the launch squad, the wonderful brothers and sisters who contributed their stories to this work, my Qur'an teachers, Ola Shoubaki who checked and confirmed grammatical and linguistic meanings, my eldest child who checked the Arabic ayat didn't miss a word or a vowel, my dear friend Sumayah who recites the verses for the audiobook version of this book, and Sheikh Asif Uddin who kindly answered queries related to tafseer. And, of course, my beautiful readers. Each one was divinely placed in my path so that this book might, I pray, inspire people to live differently with His Book. And so, while I am deeply grateful to the people, my gratitude must ultimately and always be directed first and last to Him 'azza wa jal.

When I think back to the du'a I made in 2022 – to write and publish a book before I leave this world – my eyes still well with tears. To know that Allah answered that du'a just two months later, when Penguin Random House approached me to write a book, never fails to send shivers down my spine. And to think that this is now my third book since then, subhanAllah, I feel nothing but humility before my Lord, Al-Kareem, The Most Generous. Not only did He answer my du'a by presenting me with the opportunity to work with the largest publisher in the world, granting the potential for a wider reach, but He also allowed this to be the third book released into the world. We take steps towards Allah and He comes to us at speed with so much more. My Lord . . .

I pray that Allah accepts this effort as an offering of gratitude to Him – for guiding me to Islam and for blessing me in countless ways. May He forgive me for my many shortcomings and accept this work as sadaqah jariyah for His Sake alone. Ameen.

Rabbi, I thank You.

About the Author

Aliyah Umm Raiyaan converted to Islam 26 years ago and has been involved in UK dawah for over 20 years. In 2010, she founded Solace UK, a registered charity that helps women who have converted to Islam and find themselves in difficulty. In 2019 she launched a YouTube show called *Honest Tea Talk*, which brought unscripted conversations to the table about raw, unspoken topics related to the Muslim community. In 2022, she was approached by Penguin Random House UK to write her first book, *Ramadan Reflections*, which was published in 2023 and became a *Sunday Times* bestseller. The following year her second book, *The Power of Du'a*, came out, which Mufti Menk said was 'empowering . . . of great benefit to those who wish to have their doors flung open by Allah'. Aliyah is also an international speaker and has delivered a TEDx talk titled 'The Power of Your Pain'. She lives in East London, where she home-educates her youngest children. She continues to devote her time to helping women achieve their full potential while emphasising the importance of developing a personal and close relationship with Allah.